THE IRISH

THE
IRISH

HARPER & ROW, PUBLISHERS

NEW YORK, EVANSTON, SAN FRANCISCO, LONDON

1817

Sinners
Saints
Gamblers
Gentry
Priests
Maoists
Rebels
Tories
Orangemen
Dippers
Heroes
Villains
and Other Proud Natives
of the Fabled Isle

by THOMAS J. O'HANLON

PHOTOGRAPHS BY FRANK MONACO

Grateful acknowledgment is made for permission to reprint the following:

Lines of poetry by Louis MacNeice from "Bagpipe Music" in *The Collected Poems of Louis MacNeice,* edited by E. R. Dodds (Oxford University Press). Copyright © 1966 by the Estate of Louis MacNeice. Reprinted by permission of E. R. Dodds.

Song from *At Swim Two-Birds* by Flann O'Brien (Brian O'Nolan). Copyright © 1966 by Flann O'Brien. Published by Walker & Company.

continued on next page

Designed by Sidney Feinberg

Library of Congress Cataloging in Publication Data

O'Hanlon, Thomas J
   The Irish: sinners, saints, gamblers, gentry, priests, Maoists, rebels, Tories, Orangemen, dippers, heroes, villains, and other proud natives of the fabled isle.
   Bibliography: p.
   Includes index.
   1. Ireland—Politics and government—20th century. 2. Ireland—Economic conditions—1918– . 3. Ireland—Social conditions. 4. Northern Ireland—Politics and government. I. Title.
DA959.035 1975   914.15′03′9   74-1843
ISBN 0-06-013238-8

Contents

Illustrations

AUTHOR'S NOTE

There are a number of generous people who helped make this book possible. I especially want to thank Robert Lubar, managing editor of *Fortune,* who arranged for me to obtain a leave of absence. Among those in the United States who gave me the benefit of their specialized knowledge, my thanks to Sean Cronin, William Maxwell, and Bernard McDonough, all of whom know Ireland from the inside and outside.

In Ireland, I have drawn on the advice and expertise of so many people that it would be impossible to name them all. Muiris MacConghail, head of Government Information Services, cheerfully smoothed the way. Joseph O'Malley, who ought to write a book on Ireland himself, was a tireless collaborator in separating fact from fantasy.

A special salute to my wife, Grainne, whose patience and encouragement were constant. Richard Passmore, who supervised the copy editing, is an extraordinarily perceptive professional. And without Jeannette Hopkins, editor extraordinary, this book would not have seen the light of day.

"It will, therefore, be understood
that when the Leprecauns of Gort na
Gloca Mora acted in the manner about to
be recorded, they were not prompted by
any lewd passion for revenge, but were
merely striving to reconstruct a rhythm
which was their very existence, and which
must have been of direct importance to the
Earth. Revenge is the vilest passion
known to life. It has made Law possible,
and by doing so it gave to Intellect the
first grip at that universal dominion
which is its ambition. A Leprecaun is of
more value to the Earth than is a Prime
Minister or a stockbroker, because a
Leprecaun dances and makes merry, while
a Prime Minister knows nothing of these
natural virtues—consequently, an
injury done to a Leprecaun afflicts
the Earth with misery, and justice is,
for these reasons, an imperative and
momentous necessity."

JAMES STEPHENS, *The Crock of Gold*

THE IRISH

INTRODUCTION

Illusions,
Pretensions,
and Reality

In a searching mood, I returned to Dublin to begin work on a book about Ireland. The genesis of the book lay in a strong conviction of mine, formed through innumerable visits to the country during the time I worked in New York, that the Irish had become the most interesting subjects for anyone who wanted to understand and write about the flabby human condition in the last part of the century of industrial man. My instinct told me that something big was brewing on the island, not just the prospect of an all-out, no-holds-barred, fire-and-brimstone, eye-for-an-eye religious war, although that event seemed likely ever since 1969, when the Protestant-Catholic boil of hatred finally burst in the shadows of the old wall of Derry. No. My antennae signaled that the daily murders were an overt manifestation of a universal condition. The Irish were no longer dying for a great dream; they were taking an unholy pleasure in discharging a poisonous knot of frustration in a howl of violent rage at the institutions around them. The way the murders were being committed suggested that some anarchic breakdown was taking place: a woman raped, then murdered in front of her child; a man shot and then hung on a spiked railing in a Belfast square; bombings so powerful that the victims became unidentifiable blobs of flesh to be scooped with brush and shovel into plastic bags like offal; summary executions, on the slightest suspicion of collaboration with the enemy. Murder had become so commonplace, people had become so inured to violence, that massive explosions in Belfast and Derry brought forth, as a Dublin writer put it, nothing more than the passing expression of a sigh.

The Irish have constructed, over the years, a picture of themselves which is eminently satisfying to a people who have distinct reservations about living in the twentieth century. Unfortunately, this well-known historic triptych, composed of literary genius, religion, and revolution, is coated with a thick varnish of self-delusion. The country's best writers live abroad and are banned at home. While the rest of the English-speaking world looks upon religion as a ceremonial appurtenance to life, like prayers in the White House or speeches from the throne, to the Irish, Protestant and Catholic, religion is the fundamental element of their existence. And, in a world where the nation-state is an economic anachronism, the Irish are still in bondage to the notion that political power sprouts from the gun barrel.

Such postures demand a kind of controlled schizophrenia. Churchgoers and bomb throwers insist that they live in the most refined of civilizations, yet they exit from this land of heart's desire as permanent migrants or as temporary travelers in search of the exotic: to London for banned books, Paris for sin, Ibiza for sun, Rome for the papal blessing, and Lourdes for a miracle. Politically, the Irish are suspicious of democracy, detest the egalitarianism of socialism, and view capitalism as a temporary extension of the ancient sin of usury. Every Irishman is an aristocrat at heart, as long as he is part of the elite that sets the rules for a game where everyone knows his place.

Nurtured from birth with the doctrine that they have a lien on greatness, the Irish are unable to come to terms with their own powerlessness. And by the Irish, I hasten to add, I mean both the braggarts of Belfast who profess loyalty to the British Crown and the dissemblers of Dublin who perpetuate the myth of a superior Irish Catholic race. The ten most powerful individuals in Ireland, all of whom are chronicled in this book, are collectively powerless to determine the island's destiny. The Irish live by the decisions of foreigners: the British Chancellor of the Exchequer, who determines the value of currency and sets interest rates; the Commissioners of the European Economic Community in Brussels, who set farm prices; and the executives of multinational corporations, who decide how to manipulate markets. The unfinished business about the partition of the island is the only matter left within Irish domain, and the natives have chosen to revert to an old-fashioned religious war to solve that long-standing problem.

From what I had gathered on visits, and from reading Irish publications which brought news of the latest outrages, I knew that the Irish themselves were mystified about this perplexing plunge into paranoia. There seemed to be a great deal of confusion about the aims of the combatants. Depending on the source, people were killing other people for freedom; civil rights; a Catholic Ireland; status quo in the North of Ireland; a Cubanized Ireland (this from the left-wing faction of the Irish Republican Army) ; an Ireland free from colonial domination (this was the interpretation of the right-wing blood-and-soil Provisional IRA) ; a Protestant enclave loyal to the Crown but separate from Britain, the goal of some fundamentalist Orangemen; or Wolfe Tone's Ireland, a nondenominational populist agrarian society that might have made sense when it was first proposed by Wolfe Tone, the leader of the United Irishmen, in 1791. Because the participants were advancing their views with blithe disregard for one another, the overall effect on outsiders was that the Irish, in passion, become incoherent.

The preferred manner of settling the real estate dispute in the North through violence has its counterpart elsewhere, in Vietnam, the Middle East, the Indian subcontinent. That is of little solace to people who are in the line of fire, but it serves to mask some elemental changes. Through a curious warp of time

and an accident of geography, Ireland has all at once become a
battleground of conflicting ideas, a microcosm of all the pro-
found issues that have emerged in various forms elsewhere. The
collision between rural tribalism and urban materialism has
stripped away legend to reveal conflicts that were there all
along. Just like everybody else, the Irish are faced with discontented students, women's liberation, the breakdown of family
life, crime, the real meaning of national identity, the authoritarianism of politicians and priests, distinctions of caste and
class, all those big familiar divisive themes of contemporary
society in the United States and Europe. The big multinational
corporations have arrived almost overnight, and in such
strength—Courtalds from Britain, Asahi from Japan, Snia
Viscosa from Italy, Du Pont from the United States among
many—that a few are worried not just about the destruction of
the environment but about the visible danger of foreign domination. So loaded with drama is the Irish psyche that each
subject is handled with engaging importance, generating
polemics befitting the end-of-the-world national temperament.

On the flight to Shannon, I began reading *Ireland Calling,* a
book that was distributed in New York in the early sixties, in
order to get some insight into contemporary views of the Catholic right-wingers. After a brief period of penance for supporting Hitler, Mussolini, Salazar, Franco, and Joe McCarthy, they
had, in Ireland at least, attained respectability again. The
subtitle of the book, which had been given to me by a part-time
politician who calls himself Sean Dublin Bay Christian Democrat Loftus (he had changed his name by deed poll so that his
new name became his political platform) , promised one answer
to the Irish question:

A Plan for the Political
Cultural and Economic Recovery
Of Ireland, Based on Christian Social
Principles, on Fundamental National Unity, on the
Complete Independence of Ireland, and on Justice for All Men

The flyleaf told me "that the book could be cheaply published, one of our Catholic bishops has given a personal subscription and his Lordship has granted me permission to announce this fact." It seemed a much more lively read than *Cara,* the magazine put out by Irish International Airlines with cheery articles on Portuguese cuisine and the history of the hat. Somewhere east of Newfoundland, I came across a passage on patriotism which his Lordship had imprimatured, and it seemed to contain the clues to this mental disorder. After all, religiosity and patriotism are at the root of the fighting, as Ian Paisley and the field marshals of the IRA factions kept reminding me. The relevant section went:

PATRIOTISM, THE GIFT OF GOD, IS A TRUE INSPIRATION

Patriotism is the true inspiration for every phase of national advancement.

It exercises one of the greatest and most ennobling influences on the human race.

It inspires us to make sacrifices for the common good.

It has inspired man's greatest national achievements and most noble heroism.

Great men, in every generation of our long enslavement, have suffered and died for Ireland's freedom. They have sacrificed everything in life for our release.

They have left us a heritage of hope and inspiration which we do not utilise.

"Your dead, too, live on to keep in everybody's
mind the duty of loving one's country."

This gift of God—true patriotism—is one of the strongest weapons any nation can call to its aid against internal disunion, lassitude, or greed, as well as against external attack. It is also the key to true material well-being.

And whenever in the world prosperity came, without the inspiration of spiritual values, its very opulence caused its ruin. Yet many in Ireland, to-day, pursuing opulence, apparently forget patriotism —the Gift of God.

In the words of MacSwiney:
"No physical victory can compensate for moral surrender."

Patriotism sounded like a popular patent medicine—an aid
against internal disunion, lassitude, greed, as well as external
attack: take three times a day after meals. I knew that people in
Ireland would respect the definition because it was grounded on
what they consider supreme authority, the unerring Spiritual
Leader Pope Pius XII and the revered Irish revolutionary
Terence MacSwiney, who died from hunger in Brixton Prison
in 1920. The equation "Prosperity minus spiritual values
equals ruin" nicely summarized for me the conflicting views
of the warring tribes. Unfortunately, nobody in Ireland could
agree on what prosperity really is; while the fighting continued,
politicians on both sides of the border were saying things that
boiled down to "You never had it so good," yet I knew that one
of the Protestant wild men in Belfast, Johnny McQuade, a
fellow who can bring a yelling armed mob into action against
the Catholics, boasted that he had no toilet in his house. I knew,
too, from personal inspection that the "new Ireland" of overnight millionaires, convention hotels, office blocks, night clubs,
and earnest executives who pay a lot of money to hear experts
like Herman Kahn speak about the unthinkable, or think aloud
about the unspeakable, existed side by side with the old Ireland,
a quarter of whose population lives in a state of relative poverty
that would cause a black man in Harlem to sign up as advance
scout in an Army of Liberation.

The inability of the Irish to finalize, as the students of
Harvard Business School might say, a system of priorities is
another symptom of that national breakdown. Just before I left
New York, an invitation to a dinner party had seemed providential. The three guests of honor were men who, while not
literally on the firing lines, had connections with all the feuding
factions. Dr. Con McCluskey, a tall bony man from Dungannon
in the North of Ireland, had set off the firecracker in his part of

the country by forming a local civil rights group that collected data on job and housing discrimination. Dr. McCluskey is a pure, nonviolent man; he simply wanted to publish evidence that Catholics were being denied jobs and houses by an unfair system, just as the Southern Christian Leadership Conference had done with regard to blacks in the United States in the sixties. When the Northern Ireland government tried to ignore the highly publicized evidence, the Dungannon civil rights group, which was nothing more than a typewriter, a duplicating machine, and a handful of volunteers at the beginning, grew into a mass movement that spawned radical leaders like Bernadette Devlin, caused the resurgence of the moribund IRA, brought in twenty thousand British troops, and ended a fifty-year period of one-party totalitarian government in the North.

Also on hand was Father Denis Fall, an activist Catholic priest from the North, who acted as a sort of chaplain to the Catholics interned without trial in prison camps. Both men were en route to Washington, where they were to testify before a House committee that was compiling evidence on conditions in the North; the Irish-American vote in the United States is still large enough to justify such circuses. The third visitor was Dr. John O'Connell, a member of the Irish Labour Party, who represented a working-class district in the Dail (pronounced "doyle"), the Republic's Parliament. O'Connell had other irons in the fire; as the publisher of a medical directory he was relatively wealthy, and, therefore, able to pursue his primary goal—to become a politician of international consequence. Earlier that year, he had traveled to 10 Downing Street to talk to Prime Minister Edward Heath about a plan to bring the warring factions in the North of Ireland together.

From the uneasy beginning of that night, I realized that one certain way of creating instant, insoluble confusion is to bring Irishmen of differing political views together. Dr. McCluskey gave the strong impression that he disapproved of clerical interference in political matters, an impression reinforced by the oblique verbal sniping between himself and Father Fall. In any event, the two men had philosophical convictions that were worlds apart, Dr. McCluskey being a strong civil libertarian, the soft-spoken priest a rigid opponent of birth control in any form. While Dr. McCluskey clicked off the aims of the civil rights movement—jobs, housing, and a better educational system— Father Fall talked with some passion about the tortures inflicted by the British on people who were interned in prison camps. Dr. O'Connell seemed to have a catlike suspicion of the two Northerners, a feeling that was reciprocated. O'Connell was an advocate of birth control, which made conversation with the priest difficult, while Dr. McCluskey's views of Dublin politicians made the air grow distinctly chilly. "They're a corrupt lot down there," he said with the confident air of someone who had studied the matter carefully. "I wouldn't have anything to do with them. There isn't one person in the North of Ireland that would vote for any of the political parties in the South."

What started out as a likely forum to get the consensual view of the factions ended with the three men looking suspiciously at each other as they separately outlined their formulas and theories. "It's just like the Irish," said Raymond Brady, the editor of a New York business magazine, who was expecting to hear the final solution to the Irish Problem. "Put three of them in a room together and each one forms his own political party."

I thought a lot about that breakdown in communications back in New York when I had settled in Dublin. People I talked to in Ireland seemed strangely out of touch with what was happening in the country at large, often in ways that were hilariously funny. "What this whole bloody place needs to clean things up is the father and mother of a depression," one sage told me in the Shelbourne Hotel. I looked around the lounge. The carpet was frayed, the fixtures looked as if they had not been refurbished since the Eucharistic Congress in 1932, and the tray of drinks had been brought by a boy who appeared to have reached the ripe age of fourteen. Child labor and the relics of a time when the Shelbourne was considered a classy hotel did not appear to be symbols of pulsing prosperity. A business executive who was discoursing a few days later on the economy said of inflation, which was mounting such a head of steam that the Dublin newspapers had been sending squads of reporters to keep up with the hourly price increases, "We have a long way to go to catch up with England, though."

My eyes told me that a lot of the country was still grabbed by the cold claw of poverty, but here were two responsible citizens telling me (1) that a great crash was necessary to bring the orgy of high living to an end, and (2) that hair-curling inflation was acceptable as long as Britain's inflation was even a hair higher on the charts. I sought affirmation for my view that the whole place was out of sync, finding comfort in Heinrich Böll's book *Irish Journal*. Böll had arrived in 1954, when Ireland was in the horse-and-cart age, but his penetrating—at least I thought it penetrating—analysis of the Irish character warmed the cockles of my heart whenever I needed reassurance that everybody was out of step but me.

Böll had a heart-stopping moment when he got off the boat from Holyhead, his German eye perceiving a swastika on a red vehicle lumbering through the city. It reminded him of the daily delivery in Berlin of the *Völkischer Beobachter*, the strength-through-joy paper that told the Germans how they were winning World War II. On discovering it was just a van delivering sheets from the Swastika Laundry, he settled down to discover Jameson whiskey and wrestle with the rubbery quality of the Irish psyche. His observations were a solace to me while living in Ireland, known in mythology as Tir na n-Og, the land of the young, in the popular ballad as the four green fields, and among schoolchildren as the Land of Saints and Scholars. It seemed to me that a more appropriate symbol would be a tender shamrock, representing the Republic, menaced by a particularly prickly thorn, representing the North of Ireland, where real gunmen were firing real bullets.

The passage by Böll that caught my eye went like this:

When something happens to you in Germany, when you miss a train, break a leg, go bankrupt, we say: It couldn't have been any worse; whatever happens is always the worst. With the Irish it is almost the opposite: if you break a leg, miss a train, go bankrupt, they say: It could be worse; instead of a leg you might have broken your neck, instead of a train you might have missed Heaven, and instead of going bankrupt you might have lost your peace of mind, and going bankrupt is no reason at all for that. What happens is never the worst; on the contrary, what's worse never happens: if your revered and beloved grandmother dies, your revered and beloved grandfather might have died too; if the farm burns down but the chickens are saved, the chickens might have been burned up too, and if they do burn up—well, what's worse is that you might have died yourself, and that didn't happen. And if you should die, well, you are rid of all your troubles, for to every penitent sinner the way is open to Heaven, the goal of our laborious earthly pilgrimage—after breaking legs, missing trains, surviving all manner of bankruptcies. With us—it seems to me—when something happens our sense of humor and imagination desert us; in Ireland that is just when they come into play. To persuade someone who has broken his leg, is lying in pain or hobbling around in a plaster cast, that it might have been worse is not only comforting, it is an occupation requiring poetic talents, not to mention a touch of sadism: to paint a picture of the agonies of a fractured vertebra, to demonstrate what a dislocated shoulder would be like, or a crushed skull—the man with the broken leg hobbles off much comforted, counting himself lucky to have suffered such a minor misfortune.

Thus fate has unlimited credit, and the interest is paid willingly and submissively; if the children are in bed, racked and miserable with whooping cough, in need of devoted care, you must count yourself fortunate to be on your feet and able to look after the children. Here the imagination knows no bounds. "It could be worse" is one of the most common turns of speech, probably because only too often things are pretty bad and what's worse offers the consolation of being relative.

There is no single word or phrase to describe this peculiar condition. It is a combination of pride, fear, predestination, obstinacy, indifference, timidity, dogmatism, monomania, instability, the legacy of centuries of forelock-tugging obsequiousness, cultural inversion, and exultant utopianism that have been welded together across time to form a religious psyche sizzling with paranoia. When I arrived in Dublin, the condition manifested itself in every aspect of life. The politicians in Belfast kept insisting that they were beating the living hell out of peaceful civil rights marchers in order to preserve law and order, while some Dublin politicians were threatening to launch the army across the border in a war of liberation, knowing full well that they did not have the financial resources to administer the place for a month. The totalitarian regime in the North, for by 1971 it had truly become a police state, talked scornfully about the pretensions of democracy in the South, where a citizen could not even buy a book of his choice.

The reaction in the Republic to Protestant charges that the South is a theocratic state brought some puzzling answers. Discussing the Protestant fear of domination by Catholics, Liam de Paor, in his book *Divided Ulster,* says: "It was, in other words, not so much that the majority quarreled with the doctrines accepted by the Catholics (although they did) but that they feared that if ever the Catholics should come to power in Northern Ireland, a theocratic tyranny would be instituted. *The fact that no such tyranny has been instituted in the overwhelmingly Roman Catholic state on the other side of the border appears to have had little effect in dispelling this fear.*"* Every man to his own tyranny, but when a bookseller can be prosecuted for selling not only some wild Maoist treatise on

* Emphasis added.

revolution but a mild entertainment like J. P. Donleavy's *The Ginger Man,* there is some evidence of an infringement on civil liberties that was not organized by a posse of puissant peasants demanding clean literature.

"Ireland carries memory in her mouth like an old hunting bitch," W. R. Rodgers, a North of Ireland man who spent a lot of his time in Dublin, once wrote, and a more pungent line about the love-hate relationship with the dead people who haunt the country never was written. In Ireland, a water spaniel puppy who is earmarked for work in the field is trained by throwing a ball of wire; when the dog bites the wire, it develops what hunting men call "a soft mouth." Evermore, the dog is convinced that the duck it fetches has a protective layer of spiky, blood-drawing steel underneath that deceptive soft coat of down and feathers. When Irish historians bite into a chunk of history, it almost always draws blood.

As for modern heroes, Ireland dismisses all candidates, waiting until they are safely dead before giving a final judgment, although even when a man is dead for sixty years, quarrels about his orthodoxy can hold up the decision. James Connolly, the country's only socialist of international distinction—true believers in the Soviet Union write theses on him—is still in a kind of historical limbo. He is either an agent of Satan, a blistering anti-Pope, a nationalize-the-churches-and-make-them-brothels heathen, or a prophet before his time. The jury meets every Saturday night in the pubs, but the chances of a verdict in this century are slim; because every political ideology is treated with caution as a foreign menace, the smart money is betting on a hung jury.

Lacking candidates for greatness because native politicians are slightly shop-soiled—too much is known about either their sexual peccadilloes, their drinking habits, or their slightly illegal business dealings—the Irish thirst for a national hero has transcended national boundaries. Nobody has qualified as the Man on the White Horse since Parnell was downed from his steed in the nineteenth century by that bedroom business with Kitty O'Shea. Poor Kitty is memorialized daily by people who suspect a neighbor of extramarital encounters. "A right little Kitty O'Shea, that wan," they say. The arrival of the Kennedys presented a fine nobility for national adulation. No eruption of mass orgasmic excitement exceeded that of a historic day when Jack Kennedy presented himself at Aras an Uachtarain, the President's house in Dublin's Phoenix Park. The blooming shrubs were crushed to pulp when Kennedy appeared with blind old Eamon de Valera to meet with the cream of pushy Irish society—stockbrokers, building contractors, lawyers, nuns, priests, bishops, politicians, horse trainers, and reformed gunmen, who, in their attempt to touch the hem of the hero's garment, mounted a charge of such determined wild-eyed ferocity that Jack skipped back nimbly to the drawing room. Dunganstown, reputed to be the home of the original Kennedy, is now a national shrine, a venerated stop on the tourist circuit. Having been born in that part of the country myself, I asked a relative if he knew what the Kennedys really thought about Ireland. The reply was interesting. "The first time Jack Kennedy arrived, everyone around here was bringing milk to the creamery in an ass and cart. He is supposed to have said, driving up the hill to Dunganstown, 'Jesus, this is like Tobacco Road,' so he didn't stay very long. When he became a big shot, he couldn't say enough nice things about the place." There is also a local story that when relatives to the tenth degree of kindred were posing for a family portrait, one old curmudgeon refused, complaining with the insight of an impious student of the largesse of American politicians on their own soil, "What's that fellow ever done for me? He expects us to down tools for nothing."

The hunt for "one of our own kind" abroad has intensified since then. Nixon's elevation to the White House triggered an elaborate search of the archives of old Quaker graveyards that might bring a Milhous or a Nixon to light. Many a McGovern presented credentials when the senator popped out of the obscurity of South Dakota. Even the benighted Thomas Eagleton, shock treatments and psychiatric care notwithstanding, was clasped to the national bosom. ("He's one of the Eagletons from Offaly, you know.") Visiting Americans who care about such matters check into their ancestral tree carefully, none more diligently than Muhammad Ali, who needed to drum up some headlines for a warm-up fight in Dublin's Croke Park against a journeyman fighter, Al "Blue" Lewis. Dublin had been dropped from the international moneymaking circuit by the big men of boxing after Battling Siki had been whipped by Mike McTigue on St. Patrick's Day, 1923. In order to apply a coating of local interest, Ali announced that his good left hand was the gift of an Irish slaveowner on de ole plantation, a fellow who had exercised *droit du seigneur* on his sainted great-grandmother. The announcement sent the odds on Ali to a prohibitively low level and prompted students to rush to the National Library for preparatory work on monographs about the influence of Irish capitalism on cotton prices in the Deep South in the era before Grant took Richmond.

Recently, a road mender named King claimed President Gerald Ford as a member of the King clan, registering his familial connection at a bogside press conference solemnly recorded by the Irish media. Even Charles de Gaulle, in death, has been gathered to the collective Irish breast as a son, or great-grandson, of the Old Sod; apparently Big Charlie had a dropeen of the right blood. Hibernian primogeniture is a quixotic business. It is absolutely essential that any aspirant for greatness arrange to be born abroad of Irish lineage. The rules stipulate that native-born talent is inferior, as one Irish journalist recently acknowledged:

At home the Irish film directors argue with the Industrial Development Authority about the nationality of the grandmother of a Mr. Ginna, just as in the earlier days of RTE [the Irish television authority], a Mr. Roth, newly appointed to run the place, was hailed as having had at some time or other that ubiquitous Irish grandmother. The fact that most of us at home had Irish grandmothers seems to be beside the point. Most of us haven't made the grade.

Spike Milligan, the English comedian, who claims Irish ancestry himself when in Dublin, tried to add a new dimension to the game by suggesting that Mao Tse-tung be gifted with the title "Irishman of the Year" when the Chinese hero made his marathon crossing of the Yangtze River. This was not as flippant as it seemed; a few Irish sociologists had seriously compared Ireland's condition to that of China during the Cultural Revolution. As with the Chinese, the Irish rest their claim to greatness on an ancient civilization. The young are obeisant to the elderly, the native language is impenetrable to outsiders, they are inveterate gamblers. Mao's counterpart, Eamon de Valera, has bequeathed to the nation his most precious tenets of wisdom in a chapbook, the Irish Constitution, which mostly tells the citizens what they cannot do.

The Irish like nothing better than to make-believe. This is a gerontocratic society, with all the crankiness, authoritarianism, and idiosyncrasies of old age. A lot of damage on the old body is hidden, the mental baggage of centuries is stored away in the attic. (The very thought of psychiatric examination makes the Irish tremble. Even John Huston's movie *Freud* was banned.) This leads to pretensions and illusions of a dangerous but lovable sort. Like an old person who has given up on doctors, resorting instead to the ministrations of a faith healer, such as Finbarr Nolan, the seventh son of a seventh son, the Irish don't like to talk about the harsh realities. For example, foreign writers come away with the impression that suicide is practically nonexistent. What the real suicide rate is nobody knows, because medical men, solicitous of the welfare and social standing of families, never ascribe the cause of death to suicide, even though the victim might have ingested a pint of poison or hanged himself in the barn by a stout rope.

The population of Dublin, as I can attest from experience and observation, consumes more Librium, Valium, and other forms of tranquilizers per capita than the residents of any other city, another statistic that does not appear in *Facts About Ireland,* the little book put out by the Department of Foreign Affairs. And another fact worth mentioning here, in making a preliminary examination of the ailing patient, is that the Irish spend more money on the national drug, alcohol, than any other nation—11 percent of their disposable income, three times as much as Americans. Why the Irish drink so much is a mystery that the talents of sociologists and scientists have never unraveled, but it is certainly a temporary way of closing the door on the nastiness that lies outside. Curiously, stress and anxiety, the corrosive maladies that we associate with an industrial society, are endemic in the Emerald Isle. The number of people hospitalized each year for the treatment of mental illness is astonishingly high, certainly the highest in Europe.

This book is a patient, loving, nerve-jangling, benevolent, but, I hope, objective portrait of a people who are wandering around slightly dazed after a head-on collision with the twentieth century. It is, I think, an ailment that affects us all, from the upholsterer in West Virginia whose home is about to be gobbled up by a gargantuan strip-mining machine to the farmer on the Rhine whose animals are being slowly poisoned by the effluent pouring down from a faceless multinational conglomerate chemical plant upstream. If you need a clue as to how the Irish are surviving in these stormy times, I recall a story about the confrontation of the old and the new, between the fishermen of a small village in the South of Ireland and the Harvard Business School–trained executives of a mighty United States food company. Like most American executives, the visitors were full of logical plans to expand the sales and earnings of their corporation; that prosperity could be shared, they explained, if the fishermen would undertake 180-day voyages to the tuna-fishing grounds of the South Atlantic. All the facts were presented on charts, the arrival of monster fishing boats required only a telephone call to some shipyard, the discounted cash flow was calculated down to the mill, architects' renderings of a scientific, automated canning plant were tantalizingly displayed. The fishermen listened earnestly, then retired to a nearby hostelry, where the merits of that golden cash flow were examined. The spokesmen for the villagers returned and with the hint of a smile said, "We believe every word you say, but there's just one little problem. Sure, if we went out for a hundred and eighty days we'd miss getting home for the dinner."

1

Dear, Dirty Dublin

The people who live at longitude 6°17′30″, latitude 53°20′38″, a place almost as far north as Magnitogorsk or Kamchatka in the Soviet Union, have only one predictable element in their lives, the weather. Dublin's geographical position subjects the city to the inexorable dictates of North Atlantic weather, a debilitating experience that accounts for a great deal of the moodiness in Irishmen. An occasional summer day when the low scudding clouds are chased away to Europe by a welcome sun, blinding in the clear Northern air, is hot enough to melt the asphalt on the city streets and enables the editors of the *Evening Herald* to dust off the type for the longed-for front-page headline, "HEAT-WAVE STRIKES." And in the winter there is an unexpected charge of purposefulness among the people when the frozen streets, as crisp as permafrost, ring with energy. But mostly it is rain, sweeping in from the Atlantic and across Ireland in thunderous squalls by the bucketful, falling in a jet-fine mist that enters the very bones. Every Dubliner is a meteorologist of sorts, capable of telling the next hour's weather from the look of the green fields on the Dublin mountains, the behavior of the domesticated ducks in Saint Stephen's Green, or the erratic direction of the swirling breezes.

> The glass is falling hour by hour the glass will fall
>   forever,
> But if you break the bloody glass, you won't hold up
>   the weather.

Like the poet Louis MacNeice, Dubliners endure the rain-saturated air, though they often get as moody as the Tlingit Indians. If things go wrong in the office, if, as is more likely to occur, the unreliable telephone system breaks down, the Dubliner reacts in one of two ways. He will grimly leave the office, head for the nearest bar or hotel, and, along with others who have been infected with despair, launch an impromptu potlatch, where a great deal of firewater is consumed in the course of praising deceased nobles and relatives and damning the weather. Or, if he finishes out the day, he gets an attack of "rain fever" on the way home. As he gets inside the door, he breaks things, shouts meaningless phrases, beats the children for any trifling accident. Like the Indians, the Dublin man recovers quickly. When his nerves calm down, he becomes his usual resentful but resigned self.

Nobody in the business of predicting the future could have foreseen two decades ago that revolutionary events would so transform the pattern of life that even the weather, as a subject for improvisational conversation, would become secondary. In the fifties, Dublin was, to speak kindly of the place, a small somnolent capital city of a country that had lost its nerve. Dear, dirty Dublin, as the natives called it, was a profoundly accurate description; a lot of houses, rented quarters dating back fifty years and more, had neither hot water nor a bathroom. Appropriately, the largest, though by no means the most handsome, building of the postwar era was the Busarus, an immense concrete bus terminal, conveniently located to service the country emigrants on their way to Canada, England, or the United States. A permanent form of organized charity existed; the Boot

Fund, for example, provided footwear for needy children. Legally registered, a political party calling itself "The Unemployed" managed to elect one member to Parliament, but efforts to stir up the proletariat by staging sit-down strikes on O'Connell Bridge failed. The working population was itself only a half step from poverty. It was part of the immutable law of economic survival then that nothing would be wasted; old rags, bottles, bones, wastepaper, tires, bricks, barbed wire, even the dung dropped by tired old horses hauling loads through the streets was put through what ecologists now choose to call a recycling process. Like Londoners in the blitz, Dubliners are stimulated by hard times. However poor they may be, they consider themselves a cut above the "culchies" of rural Ireland; as bad as things seem, they are worse elsewhere, and even if they are not, Dublin, with all its faults, is a better place to live. This feeling of parochial pride was embodied in the person of Jimmy O'Dea, a low-life comic of genius, who brought the ragged audiences of the Gaiety Theatre to their feet when, dressed in the drag of a long-suffering Dublin mother, he warbled the welcome words:

> You may travel from Clare to the County Kildare,
> From Galway right down to Macroom,
> But where would you find a fine widow like me,
> Biddy Mulligan the pride of the Coombe?

While the Russians were firing Sputnik I to signal the beginning of the race to the moon, Dublin was dormant in dark introspection. Those who had a little money—and the city always seemed to have a few people with the means for a taste of conspicuous consumption—spent it on a Walpurgisnacht. The antics of the tipsy guests and staff of the Dolphin Hotel went beyond eccentricity. The owner of the establishment, "as decent a man as ever stepped into shoe leather," as a waiter remembers him, provided golf clubs for everyone after the official closing hour, lethal instruments when used on the big river rats that were chased from the subterranean kitchens by the staff. Bets were placed on this grisly game, and the carcasses were neatly piled at the feet of the players like full game bags at the end of a country pheasant shoot. The scene was a minor reenactment of those bizarre events in the eighteenth century, when the bucks and rakes indulged in diabolism, dueling, or even riding horses into stuccoed drawing rooms, a style of life that was tolerated by the authorities, V. S. Pritchett tells us, "in order to keep high spirits out of political action."* In the 1950s, the authorities, in the persons of judges and politicians, were seeing and chasing rats in the Dolphin.

By the time I had settled down in Dublin in the winter of 1972, the city had made a quantum jump from that kind of spiritual and physical squalor. Although I had witnessed the physical changes while visiting Dublin intermittently over the years, I wanted to know if local experts could pinpoint a single event, or some ringing public declaration of faith, that had snapped Dublin out of its mental torpor. The question puzzled Dubliners. Not alone did they not want to talk about the past ("Sure we're a great little country now, thank God"), but the question implied the existence of an oligarchy capable of caus-ing dramatic changes, a political and business Mafia cracking the whip. Despite much evidence to the contrary, Dubliners cling to the notion that, while the city might be corrupt in some ways, democracy extends right into the tiny flats of the most scabrous tenement, a state of mind reinforced in hard times by the delivery of food or coal or medicine that is the gift of the Tammany-style political system. Even those who wrote about the change while it was taking place were annoyingly vague about the genesis of the transformation. Tim Pat Coogan, a journalist and boulevardier, in his book *Ireland Since the Rising*, published in 1966, says: "The conviction that things could be improved has dawned on a people conditioned to

* V. S. Pritchett, *Dublin: A Portrait*. London, Bodley Head, 1967. New York, Harper & Row, 1967.

believe that they could only get worse." Two years later, Garret FitzGerald, the busy economist, politician, and all-round booster of the wounded Irish ego, attributed the change to "a transformation of the outlook of the Irish people." Both men were writing about what has come to be known as the "New Ireland," but because Dublin's size and population dwarf the rest of the country, I assume that their analysis covered the capital city. Knowing the strange ways in which Irish institutions work (at one point the administration of the city of Dublin was fired by the national government following a quarrel over local taxation), I could only conclude that the most powerful businessmen and politicians had decided, by osmosis, to make a last stand in Dublin, where they would pit all the remaining human and material resources against the creeping decay that had brought the rest of the country to its knees. This collective decision was not made, I hasten to add, in such an urgent framework, for if there is one element immutable in the Irish character it is the inability to face the music, the intuitive feeling noted by Heinrich Böll that things could always be worse.

In any event, the slow process began; one apartment building erupted, one shopping center, one hotel, one school, one housing development. Pretty soon a mild real estate boom was under way, attracting capital hitherto lying dormant in London banks. Foreign institutions began to take an interest. The Chase Manhattan Bank appeared on the scene, to be followed inevitably by its big competitor, the First National City Bank, then the Bank of Nova Scotia, the Algemene Bank Nederland, Banque Nationale de Paris, the First National Bank of Chicago, London's National Westminster Bank, and a profusion of merchant bankers. The arrival of such financial giants, all, of course, in need of new accommodations, generated a little building boom of its own, but, most important, it signified that there was big money to be made in Dublin, a message to buoy the confidence of Dubliners. What the big financial houses were chasing was *not* the discovery of North Sea oil, nor the opening of some big manufacturing complex that would require a consortium of international lenders, but a real estate boom. However, the presence of the foreigners unquestionably spurred Dublin into a ferment of construction. The trade unions joined in by putting up Liberty Hall, a new office tower, still the tallest in the land. Construction was the physical proof of the transformation. It also served to hide, in dangerous fashion, the hidden wound of Ireland, the depopulation of the countryside.

The astonishing growth of Dublin has undeniably been achieved at the expense of the other small towns and cities. In Dublin, the population density is fifty times greater than that of Leitrim, a most desolate county, which is just ninety miles away but has shared not at all in the increasing wealth of the capital city. One out of every four Irish workers now lives in greater Dublin, whose population of 850,000 is twice as large as the total of the people in the next four cities, Cork, Limerick, Waterford, and Galway, with the population of all the other principal towns in the country thrown in. Real estate speculators perform wondrous deeds overnight, as the residents of London and New York and other big cities know to their regret, but nowhere is the destructive power of the speculator more appallingly evident than in Dublin. The city is the hub of every aspect of national life. It handles most of the air traffic, 90 percent of shipping; functions as the center of politics, government, law, education, banking, insurance, retailing, wholesaling; it is the headquarters town for most of the largest private companies; its supremacy is established as the gossiping and work place for those interested in the arts.

Dublin attained this lopsided eminence by gathering to itself a lot of activities which, by reason of its location, it is not really entitled to. Most of the government's rural endeavors, such as the Agricultural Credit Corporation, the Meat and Livestock

Board, the Milk Board, the Pigs and Bacon Commission, the Sea
Fisheries Board, and the Peat Board, snuggle close to each other
in Dublin's new office blocks, cheek by jowl with private enterprises like Gael Linn, which exists to help preserve the Irish
language in villages more than a hundred miles away, the
Inland Waterways Commission, and even, the final illogical
touch, the Irish Countrywomen's Association. Given the propensity of the Irish for the centralization of authority, an
eventual merger of all these enterprises, which, it must be
noted, serve a population no greater than that of Brooklyn, will
eventually take place. The surviving organization will probably
be called Bord na Bord in Gaelic, or in English Board of
Boards, like Bernie Cornfeld's Fund of Funds. During the
sixties, the government paid lip service to the idea of decentral-
izing some of its activities, and the plans were spelled out in
learned reports written by urbanologists, transport specialists,
and management consultants like Arthur D. Little and Mc-
Kinsey and Company. While the experts were studying the
situation, a small increase of 160,000 in the national population occurred between 1960 and 1971, to which Dublin contributed 133,000. To place this alarming growth in its proper
context, the population of Dublin County, with an area of 356
square miles, was, at the beginning of the seventies, equal to the
combined population of twelve other counties—Cavan, Monaghan, Galway, Leitrim, Sligo, Mayo, Roscommon, Clare, Kilkenny, Offaly, Westmeath, and Donegal—with an area thirty-six
times greater.

Dublin still preserves the intimate charm of a small town, but
the ravages of instant growth are beginning to show: noise,
pollution, crime, overcrowding, and a fouled-up transportation
system that cannot possibly function in the matrix of a town
designed two centuries ago for horse traffic. Every day, the
already chesty populace ingests some of the seven thousand tons
of effluent pumped into the atmosphere; coal is still an impor-

tant source of fuel for home heating. In the summer, when the resident population is augmented by shoppers and visitors from the country and by tourists (the Republic is visited by 1,250,000 tourists every year), traffic occasionally slows to a state of total immobility. The number of cars on Irish roads increased by 57 percent between 1965 and 1972, and on occasion it seems as if the majority of them are traversing the narrow streets of Dublin. Even the usually accommodating policemen become testy in such circumstances. A visitor attempting to find a parking place near the city center asked a policeman what a single solid yellow line represented. "It means you can't park there at all." Well, what about a double solid yellow line? "That means you can't park there at all, at all. Away with you."

The explosive growth of Dublin has brought in its wake an alarming increase in crime, ranging all the way from the pilferage of color television sets to professional bank robberies. In 1971, the number of burglaries increased by 36 percent over the previous year; more than half of those crimes were committed in Dublin, not, it should be noted, at night but in broad daylight. "Skinheads," the new breed of young urban fascists so graphically portrayed by Anthony Burgess in *A Clockwork Orange,* made their appearance in Dublin in the sixties shortly after the phenomenon surfaced in Britain. A wandering mob of skinheads in strange territory is an arresting sight, for the group carries with them an angry brooding air of imminent unpredictable violence. A pedestrian who jostles a skinhead can expect a physical response, the least damaging being a swift kick by a steel-tipped "bovver"-booted foot. Police statistics show that Friday night, between the hours of 9 P.M. and 3 A.M., when the bored working population begins the first lengthy potlatch of the weekend, is an especially dangerous time; an unaccompanied pedestrian in the center of Dublin can expect to meet violence any moment. In some districts, 60 percent of all crimes are committed on Friday nights, a concentrated period of physical clashes that strains police manpower to the limit and enables the visitor to go to bed to the musical sound of shattering glass.

Although muggings and robberies take place, a lot of the violence seems to be an explosion of anger at the system, a brooding resentment that is carried to the surface by the enormous quantities of alcohol that Dubliners consume on weekends. Heavy drinking is not confined to skinheads and slum dwellers. Most Dublin automobile accidents occur on weekends, the most lethal time to be on the road demonstrably occurring on Sunday night after the shouts "Time, gentlemen, please!" There are some powerful sexual taboos and traditions at work here, the residue of a tribal culture that urban life has not changed. To begin with, most of the drinking is a males-only affair; steady dating in Ireland is tantamount to a promise of marriage, a state that the Irish male resists as long as possible. Second, the tradition of buying rounds for the company, even if as many as twenty people are in the party, is an unbreakable one. Thus each individual is confronted at closing hour with perhaps half a dozen glasses of whiskey, to be tossed off in fast order, a test of machismo. Third, alcohol is consciously used by the Irish as a quick release from some crippling inhibitions: a deep sense of inferiority and a tribal taboo that bars sexual intercourse outside of marriage. Although enough scientific studies exist to prove the validity of all these points, few Irishmen would admit to them. Being a "good" drinker in Dublin means drinking a lot; to a father of ten children with a weekly income of fifty dollars it is, perhaps, the only release from rigid depression. The wonders of a pint of Guinness stout to the Dublinman were sung often, too often, some people would say, by the part-time writer and full-time raconteur Brian O'Nolan:

> When food is scarce and your larder bare,
> And no rasher grease your pan.
> When hunger grows as your meals are rare,
> *A pint of plain is your only man.*

> In time of trouble and lousy strife,
> You still have a darlint plan.
> You still can turn to a brighter life,
> *A pint of plain is your only man.*

The average Dublin worker closely resembles his New York counterpart in at least one other important but, for Ireland, disastrous way: he does not toil at the factory bench. White-collar workers are as ubiquitous on the South Bank of the River Liffey as they are in Wall Street; fully two-thirds of Dublin's working population earn their daily bread by office tasks or by providing services. A study by Michael J. Bannon* contains some bad news for tourists who expect to find the modern-day equivalent of Molly Malone wheeling her wheelbarrow through streets broad and narrow. Bannon calculates that the fastest-growing area of employment in the country is office work. In 1972, some 11 million feet of office space were in use in Dublin, or about seven times the footage available in New York's Pan American Building. Builders were adding another 1.2 million feet of space at the time he was writing, while proposals were on file for additional space, including an overpowering thirty-seven-story hotel-office tower on a four-and-a-half-acre site. If the trend continues, Bannon estimates that by 1991 some 290,000 people will be engaged just in office work, or about 20 percent of the total work force, the majority of those people in Dublin. Such forecasts draw speculators like barkers to a revival meeting, for there is nothing a willing financier likes to see accompany a mortgage application more than a well-documented study that promises long lines of eager, well-heeled tenants. Mr. Bannon's work promises all that and more.

New office construction is concentrated in a small area of the city, which happens to be also the most desirable residential section by far, and threatens to spread like a cancerous growth

* *Office Location in Ireland: The Role of Central Dublin.* Dublin, An Forus Forbartha (The National Institute for Physical Planning and Construction Research) , 1973.

across the South Side of Dublin within twenty years. The consequences of unchecked commercial building are obvious: high-
rise boxes will ruin the sight lines of old Dublin and make the
use of city land for residential housing financially impossible.
Already some of the old squares built in the eighteenth century
have been destroyed; others retain only a façade, the interiors of
the old russet-brick houses having been gutted for air-condi-
tioned office space. Planning and zoning laws exist that are
supposed to prohibit such plunder, but local authorities have
chosen not to enforce the law to the letter. In 1940, the Dublin
planning authority attempted to hold new buildings to a height
of eighty feet, a restriction that has been broken many times
since then. Because state and local governments are large users
of office space, a 1963 act that set out to control real estate
development was amended to exempt those bodies; apparently
the civil servants felt they, too, might want to enter the high-
rise construction business.

Financial experts I talked to said that one of the reasons for
the real estate boom was that many prominent national politicians were heavily involved in land speculation. Such a charge is
difficult to document, mainly because Irish politicians do not
have to declare their financial holdings, nor are they disquali-
fied from voting on measures that might benefit them or their
families. Under Irish law, the real owners of land and buildings
can safely remain anonymous. But the charge deserves to be
weighed carefully when one is confronted by an astounding
fact. In a country that has enjoyed almost zero population
growth for fifty years, prices for developed land for single-family
houses increased by 2,700 percent, from £1,110 an acre in 1960
to £30,000 an acre in 1973. In a four-year period the price of a
very modest four-bedroom house increased from £5,000 in mid-
1967 to £8,300 in 1971. Even the resale price of houses jumped
in spectacular fashion from an average of £2,112 in 1960 to
£5,201 in 1970. Sites for apartment buildings were sold for
£100,000, or almost $230,000, an acre in 1973. Allowing lib-

erally for inflation and the cost of raw materials, such enormous increases, especially in land prices, seem to be manipulated by factors other than supply and demand. And what is one to make of a law that defines a high building in Dublin as "a building significantly higher than neighboring or surrounding developments"? Any lawyer worth his salt could drive a Caterpillar tractor through such vague jargon.

An example of the futility of the legal restrictions is the enormous Burlington Hotel near the American Embassy; the builder-owner exceeded the mandatory height by two additional stories, while local outraged residents were unsuccessfully seeking an injunction to halt construction. In Dublin, I attended a dinner of the Master Builders Association, the fellows who were getting rich by putting up the ticky-tacky houses and the concrete boxes. The manicured master builders were dressed in a variety of midnight blue, maroon, and white dinner jackets. Accompanied by their coiffed wives, they sat through the potlatch with the jolly air of men who were looking to an endless reprise of their new-found prosperity. When the *Irish Times* asked a cross-section of citizens to write articles on the theme "Whither Dublin?" architect Niall Montgomery concluded:

So strange is Dublin in the Seventies that the Red Bank,* for instance, is now an R.C. church, and that one takes for granted the conversion into what looks like restaurants of the R.C. churches of the archdiocese, long admired as symbols of post-Emancipation Dublin. (Clearly the main effect of the Penal Laws was to close the licensed trade† to the unfortunate Protestants.)

What's better about Dublin to-day? That's just a question. Forget it.

What's worse? What's worse is the rustically operated corporation letting the developers crucify the city and blaming everyone but themselves for the mess. (What became of the City Council?)

* A restaurant.
† Bar business.

What does one miss? The Pillar blown up by the same hill tribes
that built Ballymun.*

The destruction of Dublin appears to be guided at times by
mysterious forces, perhaps some marauding band of anarchic
lepracauns whose deeds are greeted by the natives in puckish
fashion. Quite unaccountably, the new headquarters of the
Central Bank turned out to be substantially taller, by some fifty
feet, than originally contemplated. Were the architect's plans
switched at night by the little people? Eminent construction
experts assisted by the hill tribesmen with trowels in their hands
stared at the building. How, they wondered, could it be cut
down to its correct dimensions? Would it topple over? An eminent architect came up with the correct, pragmatic, Hibernian
solution: split the difference by sawing off twenty-five feet of the
excess. He was hailed as a hero.

Seen from the air, the city looks like a gray Sargasso Sea of
concrete, stretching relentlessly to embrace the market gardens
and meadows surrounding it. Outside the harbor, floating past
the Hill of Howth, the blue-green sea carries the raw untreated
sewage along the coast. The architectural legacy of the Anglo-
Irish aristocracy is almost invisible from here, as if the great
squares, wide streets, and handsome town houses that date back
to the Wide Streets Commission of 1742 had never existed.
Exuberant nationalism has attempted to deliberately erase from
history the distinctive culture of the Anglo-Irish, a rakish crew
who were lavish spenders, builders of monuments to themselves,
but, still, patrons of the arts, not patronizers as so many of the
native Irish were and are. The Anglos gave Dublin the Royal
Dublin Society, the Royal Hibernian Academy, the Royal Irish
Academy of Music, among other institutions; they fostered what
is distinctive about Irish life today, especially all the endless,

* A high-rise suburban apartment center, built to accommodate dwellers from
the city-center slums.

entertaining talk. In the twentieth century, the Irish added nothing to the graceful outlines of Dublin. The *Encyclopaedia of Ireland,* published in 1968, has pages of illustrations of the monuments of the old aristocracy, the Customs House, the old Houses of Parliament (now the Bank of Ireland), Powerscourt House, the Rotunda, the Coombe Hospital, the Law Courts, Georgian squares, and somber country houses like Castletown and Carton. Of the twentieth century the *Encyclopaedia* simply says, "Most of the house building which has taken place in the present century has not been carried out under the direction of architects; consequently, while the houses provided are a social asset, they do not exhibit any kind of architectural achievement." This is a wild overstatement. The hill tribes that built twentieth-century Dublin took their cue from the monstrosities that pass for human shelter in Luton, Coventry, Bristol, and all the other grimy factory towns of that class-encrusted country. A day spent touring the monochromatic boxes in the Dublin suburbs, each house surrounded by a concrete wall waist-high, suggests the presence of a people who are blind to the squalor of their own stultifying environment.

The intense burst of real estate speculation has created some strange kinks in the economy. For one thing, because Ireland must import most of its raw materials, plus a good deal of consumer and industrial goods, construction accounts for a sizable part of the increase in the annual trade deficit. The deficit increased by 245 percent in four years, from $36 million in 1968 to $123 million in 1972. Second, although inflation is aggravated because of Ireland's overdependence on trade with Britain, some homemade ingredients add to the wild burst of inflation. Between the summers of 1972 and 1973, the cost of living increased by 11 percent, a figure that concealed a very important statistic. Food prices, in a country that always has a surplus, went up by 13.4 percent; the Irish, while they might not eat too wisely, are used to enormous quantities of food, and the box score on food prices rates front-page treatment in newspapers. The dark news about inflation really hit home in July, 1973, when it was disclosed that the Dubliner was paying more for such staples as bread, potatoes, butter, pork, and chicken than the Londoner. The government had anticipated rising prices some years before when it devised a method of heading off the kind of national strike that periodically paralyzes Britain. The Dublin government grants annual across-the-board pay increases to everybody far surpassing any measurable increase in productivity, thus cutting the heart out of the classic labor union argument that workers deserve more money because they produce more goods. Dubliners, the vast majority of whom are employed in offices and service jobs, producing nothing but blizzards of paper, were happy to take any increase, even though Ireland is at the top of the list every year in the measurement of European inflation.

Pumping money into an already artificially stimulated economy is a dangerous business. Most classical economists believe that the technique must end eventually in an inglorious, unavoidable crash. By some measurements, Ireland seemed to be living on the dangerous edge of a cliff when I was there in 1972 and '73. The tourist business had dropped off, largely because of the fighting in Northern Ireland. Some hotels in Dublin were losing money in 1973; indeed, a few changed hands because of mortgage foreclosure. The really ominous news, however, was buried in the minutely detailed financial reports of the Central Bank of Ireland. In May, 1973, more than 20 percent of total bank credit was extended in the form of personal loans to individual customers. Clearly, those generous wage increases were not sufficient for families struggling with inflation; they were resorting to bank borrowing to balance their budgets. Moreover, the banks had given more money to real estate speculators than they had to such small but important businesses as the metals and engineering industries. The unlimited availability of credit, a newfangled idea in a traditionally conservative country, produced an impression of instant prosperity. Even with all that stimulation, though, the number of unemployed equaled the total working population in the construction industry.

Just as in the Ponzi scheme, bankers and real estate operators had come to believe that there was an unlimited number of eager investors down the line who would assume higher and higher interest charges with every transaction. Kevin Kavanagh, a Dublin engineer who had worked in New York, then moved in the sixties to Saint Martin in the Netherlands Antilles to cash in on a local real estate boom, then returned to Dublin, dismissed my Ponzi analogy with a derisive laugh. "Ponzi was ready to wait for his profit; Dubliners want to double their money overnight, and very often they do. Real estate people here have the unrealistic expectations we had in Saint Martin when we waited for all those rich New York stockbrokers to get off the plane on Friday evening to inspect a piece of land. As long as they had paper profits in their stock portfolios, they were ready to pay anything for a second home, provided, of course, it was financed by a bank. When the big bust came, the paper profits eroded, the contracts they had signed weren't worth the paper they were written on, while the land we had optioned went back to the original owners." When I asked Kavanagh if he was dabbling at anything in the building line, he looked shocked. "I'm selling the concrete panels for those buildings across the street. For cash."

It should be said that the seemingly unlimited availability of money for private construction does not carry over into government operations. Researchers in Dublin's National Library are cautioned to avoid seat number seventy-four, which lies directly under an annoying leak in the roof. Other parts of the building, which is only a stone's throw from Leinster House, the seat of Parliament, are subject to dry rot. Apart from its decrepit state, the National Library is too small to house such essential documents as maps and newspapers.

Dubliners are tardy about starting the day. As the local expression has it, a citizen will not stir from his house until the streets are "well aired," a reluctance that gives the morning streets the air of a town that is enjoying an early siesta. Life on Monday begins slowly and silently in the debris of the weekend potlatch—stout bottles, beer cans, an occasional immobilized car with smashed fenders. At seven o'clock the first suburban scouts appear, the girl with the key to the office, the man with the key to the safe. One by one, stragglers stop at the red traffic lights around Saint Stephen's Green; at nine o'clock the white-collar army appears in cars, on motorcycles, choking the narrow streets off the square. Those who place a monetary value on time have no place in Dublin; no sooner is the office force assembled than the bell rings for coffee, hot milk, and the gutting of the morning newspaper.

This is a piecework city, a price-for-the-job town, for the repair of a broken pipe, the typing of a letter, or the drawing up of a legal document threatening a slow-paying client. Time means nothing; families who have been moved to the high-rise apartments in Ballymun, near Dublin Airport, are said to be "doing time" while they wait for a one-family house. The sentence is indeterminate; a family with, say, ten children gets preference. At the office where official government publications are sold, an unctuous clerk explains that the latest statistical abstract is for 1967. "Six years ago?" He smiles. "That's the latest." Rows of clerks sitting in converted Georgian mansions are slowly piecing together the numbers telling whether the country did a good job in 1972, a task to be laid aside for another day if the Minister for Transport and Power has to answer some questions that afternoon in Parliament.

The open-air market in Moore Street is beginning to stir

around eleven, but not with sufficient activity to tear an elderly flower seller away from her task of staring at a leggy American girl in skin-tight jeans. "Would you look at that wan, for the love and honor a' God. An arse on her like two rabbits twitchin' in a sack." (Like Les Halles in Paris, Moore Street is about to be seized by property speculators.)

A thousand charitable organizations are registered, it seems; money is collected on "flag days," when tiny lapel flags are sold on the streets for churches, hospitals, athletic groups, the mentally retarded, the salvation of the Irish language. In the Shelbourne Hotel, a businessman from Chicago is nervously rehearsing a pitch he will make later over lunch to a civil servant. To the head porter he chants, "Ever hear of cable television? You know, when you pipe the picture into the home. Well, let me explain. . . ." In a meeting room upstairs, an English executive from Koscot Cosmetics, the pyramid sales company founded by the harelipped Florida wonder boy, Glenn Turner, is telling some Dublin franchise holders how rich Turner really is, how rich they might become. "He actually gave a Cadillac to the two midgets who travel with him. Naturally, they were too small to drive, but they were allowed into a parking lot where one of the little beggars worked the accelerator, while the other little chap sat on his shoulders steering." The Dubliners, tellers of tall, fabulous tales, looked dubious.

"We're destroyed by all the talk," a lot of city dwellers will say, and then spend an hour telling you why that is so. In 1964, Prime Minister Sean Lemass may have started the longest conversation in Irish history when he brought together a committee to talk over the idea of building a concert hall that would be dedicated to the memory of John F. Kennedy. A model of the Kennedy Hall was produced the following year, a sound piece of work (estimated cost $8 million), everybody said at the time, by an Australian architect, Raymond McGrath. The committee, members of all the political parties, stopped talking in 1974; Dublin, with its great musical heritage, will have neither an opera house nor a concert hall. Politicians are rated at the end of each session of Parliament by the length of time they hold the floor, an honored tradition, for it was Joseph Biggar, the Irish parliamentarian, who brought the filibuster to England when he read out meaningless nonsense at Westminster. V. S. Pritchett could not find a comparable society in the English-speaking world; he thought the Irish were similar to Russians in some respects, to the Spanish in others. "If there is a racial contact," wrote Pritchett, "it is the remote but more suggestive one with Galicia: this Biscayan province, misty and gale ridden, is populated by a cunning, thrifty, disputatious and dreamy people who are subject to long fits of despondency and self laceration in the Irish manner. They play a sort of bagpipes and sing sad and pretty ballads. They are notoriously evasive." It was not the flood of talk that bothered Shaw, when he occasionally reminisced about Dublin, but "a certain flippant futile derision and belittlement that confuses the noble and serious with the base and ludicrous."

The talk of the town can be something that happened the day before, something that never happened, or something about to happen, but always laced with the intoxicating ingredient of malice. Gossip has no yeast without a touch of spite. A few days before a national election, a magazine editor with political connections told me the big news. "The candidate is finished, done for, up the spout." He looked scornful but was ready to continue when I gave him a verbal prod. "Out near Foxrock they found him in his undershirt, rolling in the gutter. Singing away to his heart's content while half the police force was looking for him."

"Did you send a photographer out to take a picture?" I asked gingerly.

"For the love of God, we don't do that kind of thing in Dublin. Let the poor man spend his campaign funds in peace."

Men who are known as really good talkers spend hours practicing their stories, polishing up a phrase, rolling the epithets like poets, as indeed most of them are, by inclination if not by trade. One poetic Dublin version of the fighting in Belfast placed two well-known figures at the heart of the action, one a former Cabinet member, the other a retired Irish-American businessman of great wealth. "The two boyos are at the back of the whole thing. Sure, isn't it a well-known fact that the two of them have bought up half the city of Belfast and have an option on the rest? Of course, they'll sell the whole bloody city when the British get out and then get down on their knees and thank God that they had the place to sell. Not to worry. Sure it'll be worse before it's better. I hear the IRA is getting tanks from the Russians."

The machinations of the illuminati are amateurish compared with the real and imagined conspiracies that swirl about the town. Two bank robbers are caught, whereupon London admits that they have a connection with the English spy establishment. "They're not on the British side at all," explains a boulevardier. "They're double agents from our side who were put up to the whole thing to embarrass London." Conspiratorial talk can arise from the most innocent behavior. "Do you know that fella who's the foreign news editor, old what's-his-name? Never comes into the office before four o'clock. What do you think he's doing? Well, this is the way I heard it. He puts little ads in the paper. 'Refined gentleman wants a flat,' that sort of thing. So he has a handful of keys in his pocket that the landlords send in. Off with him every afternoon to the auctions on the quays. He's an expert on Georgian silver, you know. He tiptoes up behind the likeliest-looking woman at the auction. 'Grand example of a Queen Anne cup,' he'll say, giving her the oul' pinch. It doesn't always work, but when it does he always has the key to a flat for a quick bit o' work. And to look at him you wouldn't think there was a crooked bone in his body." Of a well-known actor: "You wouldn't want to bend down to pick up a penny in front of him. He's that way, you know."

Dublin may be a white-collar town because people need the

stimulation of talk; a factory hand making a four-ply radial must concentrate on his task, while an artistic consultant to the Tourist Board has no stock in trade but talk. Dubliners are not so much conversationalists as monologists; even a simple question becomes a declarative statement. Here is a man talking at lunch in a restaurant: "Will you tell me something and get me out of my pain. How did he get that job? How does a fella like that who didn't have an arse in his trousers a few years ago, and by the same token never sat behind a school desk after he was fourteen, how does he nail down a cushy job like that after doin' nothin' but sellin' sheep dip and barbed wire to Galway farmers, and by the same token, let me tell you, sportin' a pioneer pin while he was half drunk every night on potcheen? How, I ask you in the name of the livin' God, did such an unmerciful chancer get the job? I'll tell you. Pull, nothin' else. It's not what you know, it's who you know, like all them Rugby players who toured Australia."

If you miss the talk in the principal watering holes, it is sure to appear in print the next day in one of the city's newspapers, three morning sheets, two in the afternoon. A lot of the stuff is incomprehensible to the visitor, being simply a rendition of someone's monologue from the previous night. The lead paragraph in a column of political analysis in the *Irish Times* will give a fair idea of what I mean:

Of course they have the right to make eejits of themselves. Don't cry on my shoulder. I did me best last week. There I was having Jack lying on the ropes for Liam when the mere Irish had Ted Heath by the short hairs. But before you could say "Colm Condon," damme if they didn't up and make right eejits of themselves and by the end of the week Ted Heath managed to sound virtuous and the greatest friend Ireland ever had when he told the fighting Irish factions, who were still having at it, that, having played the bastard on us, he was enough of a gentleman to admit it privately. I love the cad who seduces a young thing, but even cads keep their mouths shut about it to the old people. In Ireland, of course, when you tell the old people that the daughter has lost her cherry, the father says it was the mother's fault and the mother the father's fault. . . .

A man I showed this to did not explain what it meant, but it triggered more talk. "Begod, the style reminds me of Myles na Gopaleen's parodies. Did you ever hear Myles's best pun? 'The Carmen are not so Bizet as they used to be.' Do you get it? A right wan, I thought. And then he had wan—'The Electricity Supply Board is threatening to weed out and disconnect black sheep.' Best writer we ever had."

While this familiar name dropping—Jack, Liam, Ted, and Myles—might suggest egalitarianism, Dubliners do not live in what a New Yorker would call an open society. Of course, a Dubliner will never admit as much. Ever since the promise of democracy was posted outside the General Post Office by the revolutionaries of 1916, the citizens have told themselves and the world that they indeed live in a classless town. But the great burst of proletarian rhetoric in the 1916 proclamation—"The Republic guarantees religious and civil liberty, equal rights and equal opportunity to all its citizens, and declares its resolve to pursue that happiness and prosperity of the whole nation and of all of its parts, cherishing all the children of the nation equally, and oblivious of the differences carefully fostered by an alien government which have divided a minority from a majority in the past"—was quickly forgotten by a society that, in secret, has a great fondness for class and caste distinctions. The unconscious sycophancy in references and interviews with the remaining Anglo-Irish aristocracy—the Lords Killanin, who succeeded Avery Brundage as the head of the Olympic Committee; Kilbracken, a squire who breeds Herefords; Iveagh, the maker of the pints of stout; Longford, known in England as Lord Porn, for his relentless hunt for pornographers; and the Earl of Rosse, a member of the International Dendrology Association—betrays the sly Irish peasant tip-of-the-cap to the gentry.

Dublin has preserved the stratified class-consciousness of the nineteenth century. While the Irish shun the trip to London for the Queen's Day Awards, they like titles and decorations. Prime Minister Liam Cosgrave is a Knight of the Grand Cross of Pius XI; former Prime Minister John A. Costello wears the Grand Cross of the Pian Order conferred by John XXIII; former Prime Minister Jack Lynch bowed the knee for the Grand Cross of the Belgian Order of the Crown; Eamon de Valera, the first Republican in the land, has three crosses to bear: the Grand Cross of the Order of Pius XI, the Grand Cross of the Order of Charles, and the Grand Cross of Christ. Irish titles would have a more euphonious ring: the Earl of Hackballscross, the Baron of Miltown-Malbay, Lord Lisdoonvarna. The pecking order is as important to the Irish as it is to a titled Australian sheep farmer, who, although he might be the descendant of one of the inmates of the criminal colony in Van Diemen's Land, insists that the help address him as "Sir Alfred." A bank clerk in Dublin sulks if he is not called a bank official, a press officer is a senior administrative assistant to the Cabinet Minister, while every man considers himself an Esquire.

Instead of a court circular, Dublin newspapers publish a list of the callers to Aras an Uachtarain, the stately residence of the President of the Republic. This is not so grand as it seems, however, because it is possible to buy space in the column in order to rub shoulders, figuratively speaking, with the great. Thus a column starts with the item "The President yesterday received at Aras an Uachtarain Princess Grace of Monaco, and Mme. Naida Lacoste"; which is followed by a paid advertisement: "Mary McInerney, M.C.B.T.H., M.A.B.T.H., has opened her salon at 16 Duke Street. Tel. 787352. Health Farm Treatments available. Products by Jean D'Athene of Paris."

As in Britain, the correct accent counts for a lot. Even though a man may be dressed in a tweed garment corrugated by sweat, wear, and time, a style of dress much favored by the gentlemen farmers who visit Dublin, a few words delivered in a high-pitched hoot that suggests the speaker is in the terminal stages of constipation brings the help in a hotel scurrying and heel-clicking like private soldiers to the commanding bark of a company sergeant major. So acute is the Dubliner's ear for the aristocratic hoot, real and pseudo, that he is able to identify the birthplace, school, and present residence of a speaker with unerring accuracy. North Siders are looked down on by South Siders, unless the North Sider has an estate or a title. South Siders divide themselves into the serrated ranks of Rathmines, Terenure, Donnybrook, Stillorgan, while that quaternity of neighboring castes pays homage to the South County Dublin accent, which implies that the speaker had a great-granddaddy who assisted Buck Whaley and his friends at unmentionable rites in the Hell Fire Club in 1746.

My own favorite aristocrats when I lived in Ireland in the fifties were of modest station. Gaisford–St. Lawrence (whether he was a belted earl or a lord suffering from overtaxation, I forget) bicycled down the rhododendron-lined avenue from his castle at Howth to buy the makings of his tea at the little harborside grocery store: a quarter pound of hairy bacon, a loaf, and a bottle of milk. Michael Neale declared himself royalty by rowing out to a bird sanctuary, where he put on the ermine with the title "Prince Michael of the Saltees."

When a Dubliner leaves a city where everybody knows his place, especially if the voyage takes him to the United States, he becomes disoriented, like an Eskimo in New York on the Fourth of July. Prime Minister Jack Lynch, on one of his missionary visits, was perplexed by what he felt was the unfair democracy in American dress. "Why," he asked his aide, Pat Sullivan, "do they all dress the same way?" In Dublin, it is easy to tell a man's rank by his clothes; in Chicago, Mayor Daley looked and sounded to the Prime Minister like some fourth assistant press secretary of the Department of Sanitation. This is a problem that works in reverse and has gotten Dublin an unfortunate name for being ostentatiously anti-American. To

Irish eyes and ears, Americans are like peas in a pod; the first
round of tipping marks out the Yank as either a man of distinction or a man to be ignored. Tipping early and often is
advisable for Americans who wish to be treated with the fawn-
ing gallantry that is accorded a half-pay colonel in a corrugated
tweed suit who is brushed down by Irish punkah wallahs as soon
as he hoots the magic words "I say."

Do I exaggerate? A formidable piece of sociological research
entitled *Social Status and Inter-Generational Social Mobility in
Dublin,* by Bertram Hutchinson* (not a Dubliner by his
name), presents a picture of a city frozen in Victorian obeisance
to caste and class like a fly in amber. Hutchinson interviewed
2,450 Dubliners on their attitudes toward status and success,
phrasing some of his questions not too brusquely, as he says, for
direct questions about status are considered errors of taste.
Dublin, it turns out, is almost a mirror image of Britain when it
comes to the perpetuation of the class structure. The sons of
manual workers find it next to impossible to jump to a high
rank; education is nearly useless as a tool for entry into ruling
circles; the larger the family a man comes from, the lower his
status; half the men in the most prestigious class were born into
it; 42 percent of the working class believe success can be
attained only by luck or by "knowing the right people"; and so
on. Apart altogether from the unmeasurable racial attitudes
that perpetuate class distinctions, there are potent economic
reasons why the "upper classes" in Dublin devised such a
stratified society. To achieve a higher status in a place with a
static population means "bumping" someone who is already in
the catbird seat, as difficult a task for a Dublin workingman as it
is for a black steelworker in the Pittsburgh plant of Jones &
Laughlin. Father-to-son jobs in Dublin are not skilled manual
trades but professional tasks like doctoring, lawyering, or politicking. The census of 1841 counted no fewer than 1,900
lawyers, judges, and barristers in Dublin. The census of 1961

* The Economic and Social Research Institute, Dublin, October, 1969.

showed almost the same number, 1,863 to be exact, in the Republic alone, although the population had dropped by 3 million. This probably accounts for the fact that a house buyer in Dublin must pay three sets of lawyers before he turns the key to his concrete roost.

However, there are class attitudes in Dublin, as in London, that beggar rational analysis. A scene in the Saint Stephen's Green Club, a watering hole for the gentry of the twentieth century, makes my point. The name of Conor Cruise O'Brien was put forward to a membership that included Patrick Donegan, a politician who pumped a shotgun full of lead into the backside of a tinker, and Charles J. Haughey, another politician, who was fired from the Cabinet, then charged with conspiracy in the illegal importation of arms for the IRA. Donegan and Haughey are far from having aristocratic backgrounds or the Donnybrook hoot, but, as with upward-striving New Yorkers, room has been made at the top because they are politically powerful and, by Irish standards, wealthy. O'Brien, by accent, genealogy, and outspoken criticism of shady business dealings, is not quite "one of us" to the most clannish new arrivals at the club, many of whom, on paper at least, have become instant millionaires through the property boom. O'Brien was blackballed.

2

The Devious Arts of the Country Folk

Patrick Donegan, the affable white-haired Minister for Defense in the government of the Republic, likes to tell with a hearty chuckle of the evening he discharged a load of buckshot at the backside of a tinker who was trespassing on his land. The event is worth pondering, as a clue to the state of relations between classes, and as an indication of the Irish countryman's intuitive reaction to the intrusion of any stranger.

Tinkers are the most despised minority in Ireland. Most people believe they will steal just about anything that is not nailed down, including cattle and horses, sell stolen merchandise, and sell unsound animals to the unwary. The legend says they are the descendants of itinerant metalworkers from Asia. They refuse to live in fixed dwellings, sleeping in horse-drawn caravans or motor trailers. They are a walking affront to the modern cult of respectability, preferring to keep their children with them rather than subject them to what they consider the dubious improvements offered by the national schools. Like the Gypsies in Europe, tinkers are a cultural oddity, with their own secret language, complete with cabalistic signs which they leave to guide other tinkers who might follow their path. "A right lot of bloody animals," the doorman of the Great Southern Hotel in Galway said one morning as he watched a family of tinkers cavorting on the grass of Eyre Square facing the hotel. "They all sleep together in their skins at night, like sausages on a pan. Then they come out here and beg until they have enough money for a bottle of wine." An eccentric family of tinkers who attempted to take possession of a Galway house were driven away under a barrage of stones.

When the minister shot the tinker, therefore, nobody thought of it as an extreme or outlandish act. Every farmer in Ireland approved of this sort of quick justice. Nor was this just a case of the propertied against the poor, as a group of Germans discovered when they bought some land and built summer homes in the South of Ireland. There was a good deal of local muttering about the entry of the strangers; when they erected barbed-wire fences across some historic rights-of-way, their houses were put to the torch. Mr. Donegan is very much a man of means, his political life a sort of side venture that brings him convivial friends and an additional wedge of power. He owns a milling company in Drogheda, a small town thirty miles from Dublin; he operates an enormous restaurant outside the town; he is one of the few Irishmen who owns and sails a yacht; and, above all, he is a substantial landowner, the squire of hundreds of acres with grazing herds of thoroughbred cattle.

Land has been to the Irish what hidden gold was to the hard-rock miners of the Klondike—the mother lode. To see a solemn Irish farmer walk with slow deliberate stride across a field, pick up a piece of earth, peer at it from under his salmon-tinted peaked cap, knead it, caress it, smell it, and then pronounce the verdict, "The land is in great heart," is to witness an intense expression of ecstasy. Even the way farmers walk is indicative of their calling; their feet swing very low as if reluctant to leave the comforting presence of solid earth. An Irish-American who returned found himself full of the mystical feeling when he had finally threaded his way through the tricky barriers of Irish law and stood straight-legged on what the Irish call "a great farm of land." "What was the first thing you did?" I asked him, expecting to hear great plans about plowing, crop rotation, or the cross-breeding of Aberdeen Angus and Charolais cattle. "I walked out there and looked down the road where my grandfather must have passed on his way to Boston. I thought about that for a while and about the English who wouldn't even give him a cup of water on his way. It was a great feeling." He spat on the ground with embarrassment.

The supreme attraction for visitors to Ireland, judging by the pictures and text of an elaborate folder given to callers at the Irish Tourist Board office in New York, is the antique unspoiled countryside. "In Ireland new acquaintances soon become old friends," goes the introduction. "With a smile, a wave, a nod of the head—you know you're welcome the minute you arrive in Ireland. The people are glad to see you: the man you pass carting milk to the creamery, the woman busy in her garden, the children happy in their play. You are very welcome indeed whether you stop to chat, ask directions or simply return a 'hello' for the tip of a cap or the lift of a hand. Ireland is very personable. We like it that way—we know you will too." All the likely tourist trips are there: Connemara, the Cliffs of Moher, the Aran Islands, Killarney, Dingle, and Donegal; the sporting scene "that has to be seen"; Puck Fair for the crowning of a "he-goat"; the Kilkenny Beer Festival, "merry making amid a blend of Irish, Bavarian, and international music"; the International Four-Day Walk; the Mary of Dunglow Festival; the Westport Sea Anglers Festival; the Spanish Point Holiday Festival; and the Castlebar International Song Festival, "for new pop, folk and country-western songs." Anyone who walks in from the throbbing street to be confronted by this fiesta of festivals, described exotically on request by beautiful girls with voices pitched so soft that the place has the atmosphere of a church during the confessional hour, is seduced immediately.

On the cover of the folder is a picture of a whitewashed cottage wearing a roof of fresh oaten straw, set in a green glen with a cool lake in the background and a deep-blue sky over all.

There is, however, something off-key about the scene, something that a prospective tourist would probably never notice. No evidence of life is depicted in the four-color scene, no man with a pitchfork, no wife tending the red geraniums on the windowsills, no plume of smoke coming from the low chimneys, no cows, sheep, or pigs, not even a Wicklow sheepdog. The blue gate that leads onto the narrow tar road lies crookedly open, as if the family had suddenly packed their goods and left, unexpectedly, for a long journey. Unconsciously, the art director for the Tourist Board had given a clue to the most troubling characteristic of rural Ireland, the lonely feel of a land without people.

Country people (they highly resent the term "peasant") are the living link between Irish history and the present. Sadly, one can count the fraying strands of the old traditions. The Gaeltacht, composed of small enclaves in the West and the South set aside for those who use the Gaelic language as their everyday tongue, is disappearing; the population now is down to only seventy thousand. The native language will soon be a cultural curiosity like Romany. The distinctive social life, centered around church on Sundays and house-to-house visits, or *ceilidhe,* is replaced almost everywhere with television and occasional visits to the city. The crossroads general store, the kind of place that served beer and whiskey on one side and dispensed a bewildering assortment of goods ranging from Wellington boots and farm implements to groceries, is being shunted aside by franchised chain stores. The language of Yeats and Synge, the two great writers who celebrated country life, seems oddly dated, while Joyce, the city man, sounds contemporary. Even now a few people govern their lives in ways that preserve the tie to their farm or village, but at a fearful cost. "In several parts of the country," writes Michael Viney, a Dublin journalist, "I have been told of marriages in which the husband has been working in Britain for up to 20 years, has returned for holidays and Christmases, and has begot a family of half-a-dozen children. These marriages have been described as 'extraordinarily happy.' They must also rank among the most extraordinary of the monogamous world."

In less than a decade, very little will remain of it all—the thatched whitewashed cottage, the local blacksmith, hand-churned butter, dances in farmers' kitchens, spiteful gossip, poaching, sexual secrets, down-at-heel squires on bicycles, home medicine cures, skilled odd-job men, dutiful elderly sons, eccentric bachelors. Some parts of country life will be preserved illogically and stubbornly by persistent, nostalgic farmers, some curiosities preserved quite logically for the entertainment of tourists and the strengthening of the international balance of payments. Of a vibrant, harmonious, natural life, nothing will remain.

The total effect of country life takes time to assimilate. Only after the tourists have left does the sense of decay and demoralization set in, the absence of a resilience that drives ambitious people to make an extra effort. It is not just the lack of people in villages, but the omnipresence of the aging and the very old. Not just the presence everywhere of skeleton structures that once housed families, but the new jerry-built houses. Compared to the bursting confidence of Dublin, where planners talk of a city of one million by 1990, the "Tidy Towns" campaign to smarten up the houses and streets of country towns seems pathetically inadequate. Driving through the countryside, the neat farmland of Wexford, the wet cutaway bogs of the midland counties, or the incomparably beautiful stretches of deserted land in Galway, Mayo, and Donegal, one gets little sense of confidence or renewal. The world outside has pressed too hard on tranquillity; people are worried about their economic and spiritual welfare, about their children.

Television has a great deal to do with it. Like viewers everywhere, they now can see that the outside world rules their destiny. And that world, however unreal and idealized it may appear on the screen, pulls like a powerful magnet on the

The new generation

Gay Byrne, television talker

Traditional Irish music: Tin whistles, fiddle, and spoons, Abbey Tavern, Howth

Tinkers: A dying race within a dying race

The money circles: Dublin Stock Exchange

and cattle market, Maynooth

Georgian elegance, Dublin

Irish modern, Ballymun

Seaching for the Gaelic past

Reaching out for European television

imagination of the young. The normal dissatisfaction of teen-agers with the lack of social amenities has been replaced in conversation by a tangible hatred of country life. Television has done no service either by presenting rural life in broad strokes of savage derision. The Irish bachelor has always been a figure of fun, a stock character in many of the kitchen comedies presented at the Abbey Theatre. But I missed the good-humored mockery of celibacy when I watched three old bachelors who were inveigled into appearing on a television program on which they described their daily lives and then appealed to single women to write to them. The studio audience howled in derision.

One of the most extraordinary *negative* results of a century of emigration is how little it seems to have materially benefited those who stayed behind. Indeed, it is a safe assumption that farmers who rented thirty acres a century ago were relatively better off than their counterparts are today. Although the total number of farm holdings has dropped, the majority of Irish farmers still operate on tracts of thirty acres or less. Individual ownership of these tiny holdings has meant little difference in increased productivity; indeed, the reverse may be true. In an unconscious way, the Irish are clinging to the system of subsistence farming that prevailed during the disastrous famines of the 1840s. In 1801, the population of the island was about 5 million. Most families lived on small patches of rented land which were subdivided as children reached marriage age, then about sixteen. By 1841, more than 8 million people were living on tiny holdings that produced little but potatoes. The potato blight, the subsequent famines, and enforced emigration cut the population down to 6,500,000 by 1851, and it kept dropping. The 1971 census for both the Republic and the North of Ireland showed a total population of 4,550,000.

It might seem plausible to assume that subsistence farming,

which had demonstrably failed to support successive generations, would somehow be replaced, perhaps by government fiat, or by voluntary action, or even by a combination of such methods. The change did not occur, however, even under the nine native governments that have ruled the Republic since independence. The inertia of the Irish farmer has always been masked by minor revolutions at home and major wars abroad, and always by endless talk about reforming the system. This mystery of human cussedness still draws historians, sociologists, demographers, and politicians to tiny villages where crusty old farmers are subjected to minute observation and intricate questionnaires. Anyone who has lived in Ireland knows how pointless an exercise it is to try to probe the suspicious mind of a countryman. One of the unanswered behavioral questions is why Irish farmers, when they emigrate, studiously avoid any contact with agriculture. Today, they journey to Britain, where the construction industry offers employment for the strong-backed unskilled laborer. Construction may be the only industry that offers a measure of independence. The Irish have evolved a subcontracting system in Britain called "The Lump," whereby a group undertakes to dig a hole or build a wall for a fixed amount. Technically, they are self-employed and therefore absolved from union membership. They also lose out on the substantial benefits of the British social security system.

What seems like illogical behavior today has been puzzling students of the Irish scene for a long time. In the middle of the nineteenth century, Marx and Engels had satisfied themselves that Ireland would be the focus of the great European working-class revolution.* "Give me 200,000 Irishmen and I could overthrow the British empire," Engels wrote enthusiastically to Marx in 1843 after one of his visits to Ireland. While waiting

---

* Karl Marx and Friedrich Engels, *Ireland and the Irish Question.* New York, International Publishers, 1972.

for the volunteers, Engels was compiling an elaborate Irish history. Marx, poring over statistics in the library of the British Museum, keeping an anxious eye on the bourgeois Irish delegation at Westminster, was convinced that the hour had come. In a confidential communication to the First International, written in 1870, he laid out the scenario:

If England is the bulwark of landlordism and European capitalism, the only point where one can hit official England really hard is Ireland. In the first place, Ireland is the bulwark of English landlordism. If it fell in Ireland it would fall in England. In Ireland this is a hundred times easier since the economic struggle there is concentrated exclusively on landed property, since this struggle is at the same time national, and since the people there are more revolutionary and exasperated than in England. Landlordism in Ireland is maintained solely by the English Army. The moment the forced union between the two countries ends, a social revolution will break out in Ireland, though in outmoded forms. English landlordism would not only lose a great source of wealth, but also its great moral force i.e. that of representing the domination of England over Ireland. On the other hand, by maintaining the power of their landlords in Ireland, the English proletariat makes them invulnerable in England itself.

An earlier visitor, Alexis de Tocqueville, came much closer to penetrating the mysteries of the Irish character when he visited the country after publication of the first volumes of *Democracy in America.* Tocqueville came armed with letters of introduction to the establishment lawyers, priests, and politicians, as well as with an open mind. After a number of interviews he saw and recognized something that Marx and Engels later missed:

There is an unbelievable unity between the Irish clergy and the Catholic population. The reason for that is not only that the clergy are paid by the people, but also because all the upper classes are Protestants and enemies. The clergy, rebuffed by high society, has turned all its attention to the lower classes; it has the same in-

stincts, the same interests and the same passions as the people; state
of affairs altogether peculiar to Ireland, a point one should keep
in mind. . . . in the streets of Carlow I noticed that the people
saluted all the priests who passed, very respectfully.*

Outwardly, at least, nothing has changed on the streets of
Carlow in the 1970s.

Tocqueville's description of a village near Tuam, in the West
of Ireland, gives an idea of the life style at the time.

First I followed a beautiful short-cut which led to a mansion. As
I turned to the right, I took a path to the left down a valley. Soon I
found myself at the beginning of the village which was built at the
bottom of a valley, or rather a ravine, shut in by two highish hills
covered with pasture. At the bottom of the ravine there flowed a
stream which no doubt swells in winter, but then exposed an almost dry, rocky bed. Not a tree grew on its banks which were as
bare as almost all other Irish river banks. This stream's bed, dry
or full, was apparently the only road in the village. The houses
seemed to be flattened to find room between the stream and the
two neighboring hills. I quickened my pace to hurry through this
unhappy village whose look repelled me. But in passing through I
could not help noticing what I had so often seen in Ireland. All the
houses in line to my right and my left were made of sun-dried mud
and built with walls the height of a man. The roofs of these dwellings were made of thatch so old that the grass which covered it
could be confused with the meadows on the neighboring hills. In
more than one place I saw that the flimsy timbers supporting these
fragile roofs had yielded to the effects of time, giving the whole
thing a look of a molehill on which a passer-by has trod. The
houses mostly had neither windows nor chimneys; the daylight
came in and smoke came out by the door. If one could see into the
houses, it was rare to notice more than bare walls, a rickety stool
and a small peat fire burning slowly and dimly between four flat
stones. A stranger's footsteps, kicking up the stones of the stream
soon attracted the villagers' attention. . . .

* J. P. Mayer, ed., *Journeys to England and Ireland*. New York, Doubleday
Anchor, 1968.

The fight for native ownership of land did produce one mass political movement that brought together radicals, priests, democrats, and tenant farmers through the Land League, which was founded in 1879. Headed by Charles Stewart Parnell, the League broke the power of the English landlords—and also, incidentally, spawned the word "boycott" as a term of social ostracism. Agitation reached such heights then that Parnell's sister, Fanny, was able to find women to join a separate Land League; in her spare time she wrote some blood-curdling verses which were used to whip up the crowds at mass meetings. A sample suggests Fanny may have been closer to the philosophy of Marx than her nonviolent brother.

Now, are you men or are you kine, ye tillers of the soil?
Would you be free, or evermore the rich man's cattle toil?
The shadow on the dial hangs that points the fatal hour—
Now hold your own: or branded slaves, for ever cringe and cower.

Oh, by the God who made us all—the seignior and the serf—
Rise up and swear this day to hold your own green Irish turf;
Rise up and plant your feet as men where now you crawl as slaves,
And make your harvest fields your camps, or make of them
    your graves.

There is a natural reluctance on the part of official Ireland to talk about regions where the sheep, cattle, and pigs outnumber humans by more than three to one,* where the tide of emigration continues inexorably every year. The rural population has declined by one-fifth since 1946, while marriage rates are still the lowest recorded anywhere. Demographers and economists tease the annual statistics with diligence for the key to the exodus. In the nineteenth century, rural Ireland was a place of shoulder-to-shoulder humanity, with a population density three times that of Denmark. In 1841, there were 241 people per

---

* The actual numbers in the Republic in 1971 were 5,405,000 cattle, 2,836,000 sheep, 1,155,000 pigs, and 2,978,000 people. Annual Report, Central Bank of Ireland, 1973.

square mile in Ireland; now there are just over 100. During the same period Denmark's population density increased from 82 to 276 per square mile, Holland's from 225 to 896.

One of the reasons, of course, for the decline is that no matter what any government program offered, or individual initiative achieved, it has not been enough to keep the men and women of rural Ireland at home. Again, taking 1946 as a modern yardstick, the number of agricultural workers has dropped from 594,000 to 267,000 in 1972. The opinion of experts, both Irish and European, is that this tiny work force will continue to drop at a rate between 4,000 and 10,000 annually. This may not seem like much, but those who remain in rural Ireland are either very old or very young. In 1966, six out of every ten farmers were more than fifty years old, one in seven was over seventy, one-third had not been married. The agricultural population is literally wearing out; the farms are too small to support those children who might remain. In Britain, a farm of two hundred acres is considered just about adequate to support a family; in Ireland, the average farm is forty acres, most of the holdings less than that meager number. The slow destruction of rural Ireland is certain, even though agriculture is still the economic mainstay of the country, providing 24 percent of all employment and 35 percent of the country's exports.

Minister Patrick Donegan's Monasterboice Inn, where the blue-plate special is an enormous plate of scampi, seemed a good jumping-off point for an investigation of a part of rural Ireland the tourist seldom sees. This is not pleasant country; from the rich pastureland where Donegan shot at the tinker to the low hillocks of Cavan takes less than an hour to drive, and it is a journey into the mean past. The counties around here, Cavan and Leitrim, have lost so much in population over a century that the people who remain are dispirited, angry, confused, and irritable. Each town along the way receives more mail from

London and New York at Christmas than from any part of Ireland; the local economy is propped up by remittances from abroad and by the annual visits by emigrants to their parents or elderly relatives. The land is poor; when it is not rocky, it is wet, producing crops of tall reeds that flourish in the rain that runs off relentlessly from the barren hills. The only cash crop worth talking about in Cavan is the pig business, which has become a great local benefit and a major national nuisance. Raising pigs takes little labor and a minimal amount of capital, the ideal formula in a poor underpopulated place. But the business is unregulated in one important respect, even though farmers raise and sell hundreds of thousands of the animals every year. The waste from the piggeries is rapidly destroying the ecology of the rivers and lakes, and indeed polluting the sources of human drinking water. Nobody cares very much about this, certainly not the farmers. Mechanical filtering systems, such as those used by hog farmers in the United States, are beyond the means of the small farmers, and because tourists are rare in the area, the government has refused to intervene. Anyway, political intervention that might threaten the livelihood of the farmers is likely to be met with fierce resistance.

The pig farmers often gather at the Percy French Hotel in Ballyjamesduff, a typical small market town, a likely place, it seemed, to investigate the collision between money and ecology. But no sooner had I mentioned the word "pollution" than a group of angry farmers made it clear that this, above all subjects, was *verboten*. Henry Campbell, a twinkly-eyed bachelor with whom I had struck up an acquaintance, brought me to one side and whispered, "Pigs are money around here, pollution isn't. Do you get my point?" I did. We spent the rest of the evening listening to a graphic account of Henry's adventures in the outback of Australia, where he had managed a sheep farm, with considerable success, judging by the deference shown him by the pig farmers.

It still seemed a subject worth pursuing. What, I wondered,

would happen to Lough Sheelin, a small lake in the center of the pig-producing area? After a conversation with Tom Delaney, a boat builder who lives on the shores of the lake, I concluded that Lough Sheelin would go the way of Lake Erie, the Hudson River, and every other natural heritage in the United States that stands in the path of economic progress. A decade ago, the cool, rich waters of Lough Sheelin produced the largest brown trout in Europe, delectable fish weighing up to fifteen pounds. The lake attracted expert anglers from North America and Europe, especially in the spring, when the rules required anglers to use the dry-fly-fishing method. "I have the records of the catch here," said Delaney, producing a carefully collated record from a shelf in his small workshop. "Ten years ago, you were certain of getting a catch in a day's fishing. Now you can fish for days without getting anything. The pig slurry and the runoff from artificial fertilizer is choking the lake. On a warm day, the coating of scum is inches deep. The lake will be dead in a couple of years."

Not just Lake Sheelin, either, as I discovered from the writings of George Burroughs, a fishing expert who is conducting a one-man campaign against agricultural pollution. Burroughs sees the same pattern of ecological ruin clear across the country from Lough Sheelin and Lough Ennel in the pig-producing area, to the salmon streams of Galway and Mayo in the West. In 1974, the first salmon of the season, a fish weighing ten pounds, sold for £130, or about $29.20 a pound. I could only conclude, after reading a report of a two-hour meeting of the Cavan Agricultural Committee, where farmers were exhorted to emulate the Netherlands by producing 10 million pigs a year, that Delaney and Burroughs were right.

Standing on the reedy shores of the windy lake, I realized why the destruction of Lough Sheelin, and a thousand other natural wonders in Ireland, was of no local concern. There is more money in Ireland today than there was a decade ago. I knew as I stood there that the pig farmers were in the Percy French Hotel studying pamphlets from the Department of Agriculture that promised substantial cash payments for any farmer who increased the national pig yield. Not a single boat moved on the water, some lonely crows fluttered around the ruins of Ross Castle in the center of the lake, the blooming green algae lapped the shoreline, broken up by the breeze that fluttered the water. The Irish are not enthusiastic about changing things. "Better the divil you know than the divil you don't know," they say; pigs were raised in this fashion fifty years ago and "What was good enough for my father is good enough for me." Even the talents of the great writer of the region, Patrick Kavanagh, would be insufficient to inspire any kind of social awareness; indeed, Kavanagh would be stuffed down the nearest pit of slurry if he stood between the pig men and their money.

Born on a small farm in Monaghan in 1906, Kavanagh was overshadowed by Joyce, though not in his lifelong zeal to chronicle the gradations of Irish hypocrisy, urban and rural. If invited to dinner, he made sure that he ate with his overcoat on, sitting on his battered hat. His body odor was proof of his boast that he bathed once a year. This was the theatrical pose of the country man among the Dublin literati, who knowledgeably ordered claret while Kavanagh roared for a pint or a large Jameson, the exaggerated uneasiness of the farmer in the city. Kavanagh's thought processes, too, were those of a typical farmer, centering on money, respectability, land, status, profitable litigation, and the easy way out. His one great novel, *Tarry Flynn,* which was banned on publication in 1948, is centered on the land, an autobiographical fiction of superior Tarry in a land of grubby philistines. Like the farmer, Kavanagh believed the world owed him recognition and a living:

> Where the
> Tinkers quarrel I went down
> With my horse, my soul.
> I cried, "Who will bid me half a crown?"

From their rowdy bargaining
Not one turned. Soul, I prayed,
I have hawked you through the world
Of Church and State and meanest trade;
But this evening, halter off,
Never again will it go on.
On the South side of ditches
There is grazing of the sun;
No more haggling with the world. . . .

As I said these words he grew
Wings upon his back. Now I may ride him
Every land my imagination knew.

Ireland never forgave Kavanagh for painting the country scene as a backwater of inanity. He recorded the thoughts and dialogue of life at the crossroads as they really are, breaking what he called the sociological myth so carefully cultivated by writers like Yeats and Synge and by fiercely patriotic Irish historians. "The work of Yeats which is deliberately Irish sounds awfully phony," wrote Kavanagh. "Irishness is a form of anti-art."

Kavanagh must have retched at the lines of Christie Mahon in Synge's *Playboy of the Western World,* words as artificially crafted as anything by Proust, for no country man ever courted a girl with such phrases: "It's little you'll think if my love's a poacher, or an earl's itself, then you'll feel my two hands stretched around you, and I squeezing kisses on your puckered lips, till I'd feel a kind of pity for the Lord God of all ages sitting lonesome in his golden chair." The dialogue of the characters in *Tarry Flynn* is a faithful reproduction of casual country chat—honest, earthy, and a long way from the heightened Irishness of Synge.

. . . Tarry came to a stop in the middle of the group of crooked old men who were debating the mighty feats of strength of their immediate forebears and in particular of a noted strong man known as Paddy Hughie Tom who had hurled the sixteen pound shot "from here to below the turn at McKenna's gate."

Tarry ignored Charlie's remark and tried to merge himself in the debating group by expressing a scientific view of Paddy Hughie Tom's throw.

"The world's record's well over fifty feet, but that would be well over the record. Was it the right weight or did he throw it right?"

A fellow with a long upper lip and bandy legs who was a relation of the strong man, spat out viciously and said: "Throw it right? What the hell are you trying to come at?"

Tarry regretted having made the observation. Attention was being focused on him, the very thing he didn't want. The Finnegans were only waiting for a chance to pick a row.

"I'm sure he threw it that far," he said, glancing down the hill at McKenna's gate. "He must have been a damn good man."

"He was six feet four and built according," remarked another.

"Don't be making a child of yourself, Tom," said someone else. "Did you ever see the man stripped? Chest on him, be the holies, like a barrel. Flynn," the man turned to Tarry, "did you say that the weight wasn't the right weight? Do you know what, he'd throw the breed of you over that bleddy ditch before his breakfast."

Tarry tried to sidle away, to make himself invisible, but the argument was beginning to surge around him.

"He never tried to grab anyone's piece of land," one of the Finnegans said from his sitting position.

"Huh," sniffed Tarry with contempt. "Grabbing land! That's a thing of the past."

"Here's where Paddy Hughie Tom stood," one of the crooked little hero worshippers was saying. "I was here the evening he did it."

Two girls passed on bicycles.

"Me hand on your drawers," shouted Charlie.*

A lot of the Irish middle class think this kind of writing lets the country down. Like the Russians, Irish officialdom believes that writers should be outriders for the state, crying the great

---

* *Tarry Flynn.* London, Four Square Edition, New England Library, 1962.

deeds of government departments from village to village. "He was a right ould culchie," a Dublinman is likely to say of Kavanagh, still smarting from those unerring shots. A "culchie" is the Dubliner's most wounding term for a country man, the word deriving from Kiltimagh (pronounced "culchiemah") farmers, great gangling gobshites who arrive in Dublin on the train from the West, dressed in the Sunday blue serge suit, possessions bundled in a brown paper parcel tied with binder twine, feet shod with plowman's boots tipped with steel crescents, always carrying instructions, which have to be read to the illiterate Kiltimagh man, directing him to a building site. A lot of Dublin literary men still believe that Kavanagh was a "culchie" writer, a Johnny-jump-up with the gall to elevate himself above his betters with a countryman's epitaph:

> He had the knack of making men feel
> As small as they really were
> Which meant as great as God had made them
> But as males they disliked his air.
> O he was a proud one
> Fol dol the di do,
> He was a proud one
> I tell you.

When Kavanagh was safely dead for seven years, Ireland tried to get its own back by placing a plaque on the wall of a London parking lot opposite the Plough, a Bloomsbury pub where Kavanagh liked to drink when he wasn't having lunch at Boodles or White's with some eager publisher. *"Is ioma steall do chaith se annseo,"* ran the Gaelic inscription, meaning, "Many's the stream he let flow here." Dubliners howled at the wit of it; Kavanagh's brother, Peter, traveled from New York to tear down the offending inscription.

"But Cavan is not Ireland," an Irishman is likely to say. He is right. In order to measure the mood of the Cavanmen who had elevated the pig to such heights of national importance, I traveled 160 miles south to Wexford, the model county, the home of the "Yellowbellies," so called because Wexfordmen had an inordinate appetite for great plates of imported yellow meal. By Irish standards, Wexford is a prosperous county, although its principal town, called Wexford, supports the same population now as it did at the turn of the century. This is Kennedy country, of course ("What was he but just another Yellowbelly?" the locals like to say), where a lot of the houses display a triptych of Popes John and Paul, with Kennedy in the center. In November, a visitor is likely to bump into knots of men in dinner jackets on the main street of Wexford town, an incongruous sight as they pass windows of the Co-operative store with bags of fertilizer and farm implements on display. Wexford is a proud, independent place, managing to mount an opera production every year that is comparable, in the quality of the singing at least, to productions in the provincial towns of Italy. This time-out for culture is not something to suit everybody's taste. "A person can't get a tap of work done around here with them fellas singin' their *areas*," a hard-working farmer's wife complained. "I have to milk the cows meself while the boyos [her sons] are in White's Hotel gawkin' at all the Italians." White's Hotel lies in the center of the main street, a spine of commerce so narrow in places that it is possible for people to shake hands across the street without leaving their doorways.

It is a Norman town, with names like Devereaux, yet a very Irish town, too, with the symbols of emigration and neglect embodied in a statue of Commodore John Barry, a hero of the American Navy who was born here in 1735, and the fine harbor, silted into near disuse from generations of unchecked shifting tides. Wexford emigrants were a more adventurous lot than most, some of them working their way to Latin America. "If you are ever in Buenos Aires," an old lady said seriously, "you might look up the Devereauxs from Bannow. They left here a long time ago, but I haven't heard a thraneen from them lately."

When he arrived in New Ross in 1963, John Kennedy told the welcoming crowd that had the family remained in Ireland, more than likely he would be working in the Albatross fertilizer factory. If money and image count for anything, he would have been a director of the cattle mart, the large indoor auction center where animals are sold for shipment to Britain and the Continent. The indoor mart is agriculture's bow to modernity, replacing the open-air fair where horses, cows, and beef cattle wandered the streets while buyer and seller bargained with the cute, artful seller, finally rewarded at the end of the haggling with a "luck penny." Fairs were a lot of fun, too, because they attracted tinkers, hawkers, conjurers, men who lay on beds of glass, street singers, added attractions that provided a gregarious carnival atmosphere. New Ross is blessed with an inordinate number of pubs, so the long fair day, which began before dawn and ended at midnight, was lubricated with endless frothing pints of stout for the men, ginger wine for the children. The new indoor mart system has changed all this. So serious are the Wexfordmen about the business of cattle that the mart has no bar, the nearest pub being half a mile away. Auctioneers stand on a raised platform calling out prices as each lot of cattle is led into the ring, the sums meticulously recorded on a huge blackboard.

On the day I arrived, the participants were as buoyant as boys on the first day of summer vacation. My guide was Patrick O'Brien, a big muscular cattle dealer who looked more like a stockbroker in his immaculate off-white Burberry raincoat. O'Brien did his time as an emigrant in the coal mines of Yorkshire, returning gratefully with enough money to buy a small pub in New Ross. With time on his hands, he turned to cattle dealing, a fortuitous choice.

"I was woken up by a ring from a man in Rome this morning," said O'Brien, with the air of a man who had been on the receiving end of international communications all his life. "There's a great demand for veal right now in Italy, and he wants as much as I can get him." Just to test him, I asked what the exchange rate for lire was that day. "Oh, I don't have to worry about that at all. The bank takes care of everything. I call Rome back at the end of the day, give them the numbers I bought, and they send a check to the Hibernian Bank here in town." No crisp brown five-pound notes any longer, no haggling, no ginger wine, no luck penny. The fair, almost overnight, had been transformed into a segment of the international commodity exchange, with the middleman banks standing to make a nice profit through currency arbitrage.

While O'Brien was carefully buying, inscribing each transaction in a notebook, I noticed that a few of the old elements had remained. As the cattle were driven out from the sales ring, small boys armed with ashplants gave each beast a resounding whack, an echo of the fair, when every animal had to run the gantlet. And the sellers were not very anxious to see the pleasant day end. They moved around the sales ring like guests at a cocktail party, chatting inconsequentially, yet keeping a sharp eye on the blackboard. A farmer with twenty cattle to sell tested the market by sending in four or five animals at a time. This prolonged the pleasure of the auction if the bidding was high; if it was low, he had the satisfaction of saving the rest of his herd for a better day. Since the prices seemed to be uniform that day, I asked O'Brien why the farmers were so cautious.

"Sure if everybody sold his stock when the place opens at eight in the morning, the mart would be over before the Angelus. These fellows want to make a day out of it." It seemed to me that a lot of them were preparing to make a day and a night of it, for at six o'clock the auctioneer was still calling out prices, while O'Brien was making plans to drive to another indoor mart in Enniscorthy, twenty miles away, where, he had heard, a farmer had a herd of calves for sale that would make lots of nice veal parmigiana for his Italian connection.

The euphoric air of the New Ross cattlemen has been generated in large part by Ireland's entry into the Common Market.
In anticipation of that event, cattle herds had been increased,
while prices on January 1, 1973, the day of destiny, were 60
percent higher than they had been two years earlier. The
Common Agricultural Policy (CAP), which puts a floor under
farmers' incomes, had worked well initially for the Irish, with
their enormous stocks of beef on the hoof. Just as the politicians
had promised, in a campaign designed to turn out a massive
affirmative vote for entry into Europe, the farmers were getting
an immediate injection of cash. Within a matter of months,
however, beef prices sagged because of overproduction. Farmers
are unable to resist milking a good thing.

However, the one-sided merits of the CAP system are
counterbalanced by long-term agricultural policies, calculated
to reduce the number of people living on the land, increase
farm income, improve productivity by increasing the size of
farms, and eliminate the farm surpluses that pile up, such as the
famous 400,000-ton mountain of butter and a smaller hill of
frozen beef that Brussels bureaucrats point to as the great defect
in European agriculture. It is a draconian formula, but it is
probably the only way to modernize food production. The farm
population of the original six members of the Common Market
dropped from 15 million in 1960 to less than 10 million in
1972. By 1980, most experts believe it will decline to about 6
million, an awesome drop. In a region of 240 million people,
this new order has created massive disruptions in the farm areas,
adding to the pollution and congestion of cities, while causing
political instability through inflated food prices. However,
there has been a serious labor shortage in Europe for decades;
those who leave the land are easily assimilated by industry. This
restructuring has brought real material and intangible benefits:
more money, greater mobility, better marriage prospects, a
gradual breaking down of the class system. In the Common

Market scheme of things, land is a resource to be managed for the maximum rate of return, just as in any other business.

The great political problem is whether the consumers of Europe will continue to pay massive subsidies until the comforting day when the production and consumption of food are in balance. This is a race against time, because food prices have been marching up relentlessly, no small factor in the defeat of Prime Minister Edward Heath in Britain and the return of Harold Wilson, who promised to review the terms of Britain's entry into the Common Market. Ninety-five percent of the Common Market's budget of $3 billion is spent on farm subsidies, and that huge amount is likely to grow with time. Walter Hallstein, the former president of the Executive Commission of the Common Market, pointed out the real danger of a consumer revolt in 1973. "Every citizen in the community," said Hallstein, "pays taxes from which his national budget subsidizes agriculture and from which contributions are made to the Community's agricultural fund. Must he, on top of the taxes, pay still higher prices in the shops which produce senseless surpluses, which in turn lead to still more senseless charges running into thousands of millions? Is there not a danger that the Community itself will gain the dubious reputation of being a senseless undertaking?"

This kind of talk cuts no ice in Dublin, where politicians are happy that their biggest problem has now been transferred to Brussels. Whatever they may have thought in private, on the hustings they always blamed the plight of the poor farmer on old Mother England. Garret FitzGerald, the Minister for Foreign Affairs, can say, without cracking a smile, that Ireland is only now beginning to escape from "the colonial exploitation which we have suffered so long." There may be some merit in that claim, but it is unarguably true that the Irish are among Europe's most inefficient farmers. As recently as 1969, the government was spending less ($4 million) on agricutural

research than a handful of wealthy Irish breeders were paying
for thoroughbred horses at the annual sales in Kentucky and
Saratoga. The first national soil-testing scheme was inaugurated
only in 1958. Just 5 percent of the students in higher education
are pursuing agriculture as a science. Moreover, the Dublin
government perpetuated a demeaning system by paying subsidies to farm families that were just high enough to provide
escape from poverty but too low to allow the families to pur-
chase more land. In the five-year period between 1968 and 1972,
the government spent $1,242 million on agriculture; yet the
Irish farmer is still a long way from reaching an adequate level
of income. The original European plan for 1980 proposed that
an "economically viable farm" should be one that would provide two full-time workers with incomes of $10,000 to $12,500 a
year. Fortunately for the Irish, that plan was politically undesirable, especially in France and Italy, where there are many small
farmers. Had it been adopted, the number of farms in Ireland
would have had to be reduced by at least 50 percent by 1980.

Ireland's entry into the Common Market simply postponed a
radical restructuring of Irish agriculture that was long overdue.
The industry is based on dairying—five-sixths of the arable land
is under grass—the most inefficient possible system, because a
producing cow requires two acres of grass. Occasionally an
economist will humorously suggest that one way of solving the
overproduction of butter and cheese is to shoot one cow in
twenty-five; that would bring disaster to the small Irish farmer,
who depends on milk sales for his monthly creamery check.

The emphasis on dairy farming and beef production and the
decline of crop production have produced some strange results,
like the potato shortage of 1973, when the Irish government was
forced to import the national staple from Europe, along with
most of the fruit and vegetables (a good deal from Israel) that
were required. Dairy farming requires little labor, and a trav-
eler in Ireland in the seventies finds Tocqueville's nineteenth-
century picture unchanged in some places: "I saw five or six

men of strength and health lying nonchalantly by the banks of the brook. If I had known less of Ireland, this laziness in the midst of so much poverty would have excited my indignation. But already I knew enough of this unhappy country to realize that there was a ceaseless lack of employment. They cannot earn their bread by the sweat of their brow as God intended." Underemployment is now the curse of the countryside. In County Kerry, 29 percent of the farmers are part-time workers, the average dairy herd consists of twelve cows, and the thirty-acre man makes an average of $850 a year from his holding. Kerry is typical of the part-time subsistence farming that has ruined the West of Ireland, a blighted stretch extending the length of the country from Killarney in the south to destitute Donegal in the North.

The land has, of course, other uses. While I was in Ireland, Cary Grant arrived in County Clare, total population 75,000, representing a real estate syndicate that included Raquel Welch and Jack Lemmon, which intends to build expensive retirement homes on land too poor to support the local farmers. Grant cemented his relations with the locals by drinking pints with them in an endearing pub named Dirty Nellie's, but Raquel, whose presence would have been appreciated more by the men in the tweed caps, never showed. Myra Breckenridge in Dirty Nellie's would have been theatre of a kind even the Irish Tourist Board would find hard to handle.

Over the long haul, of course, Irish agriculture will be modernized; policy is now set by the Common Market Secretariat in Brussels, whose directives on prices and subsidies are mandatory. But what might be manageable in France, where other rules and traditions exist, will be a tragedy in Ireland. Irish industry is in its infancy; the factories built since the 1950s, mostly by foreign capital seeking tax advantages, simply cannot absorb all the surplus agricultural workers. Even if additional investors arrive, the number of jobs created will not absorb the people who leave those whitewashed cottages. Ireland's problem is clearly etched in some chastening numbers: *

Year	Number of Agricultural Jobs	Number of Manufacturing Jobs
1951	496,000	184,000
1956	445,000	188,000
1961	392,000	179,000
1966	333,500	198,000
1971	273,000	195,000
1972	267,000	213,000

The exodus that has absolved successive Irish governments from dealing with a fractious and growing contingent of unemployed workers will continue as it has for generations. Emigration is the only solution for the children of the underemployed farmers with thirty acres in the West. It is not as bad as it might appear, for the Irish embark on a well-traveled route to Boston, Vancouver, London, or Sydney. The departure is less of a wrench than for the Calabrese farmer traveling to Milan for his interview in one of the Agnelli automobile plants. Indeed, in many ways it is a pleasant experience for the Irish, like a family reunion. But unlike the Calabrese, once the Irish emigrate, they never return.

* Central Bank of Ireland Annual Report 1973; Census of Population 1971.

3

The Feudal Lords

When the first ebullient government of the Irish Free State invited designers to submit ideas for a new national coinage, a wit sent along a representation of an angel pouring money from a sack. The solemn committee selected to approve the new design, especially the celebrated, prestigious, and humorless chairman, William Butler Yeats, did not appreciate the joke. The mood of the times was portentous. After centuries of colonial rule, and generations of struggle to retain a sense of national identity in the face of discrimination, poverty, famine, and emigration, Ireland, as the old rebel song had predicted, was a nation once again. Or at least part of a nation. Symbols are as important to the Irish as saving face is to the Oriental. And the glittering, handsome new coins were much admired. On one side was an etching of the small harp played by medieval minstrels, the oldest heraldic symbol of Ireland. On the obverse sides of the eight coins were the symbols of what everybody hoped would be the foundation of prosperity: a woodcock on the farthing, a pig on the halfpenny, a hen on the penny, a hare on the threepence, a wolfhound on the sixpence, a bull on the shilling, a salmon on the florin, and a horse on the half-crown.

Few questioned that agriculture, properly exploited by the Irish themselves in a civilized and progressive way, would produce an upsurge of economic activity. And in the streets of every town, in the émigré quarters of New York and London, it had always been an article of nationalist faith that without England great native industries would flourish. Swift had so implied when he advised the Irish to burn everything English except coal. Wolfe Tone and the United Irishmen of 1791 believed in the dream; the nonsectarian views of Tone are still current in Irish radical circles. The political leaders who followed—William Smith O'Brien of the Young Ireland movement in 1848; James Stephens and John O'Mahony, the physical-force men who headed the Fenians in 1858; Parnell with his Parliamentarians; Michael Davitt and the Land League farmers—did not give much thought to economic matters. If they did so, they simply assumed that the end of exploitation by England would mean the revitalization of Ireland.

James Connolly, the socialist leader who was shot after the 1916 uprising, had a more sophisticated perspective. He had seen at first hand the stirrings of industrial unionism in the United States, he was familiar with the dialectical theories of Marxism, and he could discourse eloquently on the eventual disintegration of the nation-state. Yet Connolly, too, was infected with a nationalist vision of a workers' republic, a cooperative commonwealth of farmers and workers. Patrick Pearse, the poet of violence who was shot with Connolly, predicted a few weeks before the 1916 rebellion: "The population will expand in a century to 20,000,000; it may even in time go up to 30,000,000." When harnessed against an outside power, tribal pride is a potent instrument. It is not quite the stuff on which to build a nation. The Irish personality is mercurial, moving from serene optimism to extreme pessimism like a cloud passing over the sun. Life has always been, in the countryman's phrase, either a wake or wedding, and the Irish usually had to enter by the back door. For a while, they believed that as masters of the big house they would renew the ancient culture and give birth to a national economic renaissance.

A few people, but only a few, found this brand of emotional nationalism, fueled mainly by a hatred of England, nothing more than provincial fantasy. James Joyce, for one, stood apart from the xenophobia, though he was careful to record the wild talk which he later put in the mouth of his character the citizen in *Ulysses*. In real life the citizen was a windbag named Michael Cusack, founder of the Gaelic Athletic Association, who, according to Richard Ellman, Joyce's biographer, had a habit of shouting in bars, "I'm citizen Cusack from the Parish of Carron in the Barony of Burren in the County of Clare, you Protestant dog." Joyce has the citizen pontificating on economics after a few pints:

Where are our missing twenty millions of Irish should be here today instead of four, our lost tribes? And our potteries and textiles, the finest in the whole world! And our wool that was sold in Rome in the time of Juvenal and our flax and our damask from the looms of Antrim and our Limerick lace, our tanneries and our white flint glass down there by Ballybough and our Hugueneot poplin that we have since Jacquard de Lyon and our woven silk and our Foxford tweeds and ivory raised point from the Carmelite convents in New Ross, nothing like it in the whole wide world! Where are the Greek merchants that came through the pillars of Hercules, the Gibraltar now grabbed by the foe of mankind, with gold and Tyrian purple to sell in Wexford at the fair of Carmen? Read Tacitus and Ptolemy, even Giraldus Cambrensis. Wine, peltries, Connemara marble, silver from Tipperary, second to none, our farfamed horses even today, the Irish hobbies, with king Philip of Spain offering to pay customs duties for the right to fish in our waters. What do the yellow-johns of Anglia owe us for our ruined trade and our ruined hearths? And the beds of the Barrow and Shannon they won't deepen with millions of acres of marsh and bog to make us all die of consumption.

More than a few contemporary citizens were talking that way when I arrived in Dublin. Fierce nationalists, some of them wore the native peltries mid-length style, as the yellow-john fashion leaders of Anglia dictate. The sheepskin coat seems to be the only native article of clothing that men wear with pride. Symbols of prosperity like a Swedish suit, Bally shoes, or a knit shirt from Korvettes department store in New York are much in evidence. The taste in tobacco reflects a distinct preference for foreign brands, Upmann cigars if possible, if not the long thin Schimmelpenninck or Henri Wintermann, so often crushed out on ashtrays bearing the Gaelic legend *"Deanta sa tSeapain."** In women's fashions, those few who can afford it wear couture garments made by a handful of local dress designers like Sybil Connolly, Donald Davies, and Ib Jorgensen. The rest of the female population buys off-the-peg clothes from abroad, if they can, wearing cheaper local garments not as a matter of preference but as the family budget dictates. The Irish prefer many foreign articles, for their prestige, of course, and also because most native mass-produced products are notoriously shoddy and unreliable.

On my first week in Ireland, I took possession of a car from England that had been shipped "completely knocked down," as the Irish customs quaintly say, and assembled in Cork. Every American consumer knows of Detroit's reputation for turning out lemons. This lemon (or lime) of dual nationality dropped the electrical wiring harness at my feet while I was negotiating a tricky corner in Dublin. Motorists in Ireland assured me that, while they had never experienced that particular fault, comparable defects came to light in their own cars, not to mention a lot of other consumer goods.

Marx, probably a more reliable source than Michael Cusack on the state of Irish industry, at least in the nineteenth century, wrote that "The one great industry of Ireland, linen manufac-

* "Made in Japan."

ture, requires few adult men and only employs altogether, in spite of its expansion since the price of cotton rose in 1861–66, a comparatively insignificant part of the population." Shortly after, the Ulster Protestants started a shipbuilding industry; it, in turn, spawned an engineering complex. These are perilous industries today, dependent largely on subsidies from the British government. Marx forgot to mention the alcoholic beverage business, which has prospered in time of war, peace, and depression. There are distilleries in familiar Bushmills, and in Belfast, Dublin, Tullamore, and Cork; breweries in Belfast, Dundalk, Drogheda, Dublin, Kilkenny, Waterford, and Cork; cider is made in Portadown and Clonmel. An industry, one might venture to say, that is based on agriculture. But no native venture capitalist brought forth any new manufacturing industry of significant size in the twentieth century.

As for the promise of agriculture as a basis for national wealth, that blossom perished, if it ever bloomed anywhere except in the romantic imagination of Yeats and his fellow committee members. The land has been kind to the Irish, but the Irish have been unkind to the land. It is not simply that the landscape has an unfinished look, with acres of weeds and thistles, wild high hedges, and miles of barbed wire. There is a running fight between the inspectors of the Irish Tourist Board and the farmers over the appearance of the landscape. For example, although travelers on the main road from Dublin to Galway see one uninterrupted tranquil pastureland, a tourist finds it impossible to get a panoramic view in most parts of Ireland because roadside hedges grow uncontrolled. The Tourist Board would prefer the neat hedgerows of Kent. The farmers, on the other hand, have their own reasons for preserving the thorn fences—they simply do not want neighboring families to observe whatever goes on behind them.

Otherwise, land is expected to produce a living with the minimum human assistance. The massive documentation of the famine years tells us that the way of growing potatoes then required the least possible effort. Seed potatoes were laid on the land, then covered with earth, a method known then and now as the "lazy bed." Wealth from the land is mostly produced the lazy way today by grazing cattle. If his pasture grass gets sparse, a farmer lets his animals graze the grass verge on the road outside his door, known as the long meadow. A lot of the cattle are still shipped live to Britain, one of the reasons why a big and efficient meat-packing industry has never been developed in Ireland.

This is a system that, in its way, is as primitive as that of any African tribe. Cattle grazing does not provide much employment, not even for the farmer who is, as the social scientists kindly put it, underemployed. Brought to its logical conclusion, the best way of operating this kind of business would be to run all the grazing lands as a single ranch, like Robert Kleberg's King Ranch in Texas. It could be staffed by a superboss, with a dozen understrappers to take orders, and a few hundred ranch hands to ride herd. The thirty- or forty-acre farm owned by a single individual, which is the pattern of agriculture today, is grossly inefficient, not only to an agronomist but to the farmer who must bring up a family. Still, the government dare not intervene; as long as a market, however cyclical, exists abroad for all those cattle, the small farmer is politically inviolate. Like a fortunate member of a trade union in a small inefficient factory protected by a "no-firing" clause, the farmer has a guarantee of lifetime employment. Agriculture has always suffered from a laissez-faire approach—in the methods of feeding the starving in the famine days, and in the way that successive native governments have perpetuated the tiny holdings. There was no economic plan when the first government came to power half a century ago, nor is there one today. Eventually, because of economic pressures, the system must change. Perhaps the farms will become larger, perhaps foreign companies will buy the land, for some Irish acres now cost as much as any in

Europe. For the small farmer to sell his land might be a wrench. But it is an attractive means of getting some capital together.

What went wrong with the nationalist dream? In this century, the Irish were first to break away from British colonialism. They survived the agony of a civil war, whose causes are now misted in history; they made a gallant attempt to revive the ancient culture. The misguided effort to build a self-sufficient national economy inevitably failed. Now they are in the fifth year of a sectarian war. While the fighting goes on, the pulse of the Republic quickens, the stirring martial drumbeat of nationalism muffles more ominous signals. Perhaps Ireland should not have been a separate nation. Perhaps it would have prospered as an integral part of Britain. The scorecard for self-government reads that the Irish have the lowest per capita income in the Common Market, the highest rate of unemployment, the lowest ratio of students in higher education, the highest percentage of mentally ill, the smallest contingent of workers in manufacturing, the largest percentage of children under fourteen, the highest ratio of unmarried adults, the least favorable tax structure for the lower and middle classes, the most advantageous tax system for the rich. Other nations might look to Marx, Keynes, or one of their lesser contemporaries for enlightenment on these demographic and economic mysteries. The Irish are lured by more absolute prophets. The sight of the kindly members of the Saint Vincent de Paul Society dispensing charity on weekends suggests that Irish society is still bounded by the mental frontiers of the eighteenth century—the goodness of God and the theories of Adam Smith.

"No nation in Europe is less given to industry or is more phlegmatic than this," said Cardinal Giovanni Battista Rinuccini, a papal nuncio who came in Ireland in 1645 to mediate trouble between the warring landowner factions. The phlegmatic social style was set long before His Eminence appeared.

In that feudal era only land was wealth, and ambitious men were less given to industry than to speculation. Around 1588, Richard Boyle, an English adventurer, arrived on the quayside in Dublin with just the clothes on his back and a few coins clutched in his fist. Land made him the richest man in the nation, power made him Earl of Cork, vanity made him build magnificent mansions in Ireland and in England. The ghost of Richard Boyle still haunts contemporary land deals. When another Earl of Cork needed cash in 1750 to build Burlington House in London, now the seat of the Royal Academy, he sold the castle, town, and lands of Cappoquin, in County Waterford, a thirty-thousand-acre holding, to John Keane. The scattered remains of that princely domain are now owned by a descendant, Sir Richard Keane, who controls most of the property in the town, population eight hundred, along with almost two thousand acres of mountain and farmland. Sir Richard holds leases on most of the valuable property in town, the hotels, bars, shops, houses, garages, drugstore, bacon factory, even the police station, a circumstance that the local residents compare to the landlord-tenant relationship that existed in the days of the first Earl of Cork.

The life of a British army officer stationed in a garrison town in the nineteenth century, according to the Irish novelist Samuel Lever, was spent in a round of diversion—dining, drinking, dancing, riding, steeplechasing, pigeon shooting, tandem driving, attending balls and plays. In Dublin, political corruption lifted "Copper Face" Jack Smith from a bootblack to Lord Chief Justice. Buck Whaley, the greatest of plungers, once jumped from the drawing-room window of Daly's gaming club in Dublin to the roof of a passing cab. He wagered £15,000 that he could walk to Jerusalem within a given period. He accomplished the journey on time, returning with a profit of £8,000 over his traveling expenses. Daly's club was connected by a secret passage to the adjoining House of Parliament for the convenience of members. When the British wanted to end that annoying separate legislature, where talk of real independence could be heard, most of the members sold their votes for a consideration. With the old Parliament, which now houses the Bank of Ireland, went any sense of landlord responsibility. A lot of the country gentry left for London, an exodus memorialized by a son of Charles Kendal Bushe, known as "the incorruptible" because of his vote against the abolition of Parliament.

> The worthy Esquire sells his old estate,
> Possessed with proud ambition to be great.
> And what's his view of greatness? To be sent
> An independent man to Parliament.
> And truly independent, forth he goes,
> Of all the comforts his old home bestows.
> See him in London to a chop house sneak
> To famish on a solitary steak. . . .

The landlords who remained, surrounded by their pauper tenants, became themselves prisoners of the feudal mind. The comparison between Russia and Ireland in this respect has often been made. When a factory chimney appeared in Mitchelstown, Lord Kingston, owner of the town, the land, and the people, gave an ultimatum: Either the factory would be torn down or he would leave for London. The factory owners left. Half cracked with authority, Kingston ordered his tenants to vote for his political candidate. When they refused, he mounted the stairs to the long gallery in Mitchelstown Castle, shouted, "They are come to tear me to pieces," and went mad.

The copperplate parchment leases, good for 999 years, still bind the Irish tenant to the landlord. The Earl of Cork and Orrery owns part of the city of Cork; Lord Roden owns most of Dundalk, a border town; the people of Enniscorthy are tenants of a Baron Wallop of Portsmouth; most of the charming village of Adare is owned by the Earl of Dunraven. The old rules of law, if they favor speculation, remain undisturbed. An act passed in Westminster in 1874 allows the directors of building societies, as savings and loan associations are called, to use depositors' money for their personal investments.

Only once in the twentieth century did the Irish throw off the "big house" mentality. On the eve of the August Horse Show in 1913, a correspondent for the *Times* in London gave the news that London wanted to hear of events in the Irish capital. "These are great days in Dublin," he wrote. "The weather continues perfect, great crowds thronging the city, and tomorrow what all Irishmen not unjustifiably believe to be the greatest horse show in the world will open." The following day a general strike began that was unequaled in Irish history for its bitterness. The real Dublin was the classic slum of Europe. A survey of the time showed that many families were living five to a room in stinking tenements with about three hundred cubic feet of space for each resident, far less than the law demanded, less even than the four hundred square feet provided for prisoners on hard labor in Mountjoy Prison. The death rate in Dublin was twice as high as that of London, a city fifteen times as large. Wages for factory workers were half a crown a week, not much more than the going rate a century before. The diet of the working poor was black tea and unbuttered bread. It seemed that the strike, as Sean O'Casey wrote in his first book, *The Story of the Irish Citizen Army,* was bringing Ireland to the eve of an Armageddon between capital and labor.

"Prime Ministers have fallen, and Ministers of State have been impeached for less," wrote Yeats when he witnessed unprovoked police attacks on the strikers. The leader of the four-hundred-member employers' association was William Martin Murphy, a lineal descendant of those native Catholic squires who had managed to hold on to their estates by continuing authoritarianism toward their tenants and with sycophancy to the Crown. Murphy was a central figure in one of those classic Irish debates where the slatternliness of the native gentry always seems to emerge. A group of citizens had commissioned Sir Edwin Lutyens to build an art gallery to house a collection of

French Impressionist paintings donated to the people of Ireland by a wealthy Anglo-Irishman, Sir Hugh Lane. In his own newspaper, the *Irish Independent,* Murphy took note of the excitement created by the imminent arrival of the Lane collection. "There has been much eloquence wasted on this subject over the last few days," Mr. Murphy wrote, "and all the old platitudes have been trotted out about the 'priceless collection,' the 'envy of Europe,' 'the resort of pilgrims,' the educational effect on the taste of the citizens, the answer to which may be summed up in one word—Fudge."

The leader of the strikers, James Larkin, organized the Irish Citizen Army to protect his tattered followers. Many of those who saw Larkin leading this crusade came away feeling, like Sir William Orpen, the artist who studied Larkin daily at Liberty Hall, that they had seen an extraordinary personality. "Larkin was the finest orator I have ever heard," the English writer and translator David Garnett wrote, "just as Chaliapin was the finest singer—and for the same physical reasons. Larkin was, I believe, actually taller than Chaliapin and could have out-roared the Russian. There was no fat on him. He was absolutely unselfconscious and seemed to care nothing for his audience. He was deadly in earnest and, walking up and down like an infuriated tiger, he roared out his message of defiance to the capitalist system and of death to Murphy. There striding about the platform one beheld the whole of the sweated, starved, exploited working class suddenly incarnate in the shape of a gigantic Tarzan of all the slum jungles of the West."

Communist, anticlerical, internationalistic, Larkin represented a new force in Irish politics, the urban agitator in contrast to the rural Tory. "Each for all and all for each" was his original slogan. Radicals like Bill Haywood, leader of the Industrial Workers of the World, traveled to Dublin to witness the dismantling of the barricades. French, English, and American trade unionists contributed funds to provide soup kitchens for the starving strikers, who represented one-third of the popu-

lation of the city. Mrs. Dora Montefiore, an activist in the
international socialist movement, proposed to send the strikers'
children to the homes of sympathetic English workers, a plan
that provoked the wrath and condemnation of the Catholic
hierarchy. Nothing came of it all. After eight months, the
strikers went back to their jobs, Larkin went to the United
States. Dublin prepared for the next horse show.

Years afterward, according to a story told by one of Larkin's
comrades, the Comintern called a meeting of European affili-
ates, one of those affairs where the presentation of banners
symbolizes the solidarity of the international working class. A
Russian dignitary announced that a banner was about to be
presented to the city whose workers had taken part in the most
significant proletarian uprising in the twentieth century, apart,
of course, from the heroic vanguard in the Soviet Union.
Larkin was in the audience. He walked past a bewildered Baltic
delegate who had been selected for this honor, furled the
banner under his arm, and treated the comrades to an hour of
oratory on the peculiarities of nationalism. Dublin settled
down, as Frank O'Connor wrote, to exchanging the familiar old
complaints.

> Things are much the same again, damn the thing to eat;
> Not a bloody fag since noon and such a price for meat.
> Not a bit of fire at home all the livelong day.
> Roll the stone away, Lord, roll the stone away.

Why did this eruption of suppressed anger never find any
political expression, as it did in the Communist and Socialist
parties of Europe? One good reason came to light in the first
census of the Irish Free State, taken in 1926. There were ninety
thousand domestic servants then, just about equaling the total
number of factory workers. Having a servant, often paid little
or nothing and exempt from any form of social insurance, was a
symbol of prestige for a priest, a doctor, a lawyer, a sham squire,
just as it had been for the half-pay Anglo-Irish colonel. The

tradition continues. The last available census figures show that there are thousands of domestic servants and housekeepers in the Republic, still excluded from all social security provisions. If the complex ideology of the native Irish could be encompassed in a phrase, perhaps it is wrapped in the line snapped out by a servant to her Anglo-Irish master in the 1920s: "Youse will be us now, and we will be youse."

The style of Irish living today owes a great deal to the heritage of landlord-tenant relationship that began centuries before the Earl of Cork arrived on the scene. Today an astonishingly small number of people actually produce things; less than two in ten of the working population can be classified as factory workers. The farmers, lawyers, auctioneers, bookmakers, brokers, accountants, architects, the army of self-employed people who want to be "them," who inundated the publishers of the first Irish *Who's Who* in 1973 with their lengthy biographies, complete with real and imaginary qualifications, make up 26 percent of the national work force, probably the highest proportion of any Western country. They have preserved the colonial pattern, as the Indians have preserved the tradition of tea in the afternoon and a chukker of polo on the Maidan.

Being "in trade" is still a mark of social inferiority. If two old members of the Kildare Street Club see an energetic new young member appear, one is likely to say to the other, "A bit of a counter-jumper, that lad," as if he had doffed his working clothes; just as Oliver St. John Gogarty, asked to define a mysterious change in the character of Yeats's poetry, said, "Oh, he's just evicting imaginary tenants." The Kildare Street Club has fallen on hard times now, lack of membership and money forcing the governors to allow an insurance company to occupy half of the hallowed old premises. Times have changed, but the old leather chair balanced on the weighing scales is still available for members who are concerned that they might be overweight for the Gentleman's Steeplechase at Punchestown.

The style of the up-and-coming businessman, even if he has

made the obligatory visit to Harvard or the Stanford Business School, owes much to the fops, rakes, and plungers of the past. "Cultural System Blamed for Lack of Entrepreneurs," read the headline of a story in the *Irish Times* of January 15, 1974. The story went on to describe a survey of twenty-two manufacturers and has this penetrating summary: "If there is one thing successful Irish entrepreneurs are determined not to do, it is to sacrifice their private lives to the job." Like the cavalry officers of garrison towns, a lot of businessmen find time for dining, drinking, dancing, riding, steeplechasing, pigeon shooting, tandem driving, garrison balls and garrison plays, with perhaps a little wenching on the side. In their own way they are trying to revive what a historian has described as the gaiety and gorgeousness of the Irish provinces in the early nineteenth century, when a family drove to Cashel races in a bottle-green silver-plated coach, and afterward attended a ball where the rake of the family was dressed in a "pink lutestring suit blazing brilliants from top to toe and covered with double paste buttons on cuffs, knees and shoes." The lack of industriousness that Rinuccini complained about is still noticeable, as is the presence of some foppish dressers. In battle and business, the Irish lean to the quick, decisive stroke. They may lose badly, they may be humiliated in the eyes of others, but the loss is so complete and cathartic that it clears the mind wonderfully for another adventure.

In a wry salute to the Irish-Americans,* Daniel Patrick Moynihan has suggested, with persuasive sociological chapter and verse, that, in business, the Irish are less successful than other ethnic groups. Moynihan wrote: "The curious distribution of even successful Catholics—getting ahead as bankers before making much progress as merchants—raises the question whether

* Nathan Glazer and Daniel Patrick Moynihan, *Beyond the Melting Pot.* Cambridge, M.I.T. Press, 1963.

the relatively poor showing of Catholics in the business world is not primarily a poor Irish showing. The Italians and Poles and Puerto Ricans have not really been settled long enough to make it clear what their performance in normal circumstances will be. In time they may produce a Catholic business class that is quite up to average. But clearly, the Irish have not done so."

Generalizations about racial groups can lead into dangerous shoals. However, the judgment that the Irish have no head for conventional business has an arresting core of truth. How else can one explain that the island perched on the edge of a fishing area so rich that it attracts trawlers from the Soviet Union and Japan has never developed a fishing industry? There is another tribal quirk to complicate matters: fishermen in the West of Ireland traditionally have refused to learn how to swim, preferring to drown swiftly if their frail curraghs made of laths and fabric are damaged in a storm. Well, then, why not buy a modern trawler? Because pride and suspicion make cooperative ventures almost impossible to organize. The fishermen stay close to shore, shooting their lines, while the foreign trawlers steam along the horizon. Among farmers, productive cooperative movements are so rare that when Father James McDyer brought together the poor residents of the remote Donegal townland of Glencolumbkille to form a successful vegetable-growing co-op, he became something of a national celebrity. Tourist-oriented publicity helps provide a market for traditional but small cottage industries such as weaving, knitting, and leather work; a venture into vegetable processing and canning in the same region, however, was looked on as unfair competition by larger privately owned companies.

Suspicion and secrecy characterize every form of enterprise in Ireland. In a society that cut itself off from Europe by choice in the thirties, the custom of keeping sensitive information within the family was understandable, but it bred inefficiency and arrogance. In the mid-sixties, after Ireland had signed a trade agreement giving Britain gradual entry into the Irish market, the incapacity of Irish businessmen to compete was quickly apparent. Not alone did English companies capture greater market shares, but on occasion they so weakened Irish enterprises that mergers and acquisitions became the order of the day. A lot of the native companies had enjoyed a monopoly market for decades, a profitable gift from the government requiring little or no initiative on the part of the managers. The art of manufacturing requires discipline, hard work, patience, and often subtlety, qualities rare in Irish businessmen. They prefer a more poetic approach to making money, in banking, brokering, and real estate speculation.

The atmosphere in the Dublin Stock Exchange today greatly resembles the free and easy days of the 1960s in Wall Street when Irish-Americans controlled the lesser of the two New York stock exchanges. The Dublin exchange has the ambiance of Las Vegas and is even less demanding in the information it requires of its traders. As a gambling vehicle it suits the Irish temperament, for the odds are high, anonymity is preserved, and the volume of trading is never disclosed. Antitrust laws in Ireland are nonexistent; there is no capital-gains tax (one was proposed in the spring of 1974); accounting systems are, to say the least, creative; and rules against insider stock trading are easily circumvented. Given this climate, a conglomerator can set full sail on a direct course, satisfied that no legal reefs bar his route. A listing on the Irish Stock Exchange is in some respects like having a numbered Swiss bank account. The Dublin institution, although it has merged with the London Stock Exchange, is extremely close-mouthed about the affairs of its listed companies. Stock prices are determined by private negotiations, and the exchange has a firm practice that the actual number of shares traded in individual securities be kept secret. Moreover, insiders are not required to disclose their transactions, which encourages many an incestuous deal. Nothing prevents the directors of listed companies from exchanging bundles of their own paper.

The role of a businessman in Ireland is secondary to that of a Church leader. His social role is to provide jobs, which leads to the overstaffing of many businesses and uncompetitive pricing for products. The hierarchy of an Irish company is rigidly authoritarian; the chairman thinks of himself as being the leader of a clan. Executives, office staff, and production workers are cast in the roles of lesser clan members; criticism of the chairman's decisions and orders is very rare. Companies are still small enough to preserve the outward appearance of a family business, with the name and family circumstances of each worker known to the chairman. However admirable the style may be in a world that is growing more and more impersonal, it destroys incentive. The rewards go to a few at the top, in the form of high salaries, expense accounts, stock options, and social standing; those at the bottom make barely a subsistence wage. Although many of the larger Irish companies are listed on the Dublin Stock Exchange, and therefore are theoretically "public" companies, stock ownership is not sufficiently widespread to threaten a stockholder revolt if the company performs badly. The chairman, therefore, is in an unassailable position of authority, answering to nobody, for his board members are usually friends and relatives.

It is entirely in character for Irish businessmen to have adopted with collective enthusiasm the most poetic free-form business enterprise, the conglomerate. The conglomerate is not concerned with workers, production lines, or products but with negotiations for the merger and acquisition of pieces of paper. It entails face-to-face bargaining at secret meetings in a conspiratorial atmosphere of great appeal to the wheeler-dealer. The search for the perfect moneymaking formula, the unique get-rich-quick scheme, which arrives in a providential moment of inspiration, has some interesting historical parallels. Irish-born inventors are few, and those who have made a mark in the world, like Charles Parsons, who developed the steam turbine, or J. P. Holland, who built a prototype of the modern submarine in the United States a century ago, never really brought their ideas to a practical conclusion. The great Irish mathematicians of the nineteenth century also seem to have lacked staying power, and, curiously, they left no tradition of science to the following generations. After William Rowan Hamilton scratched the formula for quaternions on a canal bridge, a breakthrough in theoretical physics, his genius seemed to dissipate. *An Investigation of the Laws of Thought,* written by George Boole in 1854, contained the essential formulae for pure mathematics, as Bertrand Russell later acknowledged. He did not progress further. Such men were rare, however, even with those limitations. Writers, politicians, lawyers, soldiers, doctors, churchmen, and minor professionals are listed in abundance in Irish directories; not a single great native scientist or man of industry appears.

When the chief of the London Bureau of *Time* magazine recently was asked to submit names of prominent young businessmen who might make a mark in the enlarged Common Market, his Irish candidate was Dermot Ryan, a slim saturnine fellow who must have seemed something of a dilettante to journalists recording the epic deeds of eighteen-hour-a-day tycoons. Ryan did not make *Time*'s list of those most likely to succeed, a loss to its readers. At nineteen, Ryan began renting used cars to his friends. That sideline gradually blossomed into a national car-rental service, then into a motel business, then into a European travel enterprise. When his businesses were firmly established, he took four hundred lessons over a two-year period in order to become an expert horseman and show jumper. His verse appeared in newspapers signed Douwl Topebe, an anagram for "Would-Be Poet."

"A man can only be expected to be professional in one area," an American banker who lives in Dublin said to me in the course of explaining his frustrations at what he felt were the casual approaches to money matters by Irish businessmen. "These fellows think they know everything. I'm expected to tag along to every art showing, every poetry reading, every cross-country race meeting." I sympathized with him, for American businessmen tend to plow a single furrow, which can be perfect, however dull.

A visitor to Gordon Lambert, chairman of Jacob's, a large manufacturing company by Irish standards, is sure to come away with the impression that Lambert has missed his vocation. Collecting modern art, to which he has devoted a lot of his time and money, seems to be as close to his heart as the market shares of Jacob's Cream Crackers. I felt distinctly uneasy listening to Lambert's erudite monologue; the Irish have a singular ability to memorize arcane details to bewilder a competing conversationalist. The numbed visitor cannot distinguish whether he is crossing swords with Renaissance men or gifted amateurs. The exhibition of superior knowledge has carried over lamentably into business conversation, especially by those who have attended crash courses at business schools abroad. "Why are you building that canning plant?" I asked Tony O'Reilly, the most flamboyant of the young businessmen. Out poured a dissertation on discounted cash flow, with a lengthy footnote on the relative merits of two- and three-ply cans. As he came toward the end of his recitation, O'Reilly's serious freckled face broke into a smile, then a grin, finally dissolving in quiet laughter. "Word perfect," I could hear him saying to himself.

Besides plunging on the stockmarket, speculators find plenty of other public facilities for striking it rich. There are 879 bookmaking offices scattered around the country for the convenience of punters, who bet $124 million on horse and dog racing alone in 1972. (Eighty-five million dollars was budgeted that year for the first-level education of 500,000 children.) A businessman is not considered well rounded unless he makes his presence felt on the horse-racing scene. Usually, representatives of most of the top one hundred companies in the United States are on hand for the opening round of the Masters golf tournament in Atlanta. The Irish business fraternity congregates almost every Saturday at one of the racetracks around Dublin.

It was only natural that out of this capricious, speculative postrevolutionary society should emerge a modern Dublin buck. No casting director could have bypassed Joseph McGrath for the part. He was larger than life, lucky as only the Irish can be, enormously rich, very mysterious, and slightly sinister, a genius who founded the world's best-known lottery, the Irish Hospitals Sweepstakes. McGrath started out as an office boy, graduated to a clerkship in the Transport and General Workers Union, where he doubtless rubbed shoulders with Sean O'Casey and other literary luminaries who were supporters of the revolutionary Dublin labor movement. In 1922, McGrath was suddenly elevated to the first Irish Cabinet. One can only speculate on the reasons for this sudden ascendancy to the Ministry of Labour. Authoritative people say McGrath was inducted into the oath-bound Irish Republican Brotherhood at an early age. The IRB, which was founded in the nineteenth century by Irish nationalists living in the United States, was tougher and more ambitious than the usual run of Irish secret societies. From the beginning, it claimed jurisdiction over what is called the "national territory"; in other words, the Brotherhood asserted *its* hegemony, not that of an elected parliament, over the entire island. Moreover, the IRB was guided by an executive whose identity was not known to the other members. This seems to have been a standard organizational tool, as much to confuse espionage outfits like the British Secret Service as to provide a mystique for the membership. The pattern has been used by Irish secret societies like the Molly Maguires in the coal fields of Pennsylvania, by Communist parties in various countries, labor unions, Algerian rebels in the sixties, and no doubt is the structure today of the various revolutionary groups in Latin America.

If he was a member of the inner circle, and McGrath later spoke in Cabinet meetings with that kind of authority, he had access to much invaluable and secret information. He was a close associate of Michael Collins, a more imposing political leader than Eamon de Valera. Collins was de Valera's superior in a sense, for he was president of the Supreme Council of the IRB and treasurer of that organization. During the negotiations that led to the formation of the Irish Free State, McGrath was commissioned by Collins as a kind of ambassador-courier on visits to the British Prime Minister, Lloyd George. After the Civil War of 1921–22, during which Collins was assassinated (Collins led the so-called Free Staters, de Valera was chief of the Republicans), McGrath popped up in the first Irish Cabinet. He is remembered less for his mastery of the legislative process than for his crucial Cabinet vote that approved the execution of four Republican political opponents suspected of murdering two members of Parliament. The official historical accounts are vague on the reasons, but McGrath later quarreled with his Cabinet colleagues over a threatened army mutiny. He resigned. Then he appeared on the public scene as the construction boss of Ireland's first hydroelectric plant on the River Shannon, a job which in those turbulent days was more important than it may now seem. The clash between opposing armed forces on the site—one side representing science and industrialization, the other the old rural Gaelic Ireland—was so symbolic of the struggle then being played out in real life that, as a literary subject, it was irresistible; Denis Johnston wrote *The Moon in the Yellow River*, for the Abbey Theatre, in 1931. In those days, McGrath was squarely on the side of science.

One must dwell a little further on the nature of the Irish Republican Brotherhood here to gain some perspective on McGrath's subsequent career. Because no official records exist, there is no evidence that the IRB was ever disbanded. Indeed, if it was to fulfill its constituted mandate of holding jurisdiction over Ireland, North and South, it could not be abolished. While it may not live on in name, it is certainly represented in Ireland by forces within the IRA and in parliamentary politics.

In the United States, the IRB tradition is carried on in public by fund-raising organizations which ostensibly collect money for Catholic families in the North of Ireland and privately by people who assume other identities and have respectable occupations as a cover for their organizational and smuggling activities. No secret organization is without its powerful public sympathizers, consisting of some who are quite aware of nefarious schemes but who balk at joining, and others who are seduced by the idea of rubbing shoulders with revolutionaries. A lot of Irish-American politicians fall into the last category. One has only to recall the many prominent American Jews who supported such underground organizations as the Irgun Zvai Leumi in the creation of the state of Israel to get the analogy. The Irgun developed an organization to raise money to buy arms in the United States and elsewhere, which were smuggled into what was then Palestine. The Irgun had copied the methods devised by the Irish Republican Brotherhood in the nineteenth century and later: secret bank accounts, assumed names, codes, various front organizations and businesses, and a powerful propaganda effort that can be measured by the sympathetic contemporary press accounts and later histories.

It was such an apparatus that McGrath was to use later for the administration and operation of the Irish Hospitals Sweepstakes. Conveniently, his IRB connection also gave him a powerful argument to use in persuading the government to support his gambling operation. The Sweepstakes would provide lucrative employment for Irish revolutionaries who were genuinely looking for employment. It would also be used, and this was the clincher, to get some discontented gunmen out of Ireland and into positions abroad where they could make a lot of money as distributors of Sweepstakes tickets. Southern Ireland was as violent a place in the 1920s as Northern Ireland is today; bank holdups, payroll robberies, and murders were commonplace. The violent flavor of the times can be measured in one of the comments of Kevin O'Higgins, the tough puritanical Minister of Home Affairs: "We have no real conception of freedom, no real conception of independence. If we had, we would be dignified enough to appreciate what democracy means, and to resent more savagely and fiercely than we do, the claim of any wretched minority to dictate to their fellow-citizens at the point of a gun. It is the slave drop in us, the slave mind lingering in our midst, which makes us bear that thing with the equanimity and complacency with which we have borne it."*

Under the financial strain of conducting a civil war and pacifying a discontented people, the Free State government almost collapsed. It was saved by a fortuitous loan from the Bank of Ireland. Although health and hospital care in Ireland were one of the great scandals of the day (the rates of infant mortality and tuberculosis were the highest in Europe), the government was not about to spend a large part of its budget on a remedial crash program. This gave McGrath a vital opening. Why not finance medical care through gambling, a world-wide gambling game that would cost the government nothing?

The idea initially ran into strenuous opposition from McGrath's former Cabinet colleague Kevin O'Higgins, who felt that there were "too many people trying to live too well out of too small production of wealth." In Parliament, O'Higgins complained that his private office had become damp from the tears of weeping promoters crying the virtues of lotteries. O'Higgins was shot dead one Sunday morning in 1927 while on his way to Mass. The perpetrators were never caught. Another opponent was Thomas Johnson, leader of the Labour Party. "The professional promoters are tumbling over themselves to get hold of a charity," said Johnson. "They are like the professional beggar who gets hold of the most decrepit child for exciting the charity of the public." That image was to inspire

* Terence de Vere White, *Kevin O'Higgins*. London, Methuen, 1948.

one of McGrath's later promotional efforts. The Catholic Church in Ireland has always reserved to itself veto power over government policy on health. The hierarchy supported Mc-Grath's lottery. Needless to say, the plan was approved by the government in 1930.

For assistance in the complexities of structuring a gambling operation with universal appeal, McGrath turned to two colorful friends. The first, Richard Duggan, was a hotel waiter who, according to a possibly apocryphal story, had run bets for customers. Noting that the odds were always weighted on the side of a canny bookmaker, he decided to go into business for himself. He became a familiar figure at the track, standing beneath a colorful sign that said, "Dickie always pays what he lays." Along with his betting business, Duggan ran a number of small lotteries in the twenties, including one for a Dublin hospital.

Spencer Freeman, the only surviving member of the trio, was born in Wales. A footloose wanderer in his youth, he traveled in South Africa, turned up in Chicago and worked, at one time or another, for Chrysler and Pullman. Freeman enlisted in the ranks of the British army at the outbreak of World War I, was quickly given a captain's commission, and ended up, according to his own account, "supervising thousands of German prisoners of war." On the wall of his luxurious office, Freeman has a framed letter of commendation from Sir Winston Churchill for his service as an executive in Britain's Ministry of Aircraft Production during World War II, for which he received the Order of the British Empire from King George VI. Freeman has all the boosterish enthusiasm of a member of the Chamber of Commerce in Zenith City. Indeed, he even looks a little like an octogenarian Babbitt. He founded something called the "Good Luck Club," which adopted "Be Deserving" as its motto. He also wrote inspirational pamphlets such as *You Can Get to the Top*. Like Stalin's writings on politics, it comes from someone who knows the real thing.

The Hospitals Trust was set up in style, by nothing less than an act of Parliament. In order to preserve the fiction that the Sweepstakes was a charitable organization, a special tax status was established for the Hospitals Trust. The corporation makes a small payment—called stamp duty—to the government. It amounts to 6.4 percent of net proceeds.

There is no public audit of the Hospitals Trust's books, and the company proffers no detailed information on its finances. Under the law, the Hospitals Trust is entitled to use up to 23 percent for expenses (a pretty generous allowance, considering that the government-run Puerto Rican lottery spends only 1.7 percent of its take). The company can also take a maximum of 7 percent for promoting the lottery and $2\frac{1}{8}$ percent as a management fee, and an additional unspecified amount for "commissions, prizes or other remuneration given in relation to the sale of tickets." Since it is not obliged to disclose the actual number of tickets sold, the reported figure for net proceeds must be treated with a certain skepticism.

Those who think of Ivy Lee, who softened Rockefeller's hard public edges by advising the old curmudgeon to give dimes to children, as the father of modern public relations might consider the staging of the first Sweepstakes. It took place in Dublin in 1930 with what can only be called a world-wide trumpet blast of favorable publicity. The stage was set with low-keyed pageantry—bishops, politicians, titled gentry, pretty nurses in starched uniforms, the Commissioner of Police, a military band, and Joe, Spencer, and Dickie watching *a blind urchin draw the winning ticket!* The blind child brought forth a single winning ticket for three poor fellows in Protestant Belfast, who won the top prize of $584,617.60. A Mr. Dawe from Vancouver won $233,847.60, and a Mrs. Thompson of Worksop, England, won $116,922.40. Ah! Lady Luck brought fortune around the world. What would have been the result of future lotteries, one wonders, if the three winners happened to be from, respectively, Dublin, Cork, and the townland of Jack's Hole? In those

Depression days, the magical arrival of $233,847.60 in Vancouver was good for stories in every North American newspaper, while the Worksop lady's windfall took pre-eminent spots in the European dailies. The three Belfast winners proved, above all else, that no element of sectarian bias was present; Catholics would receive no favor from Joe, Spencer, and Dickie. People who bought tickets on that magical Manchester November Handicap of November 22, 1930, read the news, checked their tickets, and read once again that the whole business was under the supervision of Viscount Powerscourt and some other people with resoundingly respectable names. It just had to be on the level.

The flavor of honest charity is somewhat deceptive. Despite its eleemosynary title, the Hospitals Trust is a private company run for profit. Its handful of stockholders have used their earnings from the Sweepstakes to build a group of industrial enterprises that loom important in Ireland's economy. Since the lottery was organized forty-five years ago, it has grossed between $2 and $3 billion. Some of this money has truly gone to assist hospitals, though there is a question about the precise amount; company executives give out one figure, while the Irish government gives another. Whatever the amount, which ranges from $200 million upward, it is a small fraction of the Hospitals Trust's total receipts and less than the company would have had to pay in normal corporate taxes were it not blessed with official exemption. "The worthy cause of helping the hospitals is used as a cloak of covetousness," said the Church of Ireland Temperance and Welfare Society in one of its periodic attacks on the Sweepstakes. But the Society, which speaks for the country's small Protestant minority, is practically alone in its criticism. The Sweepstakes can always counter with a clerical reference like this panegyric from the Right Reverend Monsignor Donald A. McGowan, who was at one time a director of the Irish Bureau of Health and Hospitals: "Thus, through the efforts of the Irish people and in their own characteristic way, the sick in

Ireland have come into their own and are treated as human beings and Christians."

In a nation where gambling is a legal and socially acceptable form of recreation, an accepted vice of the rich and the poor, the Sweepstakes enjoys the respect of the public and the benevolent protection of the government. The prize drawings in Dublin are festive occasions that make the front pages of the Irish press and, by some mysterious method of editorial selection, are publicized in many other countries, including the United States, where the lottery is illegal. Counterfoils bearing the names of ticket purchasers the world over are mixed, and in an elaborate ceremony officials draw the winning numbers. An added ring of respectability comes from the printed assurance that the drawing for winning tickets is held under the supervision of the Commissioner of Police. Each Sweepstakes is based on a specific horse race—such as the Lincolnshire Handicap, run at Doncaster in England in the spring; the Cambridgeshire, at Newmarket in England in the fall; and the Irish Sweeps Derby, at the Curragh, near Dublin, in the summer. Winning tickets plucked from the revolving drum are matched with a horse in the race; the big prizes go to those whose horses win, place, or show. The top prize now is $500,000, enough, even after taxes, to change a man's life overnight. Hundreds of consolation prizes are awarded to ticketholders whose horses were also-rans.

Sweepstakes officials boast that they will make payments in any currency—yen, dollars, rubles, pounds, dinars, leks, pesos, francs, schillings, rupees, rands, levs, kyats, riels, sangs, kroner, pesetas, quetzals, drachmas, even the gallant gourde of Haiti, the winning won of Korea, the capricious cedi of Ghana, or the lordly Laotian kip. Precisely how this currency problem is handled if, say, a seaman from Vladivostok or an Irish-Catholic missionary in Laos wins the big prize is proprietary information that the Sweepstakes clan holds to its collective breast. The Russians never tell us how they manipulate international markets in gold and wheat, nor does the board of directors of

Coca-Cola allow the secret recipe to be whispered outside the board room in Atlanta. If a carload of kips has to be shipped to that Catholic missionary in Laos, the details are worked out in some sanctum of the Sweepstakes building in Ballsbridge, Dublin, which, when it was put up in the thirties, was one of the largest office blocks in Europe, covering God only knows how many acres. Like a true Irish revolutionary, Joe McGrath located his building directly opposite the great monument of the Anglo-Irish aristocracy, the ancient august quarters of the Royal Dublin Society, which was, not so long ago, considered such a hotbed of Protestant intrigue that Catholic children were forbidden to use its excellent library.

To date, citizens of forty-one countries have won a total of more than $850 million. Three times a year, several million Americans—and millions of citizens in 146 countries—pay three dollars a ticket to participate. They are investing their small sums in the age-old dream of getting rich quick. And those who lose carry away the soul-satisfying thought that the proceeds of their little gambling fling are going to finance medical care and hospitalization for the poor people of Ireland. In any one drawing, perhaps half of the net proceeds is set aside for prizes. To ensure a large number of winners and thus get maximum publicity, the sponsors divide the prize money into ten units, each of which is distributed among a complete set of winners.

Though perfectly legal in Ireland, the sale of Sweepstakes tickets is outlawed everywhere else; in some countries, police put it in a class with drug peddling. The Hospitals Trust, therefore, has to conduct its foreign operations with the stealth and secrecy of the old Republican Brotherhood smuggling techniques. Sweepstakes emissaries abroad must labor in anonymity, like operatives of the KGB, Britain's M15, or the CIA. The company's man in Montreal, for example, was known at one time as Agent 4268. No doubt the number is changed every quarter. Agents communicate with Dublin by an elaborate code system, often through a circuitous route that takes in four or five other cities. Tickets are smuggled through customs and then distributed by an underground network. The counterfoils of the sold tickets go back to Dublin headquarters by a similar route, emerging in blissful respectability on the day of the drawing before the stern gaze of the Commissioner of Police.

In the United States alone, an estimated $60 million is wagered each year on the Sweepstakes. Despite the best efforts of the FBI, the Department of Justice, the Customs Bureau, the Post Office Department, and the local police, tickets are freely available all over the country. "It's like Prohibition," says a Post Office official philosophically. Police in Canada have been somewhat more successful, and there a series of successful prosecutions has provided the most revealing glimpse to date of the scope and methods of the Sweepstakes underground sales organization. In September, 1965, state and local police throughout Canada seized $25 million worth of lottery tickets, arrested the main distributors, and succeeded, as a police spokesman put it, "in messing up the organization." The tickets had been shipped from Ireland into Montreal in numbered crates with a bill of lading describing the contents as "table jellies." From Montreal the tickets were distributed to cities as far away as Vancouver. During the raids, police discovered lists of agents and a code system identifying distributors.

U.S. law-enforcement agencies are continually frustrated in their attempts to break up the Sweepstakes sales operation. On occasion, large shipments of tickets are seized. In 1974, the Treasury Department intercepted a shipment in New York worth $15 million. On one occasion, Norfolk, Virginia, customs agents did score a coup of sorts when the *Irish Elm,* a freighter from Dublin owned by a government agency, steamed into the harbor at Newport News and in the cold dawn light unloaded fifty cases, containing a million and a half lottery tickets, into a waiting launch. Two men who were taking the tickets to dockside were arrested; a three-day trial resulted in a hung jury. Some crew members were also arrested, but they, too, were

released. "These men were pretty small cogs in the machinery,"
Roger T. Williams, the Assistant U.S. Attorney in Norfolk, told
me at the time. "They were making a maximum of two thousand dollars a trip." The U.S. chief of the Sweepstakes, whose
income must have been at least in the six figure range, was
sleeping comfortably in his Manhattan apartment when the
ship was seized.

The original investment in the Hospitals Trust, a mere
$201,500, has since multiplied perhaps as many times as the
Biblical loaves and fishes. Over the years, undistributed profits
were capitalized and distributed to the twenty stockholders as
fully paid shares. (Cash dividends were also declared.) Joe,
Spencer, and Dickie did handsomely as Irish law allowed. The
company did not allow its accumulated funds to sit idle in a
vault, waiting for conversion to kips or kroner. It transformed
itself, in effect, into a holding company with investments in a
host of industrial enterprises—container manufacturing, metals,
plastics, carpets, offshore oil, postcards, and, as Dubliners say
with pride, "The divil knows what all." The McGrath family's
particular pride and joy is Waterford Glass Ltd., founded with a
large infusion of lottery profit, and now one of the world's largest
crystal manufacturers. Waterford chandeliers hang in the British
Embassy in Moscow and in Westminster Abbey; the Irish government gave one to the John F. Kennedy Center for the Perform-
ing Arts in Washington. The original investment in Waterford
Glass was $870,750; in 1973, profits amounted to more than
$6,300,000, and the company has a two-year backlog of orders.

The Freeman and Duggan families used their earnings to set
up numerous investment companies for a plethora of ventures.
Spencer Freeman was a director of a large finance company in
the sixties; the Duggan family runs a prosperous insurance
business. So influential have the families become that their
members are invited to sit on boards of directors of companies
where they have little or no investment. In a country strapped

for native investment capital, the Sweepstakes sponsors are looked on as big investment bankers.

The business successes of the lottery promoters are not trumpeted to the multitudes. "What they don't know won't hurt them" is the attitude of most wealthy men in Ireland. As far as the Irish public is concerned, Spencer Freeman lives quietly in Knocklyon House, located in a fashionable suburb. The McGraths patronize racetracks in Ireland, with occasional forays to England, France, and the United States. The sons of Richard Duggan are eminently respectable clubmen who take their ease in the privacy of the Royal Irish Yacht Club or the Saint Stephen's Green Club. This near-anonymity does not reflect a lack of curiosity on the part of the public, who are well aware that there dwell among them a few people whose wealth is comparable to that of people listed on the *Fortune* list of the world's richest, and therefore, presumably, most powerful, men. Rather, it is a retention of the "God bless and keep ye, yer honor, and all that belongs to ye" style of the peasant, who lives in fear of the boss and never, never looks a gift horse in the mouth. Anyway, there is always the possibility that some Irish buyer will win the Sweepstakes. In the superdemocratic *Who's Who* in Ireland, a mailman named John B. McGowan lists as his ambition, "to win bonanza Irish Sweeps." He speaks for the multitude. Recently, an elderly tenant of the McGrath family won the jackpot $500,000 prize, one of the few native winners in Sweepstakes history. Who else would he trust the management of his windfall to but a McGrath-owned bank?

When I wrote a story on some aspects of the Sweepstakes for *Fortune* in 1966, the Hibernian version of hell broke loose. I knew the identity of the chief executive of the Sweepstakes in New York, a former IRA activist who was operating under a quite respectable cover as an importer of Irish products. He did not condescend to see me. Instead, I was directed to the fellow who legitimately handled the importing business from an enormous loft off Fifth Avenue. It was like being in the entrance

hall of Boscobel, the restored home of States Dyckman, one of
the original Dutch settlers on the Hudson. Dyckman put together a great collection of heavy old Waterford Glass, which is
on exhibition at Boscobel. In the loft we talked about various
Irish products. I told him that I particularly liked the cuts of
crystal named Kylemore, Glencree, Ashling, Deirdre, Hibernia,
and especially Innisfail, the old Gaelic name for Ireland, which
translates as Island of Destiny. It appealed to me, I told him,
because it reminded me of the name Eamon de Valera gave his
political party when he decided to put away his gun and become
a parliamentarian: Fianna Fail, or Soldiers of Destiny. Since the
fellow's previous job was that of a hard-goods buyer, I'm not
sure he understood the conversation.

Talking to people in Ireland about the Sweepstakes is quite a
different and, indeed, a dangerous matter. As a subject for public debate, the Sweepstakes was long ruled out of order. With
his excellent public-relations judgment, McGrath had made the
Sweepstakes into one of the largest national advertisers, and not
until 1973 did a newspaper print any original material about
the lottery, its purpose, or its founders. One can hardly say that
abstract questions of morality troubled the impoverished Irish
intellectuals when the lottery was started, certainly not the
distinguished writers who appeared in *The Bell,* with its handsome subsidy from Joe McGrath. While the press abroad helped
promote the lottery with human-interest stories about impoverished families who were rescued from the poorhouse by spending their last few dollars on a Sweepstakes ticket, not a hard
word was said about the three charity buffs who ran the lottery.
The kind of stuff that appeared in the United States about
McGrath read like an encomium for a king. In her book *The
South and the West of It,** Oriana Atkinson, wife of former
New York Times drama critic Brooks Atkinson, compared him
to King Guaire, the seventh-century King of Connacht, whose
right hand grew longer than his left from the continual strain of

* New York, Random House, 1956.

giving handouts. Mrs. Atkinson told her readers: "No trouble is spared to make certain that everything in connection with the Sweepstakes is completely honest. In fact, the system used in collecting the tickets and storing them, and in the final selection of the winning numbers is so involved and inviolate that it makes me dizzy just to read about it. It is enough to say that even Willy Sutton, the famous American bank robber, could not figure out a way to beat the absolute integrity of the process."

Joe McGrath had just died when I began to look into the story in Dublin, more as a matter of curiosity than an intention of publishing anything. In death, the old warrior had become a national hero. Not only had he left the Irish Sweepstakes, Waterford Glass, and so many other monuments of honest toil; Ireland remembered him best because he had cocked a snoot at the English Crown through his successful horse-breeding business, a little sideline that ranked in size with the largest establishments of its kind in the world. He had lived near Dublin in the largest walled estate in Ireland, but when the Sweepstakes machinery was well oiled, he had devoted his energies to Brownstown Stud, a magnificently appointed five-hundred-acre farm. There he experimented with bloodlines, producing some of the finest thoroughbreds. One of the reasons for the success of American bloodstock is that McGrath mistakenly sold his great sire Nasrullah to a U.S. syndicate in the fifties. He must have talked about that slip when, as chief steward of the Irish Turf Club, he was given honorary membership in the American Jockey Club. Still, he managed to outperform Richard Croker, the Tammany boss who ran to Europe with millions and set about winning the English Derby to disconcert aristocrats who wouldn't raise a glass with him. McGrath won his first English Derby in 1951 with Arctic Prince, a colt he bred himself. As he led his tough little horse into the winner's circle at Epsom, it was more of a national celebration for Ireland than a personal triumph. Under his slouch hat, McGrath's face was a picture of honest ecstasy. His puckish smile was directed toward young Princess Elizabeth, seated in her box with the Court entourage, a smile sufficiently theatrical that all his countrymen could tell that he was about to frame the words that any decent Irishman would say on that occasion: "There y'are now, Ma'am. It takes an Irishman to beat yez at yer own game." (There are some solemn IRA fellows who insist that Joe would never recognize royalty. But I think he had become so lordly himself by then that he might have expected the members of the House of Windsor to bow to him in return.)

"Don't say a bad word about old Joe," a journalist friend in Dublin told me. "He's done an awful power of good for this little country." The country had done nicely by Joe, too, I thought. Patrick McGrath, one of Joe McGrath's three sons, had become chairman of the Sweepstakes, but Spencer Freeman was delegated to do all the talking. He was overcome with a passionate zeal for the respectability of the founding fathers. "Some people say that Joe was a gunman and I was a racing tout," he complained with all the vigor of a bookie who has been taken by a bandit. "It's not true. We are respectable businessmen." Otherwise, he was as noncommunicative as the Pope must be after hearing the confession of a bishop or a cardinal. To unearth the legislative maze that protected the Sweepstakes, I spent a dusty week in the bowels of Dublin Castle, a repository for important documents, like secret treaties and the tax agreement between the Sweepstakes and the government. I emerged parched, but full of knowledge and eager questions. They were not to be answered in Dublin.

Spencer Freeman pursued me by long-distance telephone to New York, where his tremulous voice echoed daily in my office with alternate fulminations and pleas for fair play. "Facts are facts," I told Spencer whenever I could get a word in edgewise, for he is extremely voluble when the humor is on him. The trail in the United States led to some odd conversations.

I began by exploring the matter with one of New York's

finest policemen, Deputy Inspector Joseph Walsh, who stared at me with the disbelief of someone who had just heard that a brothel was operating in the basement of Saint Patrick's Cathedral when I asked him how many Sweepstakes operators the New York police had arrested. He recovered quickly and said nothing. It would be more correct to say that he said a lot but never got around to explaining why the department had never bagged any of the well-known lottery men. An encounter then took place in Washington that proved more puzzling still; one could expect a New York cop to take it easy on the Irish, but the criminal expert this time was Henry Petersen of the Justice Department, who subsequently appeared in the Watergate investigation. When testifying before the Ervin Committee, Petersen portrayed a man in anguish, a professional Department of Justice man who had been raped during the cover-up conspiracy. When I asked him about the curious immunity that the Sweepstakes operators seemed to have in the United States, he had an interesting but rather puzzling explanation. Petersen suggested that the Department of Justice had better things to do than tracking down the sellers of Irish lottery tickets, such as arresting and convicting various alleged Mafia figures. He named three or four people whom I recognized. Still, whatever the manpower restrictions in the Department, it seemed a curious distinction, almost like the line that is usually drawn between white-collar crime and the other kinds. Just as people find it hard to credit that a man of standing in a Wall Street brokerage house has been stealing the customers' money, law-enforcement men in the United States, when they hear the words "Irish Hospitals Sweepstakes," never, never picture the possibility of large-scale fleecing.

When the story finally appeared in *Fortune* in November, 1966, an Irish-American who had been persuaded by the Irish government to invest some millions in the faltering economy was so outraged at what he felt was a gigantic, government-protected, floating international crap game that he sent copies

of the story, not at my suggestion, to every member of the Irish
Parliament and many other prominent Irish citizens. One brave
fellow asked a question in Parliament of the then Prime Minister, Jack Lynch. Lynch's manner of speaking when under
pressure is less than magisterial; it is closer to that of an
exasperated schoolmaster who, after the third verbal warning to
an errant pupil, is about to reach for an instrument of corporal
punishment. The Prime Minister cut off the debate with a
sentence or two. He was not quite as snappy as Eamon de
Valera, who in the thirties had silenced Leinster House by
declaiming to a questioner about the operation of the sweepstakes: "Might I suggest that it is not in the national interest to
pursue that? The less the Deputy talks about it the better."

In 1966, the questions in Parliament gave the Irish newspapers a chance to comment. The best effort the entire corps of
Dublin journalists could manage was a story in the *Irish Press,*
the house organ of Mr. Lynch's political party, which began:
"Irish Americans are indignant about an article in the current
issue of a big business magazine 'Fortune' which carries a biting
attack on the Irish Sweep." I locked the door, called the chief of
security in the Time-Life Building, and asked him to tip me off
if anyone on his staff saw Jim Farley appear in the lobby with
his ashplant. It was Farley who, as Postmaster General in the
first Roosevelt administration, had given the green light to
newspaper editors who were anxious to print all the news that
was fit to print about the Irish Sweepstakes. Farley said it was
perfectly fine with him to print news about a charitable enterprise like the Irish Sweepstakes. As for the morality of it all, Jim
said, perhaps after consulting some eminent theologian, "If it is
going to impair our morals to know what is going on in the
world, that is a problem for our pastors, not the Post Office."
Farley liked to visit Ireland, where he cut up touches with his
old friends.

As a coda to the dirge of Spencer Freeman, the Irish government, or at least somebody of importance in Dublin (I never

did get to find out who gave the orders) , sent a delegation to me in the person of Cathal (Charles) Loughney, who was then top executive of the Irish Industrial Development Authority, an agency that smooths the way for foreign companies who want to invest in Ireland. At one time Loughney was the head of a trade association representing all the grocers in Ireland. When he asked me over lunch to retract the *Fortune* story, he had the solicitous air of a man who had overstocked badly on a bargain sale of Buttevant butter or Limerick bacon and was ready to unload fast. He told me that Joe McGrath had sent him to Switzerland when he was a lad, and that his tubercular condition had cleared up nicely in the Swiss sanitarium. I liked Mr. Loughney a lot. His story came across as fresh and true as anything out of Thomas Mann's great sanitarium novel, *The Magic Mountain*. I left him on the steps of the University Club, wondering what he would say to the mysterious chief who had sent him all the way to New York.

Some time after that visit, the Irish Sweepstakes became the subject of some comment in a Supreme Court case, *U.S.* v. *Fabrizio*. It turned out that Mr. Fabrizio had bought seventy-five tickets in the legal New Hampshire state lottery, but had committed the heinous crime of shipping them across state lines into Elmira, New York. When the Justice Department brought a case against Mr. Fabrizio in Rochester, New York, it was dismissed on the grounds that a federal statute did not apply to the legal New Hampshire lottery. The Justice Department was so concerned about this ruling that it appealed to the Supreme Court. The attorneys for the Sweepstakes Commission of the State of New Hampshire directed the attention of the then Chief Justice, Earl Warren, to the *Fortune* article. Warren asked the Justice Department attorney if he knew of any similar prosecutions against the Irish Sweepstakes. When the answer was no, Warren directed the Justice Department to submit a list of all prosecutions starting in 1961 involving the Irish lottery. I never did see that list, but I suspect, as did Edward Powers, the director of the New Hampshire lottery, that it fell a little short of showing great prosecutorial zeal.

Clearly the McGraths have some mysterious benefactors operating on their behalf in the United States. Some light was shed on the matter in 1973 by Oliver Pilat, the unofficial biographer of Drew Pearson.* Pilat claims that in the thirties Pearson accepted a $30,000-a-year contract, along with a chauffeur-driven Lincoln Continental, to handle the Sweepstakes public relations in Washington. The reaction in Dublin to a short review I wrote of Pilat's book for a magazine called *Profile* shows how tough the Sweepstakes people can be on their own turf. The entire issue of the magazine was destroyed at the printers, on what grounds I am unable to discover. Although the news soon reached the other Irish publishers, there was no outcry about freedom of the press, not even a smidgen of an editorial. I was rather disappointed, because Irish newspapers have an old tradition of editorial integrity, dating back to the turn of the century when the Skibbereen *Eagle* addressed itself to the Czar of all the Russias, warning him that news of the knouting of serfs had reached Ireland, and that it would continue to keep a stern eye on affairs in Russia. The latest news about Joe's son, Patrick McGrath, is that he has been elevated to the Irish Senate. I consoled myself by buying a Sweepstakes ticket for Patrick McGrath, which I mailed to his office in the hope that, should it win, he would be able to afford another Arctic Prince for another Derby. He never thanked me for the gift, but then the ticket I sent him never won a prize.

---

* Oliver Pilat, *Drew Pearson: An Unauthorized Biography*. New York, Harper's Magazine Press, 1973.

4

The Wild Geese Are Still Flying

Sean Kenny, a distinguished Irish architect who worked with Frank Lloyd Wright, was asked once if he could practice his profession in Ireland. Like Wilde, Joyce, O'Casey, Beckett, and so many before him, Kenny had a familiar answer. "You cannot survive in the climate of Ireland that has a false idea of religion and a false idea of God," he said, starting, as Irish emigrants always do, with clerical control of the state. "The Church puts a curb on the feelings of people as though she were afraid that there may be another revolution and that this revolution will be against the Church itself. By working in London, we can do more for Ireland than we could at home. We fight against our own limitations and against the idea that Irishmen are always drunk, never on time and unable to produce anything."*

The Irish are citizens of the world. When the time is propitious, they migrate with the natural instincts of wild geese, traveling ancient routes to Boston, London, Vancouver, or Sydney. Not all of them leave Ireland for the high-minded reasons advanced by people like Sean Kenny, who felt suffocated artistically because he saw Ireland as a place of "little men selling leprecauns made of bog oak." Within ten minutes' walk

* Des Hickey and Gus Smith, *A Paler Shade of Green*. London, Leslie Frewen, 1972.

of my home in New York live a diverse collection of Irishmen and their families, all of whom left Ireland in the past twenty years. We meet regularly—three doctors, a telephone technician, a trade-union officer, two lawyers, and a master plumber, Anthony Ward, whose artistic conscience is as pure as that of any architect. Ward returned to Ireland a few years ago, where he opened a central-heating business. The reverse emigration was a failure. "I didn't mind the employees taking seven tea breaks a day; that's standard procedure. But how can you do good work when the Irish plumbing system is still in the lead-pipe age?" An artist cannot live without a patron, a plumber without customers, a doctor without patients. Migration is the ultimate solution, as it was a century ago.

At least five out of every ten babies born this year in the Republic of Ireland will eventually leave the country to find employment, to marry, to raise families, and, sometime in the twenty-first century, to die abroad. This exodus, without parallel anywhere in the world, has led some serious scholars to suggest that the present population of Ireland should be examined as a refutation of Darwin's theory of the survival of the fittest.* "There's only a few of us left" is the standard greeting when Irishmen meet in New York. It would be just as appropriate in any town in Ireland.

* The following table shows the changes in population since 1841, for what is now the Republic of Ireland and for the North of Ireland. The Republic published its first census in 1926, and the latest enumeration, conducted in 1971, shows that the population has remained static since then. The North of Ireland, on the other hand, has shown substantial growth since 1926. Altogether, some 1,700,000 people left the Republic and about 460,000 left the North between 1901 and 1971.

	Republic of Ireland		Northern Ireland	
	Population	Percent Increase or Decrease	Population	Percent Increase or Decrease
1841	6,528,000		1,648,000	
1901	3,221,000	−50.7	1,236,000	−25
1926	2,971,000	− 7.8	1,256,000	+ 1.6
1971	2,978,000	+ 0.2	1,527,000	+12.1

Judging from migratory patterns since 1946, the Irish will continue to emigrate at an average annual rate of 24,000. From 1971 until the end of the century, about 720,000 will probably leave, most of them unmarried and in their twenties. Unending emigration is a mortal wound. As an endemic part of Irish life and culture, the causes of emigration should engage the energies of at least a few scholars. One waits in vain for enlightenment. There is no work comparable to Oscar Lewis' classic studies of Puerto Ricans who emigrated from the slums of San Juan to the barrios of East Harlem. While the rest of the world shudders at the apocalyptic vision of population explosion, by the year 2000 Ireland is likely to have one of the lowest population densities in Europe, an island of peace and emptiness for tourists to visit in the summer.

Some popular myths about Irish emigration need to be demolished. It is not confined to unskilled people from rural areas, but infects professional and managerial types from Dublin as well. Nor did the level of migration gradually taper off after the great waves of peasants left their potato patches in the nineteenth century. In the twenty-year period 1946–66, emigration was 13.2 percent higher than the natural increase in population. In layman's language, that means the excess of births over deaths in those decades was 537,834, but emigration of 608,939 reduced the population by more than 70,000. Literally, the Irish were a dying race. Almost 15 in every 1,000 were leaving the country during that period, the highest rate since the 1880s. In fact, the 58,200 people who left in 1957, the peak year of the post–World War II emigration, were more than the 54,200 who migrated in 1844, when the population was twice as great and impoverished peasants were deserting a blighted land.

Stagnation and unemployment alone could not have caused such flight. The miserable surroundings drove many people out; could anything in Coventry or Boston be worse? The air of despondency, lassitude, even despair, as I drove in to my office

in Dublin each morning in the fifties had a great deal to do with
my decision to leave. What was good enough for my contemporaries was decidedly not good enough for me. The country
looked and smelled like one enormous slum. Of the 676,402
dwellings in the Republic in 1961, only one-third had a bath, a
third had hot water, less than half had an indoor toilet. More
than half of the houses then dated back to the nineteenth
century, and 160,000 of them were crumbling slums more than a
hundred years old.

Some experts in Ireland believed that the tide had turned
when the census years of 1966 and 1971 showed a slight increase
in population. A closer reading of those numbers should elicit
concern, not celebration. The departure of young people after
World War II led to a decline in the work force of almost 14
percent. Between 1951 and 1971, three out of every five people
seeking jobs left the country. Fewer than four people out of
every ten were working in 1971, the lowest ratio in Europe.
The loss would have been greater still had it not been for the
inclusion as workers of two unlikely groups, making Ireland
such a demographic oddity: more than one-fifth of the
1,108,000 workers were boys and girls between the ages of
fifteen and nineteen, or old men over sixty-five. Such an oddly
tilted work force usually means that a country is either at war or
in the midst of a booming economy that has drawn every able-
bodied person to workbench or the office desk. In fact, Ireland
was then experiencing its worst rate of unemployment since the
fifties, a rate higher than any other nation in Europe. If anything, migration had exacerbated the vexing, seemingly insoluble problem of joblessness.

Economic experts were baffled. They had expected the country to reach a point of equilibrium after the massive postwar
emigration, with the shrunken labor force fully employed. The
80,000 unemployed in the winter of 1972 almost equaled the
total number working in the construction industry.

Annual wage increases of 16 percent and more reflected a

degree of inflation greater than in any of the seventeen nations of the OECD, including the United States and Japan. The Central Bank of Ireland, in its 1972–73 Annual Report, concluded: "This country is, therefore, experiencing the worst of both worlds; it has the highest rate of inflation in Western Europe and, at the same time, a major unemployment problem."

The paradox is explicable if one looks at the effects of emigration. Generations of young people are missing. Between 1946 and 1966 the number of people in the 15–29 age bracket had declined by almost 100,000. Reflecting earlier emigration patterns, the groups between the ages of 30 and 64 dropped by almost 60,000.* The absence of a generation of workers in their twenties and thirties means that a lot of the unemployed were unemployable. Many were old, unskilled men and, as applications for social-welfare benefits show, were suffering from diseases and disabilities. They had registered for unemployment benefits because the weekly disability payments were too low. Other unemployed included a large number of young people who had left school at fourteen, unskilled and frequently semiliterate.

Entry into the European Common Market, far from stemming emigration, may stimulate a fresh Irish exodus into this new territory. Until Ireland joined the Common Market in 1973, most European economists had considered the Italian Mezzogiorno the poorest area in Europe. For generations these southern Italians had sought escape from poverty through emi-

---

* The distribution of the population by age reflects heavy emigration by young people throughout the century. In 1901, the 15–29 age group made up 28.9 percent of the population. In 1966, they represented only 21 percent of a much smaller population.

Ages	1901	1926	1946	1966
0–14	972,900	867,800	822,900	900,000
15–29	931,200	741,700	690,700	594,000
30–64	1,108,000	1,090,500	1,126,500	1,067,000
65+	209,100	271,600	314,200	323,000

gration. In January, 1974, Professor Guglielmo Tagliacarne, an Italian economist and statistician, published some surprising findings.* Calabria was indeed poor, but four Irish regions along the western Atlantic coast were poorer still. Eight of the ten poorest areas in the Common Market's 120 regions were in the Republic of Ireland. (Only one Irish region—Dublin—did not make the list, although the per capita income there is about half the Common Market average.) The average per capita income for these eight poorest Irish regions was perhaps one-third of the Community average of $2,469.

This highly significant news may signal a new direction for future Irish emigration to countries like France and Germany, which are more prosperous than Britain, the traditional goal of the Irish emigrant, and which have economies growing at a much faster rate. Moreover, some of the Common Market countries are growing nervous about the millions of Algerians, Turks, and other Mediterranean peoples who have congregated in their cities, creating ethnic rivalries and social tensions. Some European politicians have suggested that quotas be established for emigrants from nonmember countries. The Irish, as full-fledged citizens of the European Community, are free to seek employment in any member country, and they are more than welcome, as anyone can see who reads the help-wanted columns of the Irish newspapers. A typical advertisement published in the *Irish Times* in July, 1973, read as follows:

Thrige-Titan Ltd., Odense, Denmark
require
FEMALE WORKERS
FOR ERECTION OF COMMUTATORS

Thrige-Titan Limited is one of the
largest factories in Denmark in the
electro mechanical line.

* *Irish Times,* January 14, 1974.

We primarily seek young, unmarried
women between 20 and 30 years. No
previous training necessary.

Employers in mainland Europe are anxious to recruit unskilled Irish workers for a number of reasons. The Irish have a
reputation for working harder abroad than at home, and because they are usually single they do not add to the burdensome
housing problem. One Danish advertiser recently received more
than four hundred applications for twelve jobs. Skilled and
professional Irish workers may well be drawn to the heartland
of the Common Market in the next few years. Irish schoolchildren prefer the study of German, French, and Italian to the
traditional Gaelic and Latin; the language problem will disappear within a decade. Unless the Irish government can find
some technique to improve the standard of living at home, the
attractions of European living may prove irresistible for young
people. Many of them have sampled the Alpine ski slopes and
Mediterranean beaches; they have returned home starry-eyed.

The shifting Irish population is literally moving closer and
closer to Europe, leaving the already depopulated area of the
West of the island and moving to the growing and comparatively vibrant city of Dublin. The outward trek continues from
there, as if people make the first move to Dublin, pause for a
time to gain some skills, and then move on to Europe, Canada,
Australia, and, occasionally, to the United States. Eventually,
inexorably, the coastal stretch between Dublin and Belfast will
become a megalopolis of sorts, not from choice but because the
economics of transportation and modern industry demand such
a configuration. The Irish government hopes that payments
from a special regional Common Market fund will enable it to
build up the underdeveloped rural economy of Western Ireland
and, indeed, of the whole of Ireland.

Even if the taxpayers of Europe come to Ireland's rescue with substantial subsidies—and the rancorous debates in Brussels suggest a great reluctance to hand out money without some controls over its spending—nobody seems to know how to tackle the country's economic and population problems. With the cumulative and devastating effect of emigration perhaps no solution is possible. As the working population grows smaller, as the tax base shrinks, the total income becomes smaller and smaller, investment that would provide job opportunities dries up, and the government ends up with less money for welfare programs.

If internal political pressure forces the government into two actions long overdue to lift Ireland's education standards and social-security provisions to match those of most Common Market countries—raising the school-leaving age to sixteen, and providing state pensions at age sixty-five—the working population would drop to a dangerously low level. This small productive group could not possibly provide the tax revenues necessary to finance the basic necessities of a modern society, and the Irish are now among the most heavily taxed citizens in Europe. Ironically, any improvement in the archaic methods of farming would make things even worse, for chances are that the 80,000 or so who will leave the small farms in the next ten or fifteen years will not be employed in Ireland. Since 1946, agricultural employment has declined by 300,000, while only 60,000 new jobs in manufacturing have been added during that twenty-seven-year period, an average of 2,200 jobs a year. Despite the best efforts of the government, the overall job market is contracting.

Like young people everywhere, Irish teenagers are far more politically minded than their parents. They are less nationalistic, more radical, and fiercely demanding in their approach to education and the job market. Their morale was not helped when they heard Michael O'Leary, the deadly serious, totally dedicated young Minister of Labour in the government of the Republic, and no Marxist, unconsciously echo the pure theory of surplus labor when he opened a debate in 1973 by saying, "It is, unfortunately, true, that no review of the Irish work situation can start at any point other than that of unemployment." With that factual statement, the impetus to emigrate, implanted in the mind of every Irish child as soon as he becomes old enough to think of his future life style, becomes too powerful to resist.

The government of the Republic has no policy on emigration and population. The official handbook distributed abroad by the Department of Foreign Affairs contains photographs of four famous emigrants: Luke Wadding, who founded Saint Isidore's College in Rome in the seventeenth century; Commodore John Barry, "Father of the American Navy"; Admiral William Brown, "founder of the Argentine Navy"; and His Grace, the Most Reverend Daniel Mannix, D.D., Archbishop of Melbourne, who died in 1963. Two priests and two sailors out of six million. The text mentions the flight of the Jacobite soldiers, the Wild Geese who sailed for France in 1691 to "die on far foreign fields from Dunkirk to Belgrade." A short section on the Irish abroad concludes: "As a majority of the Irish emigrants were Catholics it was natural that their dispersal should lead to a strengthening of the Catholic Church in their new homelands. Many present-day Church leaders in the United States, Britain, Australia and Canada are of Irish birth or descent. In the tradition of the monks of earlier centuries, Irishmen and women continue to leave Ireland as missionaries and educators. Irish bishops, priests, religious brothers, nuns, doctors, engineers, teachers and nurses are tending to the spiritual and temporal needs of their fellowmen on the five continents of the world to-day."

Quite possibly that paragraph was written by a priest, or a former priest, since it reflects so closely the view of the Irish Catholic Church that emigration is beneficial because it spreads the faith. Coincidentally, it also reflects the view of Henry Luce, the founder of Time Inc., who had a chance to observe some

Irish emigrants while he was growing up in a missionary compound in Tengchow, China. These Irishmen were priests, of course, single-mindedly converting the heathen Chinese, in contrast to Luce's father, who had to devote a good deal of time to his growing family. "The Irish make the best missionaries because they never married," Luce said to me once with the air of a man who had studied the question from all sides. "That's why they were the last Westerners to leave China." It's a good theory. However, it tells us nothing about the motives of lay emigrants. Anyone observing the behavior of the Irish living in New York or London would hardly say, as the Irish Department of Foreign Affairs does with such certitude, that they are "tending to the spiritual and temporal needs of their fellowmen."

The Irish government appointed a Commission on Population and Emigration, which published a lengthy report in 1954, a document bulging with statistics but empty of recommendations. The Commission saw emigration as a religious expression of free will. "As to emigration," went the report, "the individual exercising his free will is in normal circumstances free to leave when he wishes. Consequently, we believe that those who wish to and can emigrate have the right to do so, and that the State should not consider interfering with the exercise of this right, except in the case of a national emergency or where the survival of the nation is in jeopardy. We do not consider that our present demographic circumstances would justify such interference." Although the Commission did not concern itself with the political and economic consequences of emigration (why not? one wonders), it might well have appended Marx's observation, written in 1866 when the population of Ireland was 5.5 million, a million more than it is today. "England, with a fully developed capitalist production, and pre-eminently industrial, would have bled to death with such a drain of population as Ireland has suffered. But Ireland is at present only an agricultural district of England, marked off by a wide channel, to which it yields corn, wool, cattle, industrial and military recruits."

No historian has been able to explain why the Irish population grew at such a rate, from 550,000 in 1600, to 2,500,000 in 1700, to 5,000,000 in 1800, to 8,175,000 as enumerated in the official census of 1841. We can only surmise that the Irish must have married at puberty, or shortly afterward, and that the rented land was divided, subdivided, and subdivided again until families of ten and fifteen and twenty were existing on patches of land that produced nothing but potatoes. Even in those simple days, no other people had such faith in Providence. Hardly a shot was fired in anger. The people were meek, submissive; they had great respect for authority, which in those days was the local priest. Hundreds of thousands starved; they ate grass, weeds, nettles, sucked stones, and expired on the roadside. They went to their death like so many Jews in World War II, hoping against hope for salvation from some external power. In the decade of 1840–50, a million people died from starvation and a million and a half others took to the fever-ridden coffin ships for North America.

Before sailing for the New World, the emigrants had headed for the nearest English ports, ragged, ignorant, illiterate peasants striking terror in the hearts of the English politicians. The population explosion in Ireland was serious enough by the early nineteenth century for the British government to take notice. Flocking by their hungry thousands into the mill towns, the Irish provided a cheap, endless, docile supply of laborers. They came in such numbers that the population of Lancashire doubled between 1800 and 1823. Malthus, the recognized expert on population matters at the time, felt that the Irish were subhuman and, therefore, did not fit his theories on food and population. As food became scarcer, the population grew larger. He did side against the English millowners, who were more than happy to have a substitute for the indigenous industrial worker. "I really cannot conceive anything much more detestable," wrote Malthus, "than the idea of knowingly condemning the laborers of this country to the rags and wretched cabins of Ireland, for the sake of selling a few more broadcloths and calicoes."

The presence of this ragged, restless, growing foreign population was debated endlessly. Should the Irish be excluded from England, even though the Act of Union, passed in 1800, had made Ireland an integral part of Great Britain? Or should the government ship the wretches out to the colonies? A parliamentary committee sat for two years, in 1826 and 1827, listening to the expert witnesses. The committee thought that if English workers were given subsidized passage to the colonies, the Irish workers would quickly take their place in England, a horrible prognostication of pauperism and popery. The committee asked Malthus to appear; some of his answers would be as relevant today as they were then:

Q: If it be an admitted fact, that there are a great number of labourers for whose labour there is no real demand, and who have no means of subsistence, does it not necessarily follow that as far as the wealth of the country is concerned, these labourers are of no advantage?

MALTHUS: Certainly.

Q: In point of fact therefore if a thousand labourers, supposed to be under these circumstances, were to die, the wealth of the country would not be diminished by their decrease?

MALTHUS: I think not.*

The philosophers of the doctrine of laissez faire carried the day. Daniel O'Connell, the Irish leader who fought for Catholic emancipation, eventually granted in 1829, was as conservative as Edmund Burke when it came to such practical matters as emigration and labor. During a debate on a bill designed to improve the conditions of English child laborers, O'Connell

---

* Brian Inglis, *Men of Conscience*. New York, Macmillan, 1971.

expressed the wish ". . . would to God that children under thirteen years old in Ireland could earn the money the English factory children could have earned." The Irish leader died in Genoa in 1847 on his way to an audience with the Pope in Rome. He wished his heart to be buried in Rome and the rest of his embalmed body to be returned to his native country for burial. As the body of the Great Liberator was carried up the mouth of the River Liffey, the emigrant ship *Birmingham* sailed outward bound with a cargo of emigrants. O'Connell's last plea in Parliament for his countrymen was pathetic: "Ireland is in your hands. . . . If you do not save her she can't save herself."

England did not save her, and the Irish never forgot. In *Man and Superman,* Shaw has Malone, whom he describes as having "the self-confidence of one who has made money, and something of the truculence of one who has made it in a brutalizing struggle," talk about the famine.

MALONE: Me father died of starvation in Ireland in the black 47. Maybe you've heard of it.
MISS VIOLET: The Famine?
MALONE (*with smouldering passion*): No, the starvation. When a country is full o food, and exporting it, there can be no famine. Me father was starved dead; and I was starved out to America in me mother's arms. English rule drove me and mine out of Ireland. Well, you can keep Ireland. Me and me like are coming back to buy England; and we'll buy the best of it. . . .

England saw very few Malones, although they believed that Ambassador Joseph Kennedy acted a bit too much like a truculent Irishman in the early days of World War II. Ireland was neutral, of course, and the IRA was sending characters like Brendan Behan across the water to bomb civilians. The Irish did contribute just a little to the war effort; the British government recruited miners, laborers, and a few skilled hands for arms factories, and C. P. Snow persuaded some scientists from

Trinity College in Dublin to work on nuclear physics. Economically, the war was good for Ireland in at least one respect: the marriage rate increased slightly. Many temporary war workers stayed in England after 1945. Between 1946 and 1959, they were joined by some 350,000 others; the traffic has continued: by 1961, there were more than 170,000 people of Irish birth living in London, the second largest Catholic Irish urban population in Europe, Dublin, of course, being the largest.

The most recent British census, taken in 1971, shows that 720,985 people who were born in the Republic now live in England. Experts believe that the actual number is far greater than this, possibly as high as a million. The missing Irish absent themselves on the night of the census for a variety of reasons. Many of these migrants, who are, of course, free to enter England and to depart without passport or visa, are self-employed workers, mainly in the construction industry. In order to avoid paying taxes, they do not register with local unemployment offices. And for that reason they are excluded from all social-security provisions, including free medical care. Others are moving from one job to another. Some leave England the night before the census, especially husbands who have deserted their wives. And not a few have preserved their belief, nurtured from the cradle in Ireland, that any information, however little, given to any government official of any kind is too much. These independent souls are absent when the enumerator calls. They burn the questionnaires if the information is requested by mail. But even if the low figure published by the British government is accepted, it still represents about 23 percent of the Republic's population. The Irish work force of 442,430 is the largest "foreign" element in the British working population, larger than the contingents from India, Pakistan, the West Indies, Cyprus, and the old African colonies, a vitally important part of the British economy. During the sixties, when the British government passed strict laws against the entry of certain people from Commonwealth countries, Ireland was not included.

The Irish builders' laborer in England is a fixture of the urban scene. Donal MacAmlaigh, a perceptive laborer and part-time journalist, keeps the folks back home abreast of conditions. In August, 1973, he described, in an article written for the *Irish Times,* how he joined a group of nonunion Irishmen on a New City development in Milton Keynes, near the city of North-ampton. Wages were paid by the day, nine pounds, or about $108 a week, far more than any other industrial worker. The Irishmen worked from 8 A.M. to 6 P.M.; no safety precautions were observed, nor did they participate in any social-welfare or pension benefits. On one of the toilets on the site, some IRA-inspired graffiti reads: "1 Anglian, 2 R.E.M.E., 1 Light Infantry, 1 Scots Guards, 3 Green Howards, 1 Para = 1 Provo." The work gang, MacAmlaigh wrote, was made up of Irish and Jamaicans; the Jamaicans were skilled carpenters. "Culturally, of course," the Irishman wrote, "they differ widely from us and are in lots of ways more close to the English. . . . Otherwise they are very like most of the Irishmen you meet on building sites with their love of gambling, ready laughter, and in the certain knowledge that, no matter how polite a front they encounter on the part of the indigenous population, they are still regarded as being very much bottom drawer."

The "other" Irish in London—the doctors, lawyers, brokers, real estate speculators, and advertising men who drink martinis in the Irish Club—like to pretend that they are a different breed from the Paddy in the salmon-colored cloth cap. They read *Private Eye,* clown around at fashionable clubs like Annabel's, and hire striped pants and topper at Moss Bros. for a day out at the Ascot races. When these superior Irishmen gathered on St. Patrick's night to hear an address by Edward Heath, the world's most insensitive politician, they got an earful of what the son of a working-class Englishman thinks of the Irish. Looking, as always, as if he had just been scrubbed and starched in a public school laundry, Heath began by saying, "I know a great deal about the Irish. After all, my housekeeper is one."

The American WASP has *his* stereotyped view of the Irish character. On one memorable occasion, I got a taste of the "You may be Irish, but you're one of us" touches of Midwestern Protestant patronizing. When I visited Akron to interview a gentleman named J. Ward Keener, then board chairman of B. F. Goodrich, Keener leaned back in his leather armchair and asked me, "Do you know what my name means in Gaelic?" I pretended ignorance. "It means that I'm a professional mourner." It was a nice welcoming touch for a rubber manufacturer in the Midwest to know such trivia; he apparently thought that the keeners, the professional mourners who cried at funerals in the West of Ireland, were still extant. Keener looked as if he was about to break into a wail himself, because his company was being raided by two Jews, Laurence Tisch from New York and Ben Heineman from Chicago. He looked on me as a sympathetic confidant as he explained the machinations of these foreign invaders. On the way to his country club outside Akron, he pointed to the extraordinary number of golf courses along the way, turned to me, and said, "We even have one for the Jews." When I told the story to Tisch, he laughed bitterly.

The assumption that some of the 16.4 million people of Irish descent in the United States are anti-Semitic is, I suppose, a regrettable sign of progress. It confirms the latest data of the Census Bureau, which portray the Irish as being average Americans, earning average incomes with average-sized families, and, no doubt, with the same foibles and prejudices as every other ethnic group, including WASPS like J. Ward Keener. Perhaps something has been lost along the way in this assimilation, though, for in the role of the underdog the Irishman brought to the American scene the best and the worst of his volatile, charming, vindictive, mercurial personality. An Irish presence is still evident in the United States, though, at wakes, weddings, sporting events, and social clubs that attract some of the Irish-born and their children.

In 1970, the U.S. Census Bureau counted 1.5 million residents of Irish stock, meaning that they either had been born in the Republic of Ireland or had at least one parent who had been born there. By Irish standards this is a substantial number, equal to more than half the resident population of the Republic. Irish emigration to the United States slackened somewhat in the 1920s, when annual ethnic quotas (15,000 a year) set by Congress were never filled. By 1965, when new immigration laws were passed, the movement from Ireland to the United States was down to about 5,000 a year. Irish-American organizations claim that the new laws discriminate against the Irish. In 1973, fewer than a thousand visas were issued by the American Embassy in Dublin to prospective immigrants. Irish-American newspapers like the New York *Irish Echo* claim that a substantial number of people in the Old Sod want to live and work in the United States, but have neither close relatives there nor the requisite skills required for entry.

About half of all those now living who were born in Ireland live abroad. This estimate is far from precise, for governments have an annoying habit of using different methods of counting their resident populations at census time, and the Irish government has better things to do than count the "wild geese." The Irish are, however, dispersed widely: perhaps 1,000,000 in Great Britain, about 500,000 in the United States, 65,000 in Australia, 50,000 in Canada, with a scattering in New Zealand, the Union of South Africa, Rhodesia, and in Latin America. In the eighteen-county New York metropolitan area live 250,000 Irish, more than twice the population of the Republic's second city, Cork. If all the Irish in Canada decided to return, they would constitute, as a group, the third largest city in Ireland.

Those of Irish birth who live in the United States, their numbers dwindling year by year, nevertheless manage to keep Irish
International Airlines in business.

The decline of the Irish as a clannish, homogeneous group
who took care of each other is especially noticeable in New
York. In the thirties, clubhouse politics, the teaching profession,
the police, and the unions were dominated by Irish. As emigration declined, so did their influence. Only the Catholic Church
remains as a monument to the Irish emigrants, although
Church directories show an increasing number of priests and
bishops with Italian names. The Irish-American family is less
likely to produce a priest nowadays; more likely the oldest son
will become a lawyer, doctor, or Wall Street broker. The broad-
loom-carpet Irish are eminently respectable, drawing a clear
distinction between themselves and the likes of the bellicose,
agitating agin-the-law labor leader Michael J. Quill. When
Quill was sentenced to a jail term for calling a city-wide transit
strike in 1964, the respectable Irish blanched when they saw
him on television shouting, "May the judge, in his black robes,
drop dead." Quill died shortly afterward, and his Irish union
membership and leadership are gradually being supplanted by
blacks and Puerto Ricans.

Quill's last hurrah at the city jail was demeaning. I prefer to
think of a more typical Quillian farewell, an occasion a few
years earlier when he crashed the Saint Patrick's Day parade.
Judge Comerford, the stuffy little leprecaun who examines the
credentials of paraders, had banned Quill, apparently fearing a
demonstration. In masterful fashion, union organizers had
gathered about a thousand strikers on a side street. Unable to
walk the long route, Quill had hired what he called an "Irish
mail coach," drawn by two dispirited horses, that looked like a
vehicle occasionally used in Dublin for solemn funerals to
Glasnevin Cemetery. It was sturdy enough for Quill to sit on
the buckboard with the driver, a theatrical gentleman named
Hopalong Abramowitz, and spacious enough inside for about a

dozen excited children, who were waving flags and banners from the windows. When Quill gave the signal for the entry into Fifth Avenue, the union members, who had been lounging around for hours with little to do except toast the Saint in local bars, gave tongue with a Hibernian cheer probably unequaled in volume since Thomas Francis Meagher, another Irish immigrant, shouted *"Fag a Bealac"* ("Clear the way") to the Irish Brigade at the Battle of Fredericksburg. Quill tipped back his off-white Stetson, gripped his silver-tipped blackthorn stick, and shouted at his permanent photographer, Sam Reiss, "Sam, make sure you get me when I salute the little fellow with the purple slippers." His Eminence Francis Cardinal Spellman stood on the steps of Saint Patrick's Cathedral flanked by a solemn guard of Knights of Columbus, resplendent in their plumage and thin-lipped at the desecration of it all. It was said that Quill and Spellman had not talked for years, but the cardinal understood. When Hopalong Abramowitz stopped the coach opposite the Cathedral, Quill tipped his hat and waved his blackthorn, the thousand marchers doffed their hats, and Spellman laughed like an altar boy. He actually moved his right hand in what looked like a blessing. For one brief moment, the Irish owned the city.

There are no Mike Quills in Ireland, no great agin-the-government battling organizers who get things done. The country could do with a few of them, for the Irish at home never had the pugnacity or the audacity they display abroad. An almost religious stoicism prevails.

In Donegal, the wild, beautiful mountainous county at the northern tip of Ireland, the people have a saying: "There is no such thing as unemployment in Donegal as long as a man can pick potatoes in Scotland." For generations, the men from Donegal set forth for their annual summer seasonal jobs as "pratie" pickers to the crofter counties of northern Scotland. Even they are now a vanishing breed. However glorious the

glens of Donegal may be to a visitor, they have little attraction
for a boy or girl who leaves school and finds no job. The working population of that county has dropped by one-third in the
past twenty-five years; 37,887 farmers and fishermen made a
hard living there in 1946; fewer than 17,000 remain. In 1971,
the unemployment rate, in a total work force of 43,200 people,
was 11.7 percent, the highest in the land.

Donegal is one of the eight counties that stretch along the
Atlantic and hug the border of Northern Ireland, the area most
badly affected by emigration. Donegal, Cavan, and Monaghan
are the three counties of the divided province of Ulster; the
other five counties—Galway, Mayo, Leitrim, Roscommon, and
Sligo—compose the province of Connacht. These provinces are
not administrative areas; the Irish claim that they represent the
domains of ancient kings.

Census figures show the startling decline in the population of
this eight-county area.

	Population	Percent Decline
1841	2,158,907	
1901	992,806	54
1926	852,998	14.1
1971	598,000	29.1

Out of a population of 598,000, 230,000 were listed as being in
the work force.

I talked with the most famous living native of Donegal,
Peadar O'Donnell, about the problem of emigration. O'Donnell is an unsung Irish genius, an octogenarian who in his time
was perhaps the most forceful political agitator in rural Ireland
and a writer of power and eloquence. His novels, such as *The
Islanders,* written in 1927, are classic evocations of the pastoral
life of rural Ireland. Appropriately, considering the subject, my
conversation with Mr. O'Donnell took place in New York.
Peadar is as spry as a sparrow, and he journeys to New York as
casually as a Brooklynite takes the subway to Wall Street. He

turned down a recent invitation to visit North Vietnam, not because of age or infirmity but because he had a shrewd suspicion that he might be used by the highly professional propagandists in Hanoi. On occasion, O'Donnell has a tart, acid tongue. At a literary gathering in London, after listening to a harangue by H. G. Wells, whose emotional anti-Irish feelings were notorious, O'Donnell asked him in his soft, guileful Donegal way, "And is it true, Mr. Wells, that your father was an Orangeman?"

"Certainly," said the snippy, superior little Wells. "And what's wrong with that?"

"I hate to tell you this," said O'Donnell with his coy smile. "But everyone in Ireland knows that it takes seven generations to get rid of that kind of ignorance."

On the subject of Irish emigration, O'Donnell is less forthright. "The Irish politicians, ever since de Valera, have developed this 'push-pull' theory," he said. "What it all boils down to is this. The party in power says that the emigrants are pulled away by the fleshpots of London and New York. The party out of power roars that the poor people are being pushed out of the country by the lack of opportunity. The debate never goes much further than that."

"But why have the Irish got this urge to leave in such numbers?" I persisted. "They're a dying race. The West of Ireland is like one big deserted village."

O'Donnell has been pilloried all his Irish life for advancing radical political notions, and he was not about to resurrect the memories of those unhappy days for me. "The Irish are no different than anyone else, and I've talked to farmers around the world who are just as conservative as the fellow in Donegal." He went no further. And I understood. The farmer detests change, and he ignores those who suggest that life should be something more than a small box of money under the bed, a few cows to milk, and a nightly visit to the pub. He has persuaded himself that as long as he lives, the thirty-acre farm will be the rock on which his little world will survive. He is unaware that the rock has cracked, a foundation that cannot support the children he has fathered, an economic unit whose value, except to the man who works it, is nil.

Peadar O'Donnell loves Ireland with a passion that is almost tangible. He has survived as a good-humored philosopher because he concluded that a single individual cannot change things. He has made a pact not to annoy himself about the mad, illogical paths of the Irish mind. "A fellow like you wants to destroy the grand life that you can still find in Ireland," he said between chuckles. "You want everybody out of bed at six in the morning, working his heart out, and for what?" To keep the Irish in Ireland, I thought, but I dropped the subject.

O'Donnell, who has jousted with every Irish bishop of the twentieth century, told me that he had quietly made arrangements for his burial. "I went to see this bishop and I told him, 'Now, I want to go in an urn. Ashes to ashes and all that stuff.' " It is unheard of for an Irishman to favor cremation. "Do you know what the bishop said? 'I'll do it, Peadar, but for the love of God keep it quiet!' "

A sociologist could pick almost any town at random in the West of Ireland and witness the decline and death of an English-speaking community. Each town, village, and parish has the same characteristics: an aging population, few marriages, high emigration, and a sense of hopelessness on the part of the few people who are left. To drive through the region in the winter, from Shannon Airport north to Donegal, is a pilgrimage into the past. In the largest town in the area, Galway, a hotel owner is putting up Irish Army cadets, students at Galway University, in order to make ends meet. Few of the other towns have a cinema or any kind of entertainment center. The pub is the center of social life for the men, television the only connection with the outside world. The tiny fields of Connemara, with their neat stone walls, the faint outlines of the tiny fields that were tilled a century ago, the ruined cottages, bear witness to the enormous population that lived here in the past. There are other monuments to the emigrants. Between Lough Mask and Lough Corrib lies a useless canal that took four years to excavate during the famine years, a vain attempt to hold the restless local tenant farmers. The island of Inishmurray off the coast of Sligo was abandoned in 1937. Inishglora, off the Mayo coast, is the site of a ruined monastery built in the sixth century, by Saint Brendan the Navigator, who, according to Irish legend, set out from here and discovered America.

On the Aran Islands, the life of the fishermen, immortalized by Robert Flaherty in his *Man of Aran,* still goes on; they fish for sharks in their curraghs, the flimsy boats, but it is mainly tourist income that now keeps the population on the island. The majestic scenery, the presence of a region of such total solitude just an hour or so from an international airport, is a unique tourist attraction.

I suspect that one of the reasons why so many tourists visit the West of Ireland is that it seems a familiar place even to those who have never been there. Yeats, Synge, O'Flaherty, O'Donnell, and at least a score of regional writers have made it come alive on the printed page. The scenic beauty of the West can be seen in movies like *Man of Aran, The Quiet Man,* and *Ryan's Daughter,* which are only three of the many films photographed in the region that are seen practically every night in a theatre or on television somewhere in the world. The artists' versions of Irish people's lives are seductive, but quite unreal.

One of the latest studies by a British sociologist, Hugh Brody,* examines an isolated village twelve miles from the nearest bus stop, eighty miles from a railroad station, populated by a "demoralized" people who have lost faith in the social system. Inishkillane is a fictional name, but the place is real enough. The village church register records that 209 baptisms were performed in 1843. In 1963, only 19 children were born.

* Hugh Brody, *Inishkillane, Change and Decline in the West of Ireland.* London, Allen Lane, The Penguin Press, 1973.

Four marriages a year were celebrated annually between 1954 and 1958, none in 1959. Only a fifth of those born between 1940 and 1945 have stayed at home; almost all the young women leave, despairing of the possibility of marriage. Among the 231 households, there is an inordinately high number of old people, lonely people, widows, spinsters, bachelors and widowers. Twelve households include people suffering from mental illness. Three suicides have occurred in the past four years. Brody concludes his analysis of Inishkillane with this forecast:

The parish schoolteacher believes that the future will bring mechanization to the few best farms and tourist facilities to the more enterprising households. The priest is more pessimistic, and sees only an irreversible decline of everything, including all farming. The statistics suggest that very few people will be in the parish in twenty years. Perhaps the tourist industry will continue expanding, and will maintain a few families in the countryside. But there are no children in Inishkillane under school age. The pattern of traditional community and the distinctive farming it has sustained have been ascendant since the last disaster in rural Ireland, which had run its course by 1852. This life in Inishkillane is finally expiring.

The children of all the Inishkillanes are scattered around the world. John Healy, a journalist, went back to his native village of Charlestown in County Mayo to see what had happened to the twenty-three boys who attended school there in 1944. Only three were still living in the area, and one of those was unmarried. The remainder had scattered to the United States, England, Australia, Canada, a few to other parts of Ireland. Charlestown was built in 1846, a famine year, by Charles Strickland, a landowning justice of the peace. Today its only claim to national fame is that, because of Strickland's liberal rulings from the bench, Charlestown has more pubs per capita than any other village, town, or city in Ireland. Most of the pubs are open only one day a week, when the welfare checks, the "dole" money, are handed out at the post office. In an angry booklet, Healy said farewell to Charlestown and to the decaying region:

> The game is lost: it was over and finished before they knew it had started. Today a few leave Charlestown every year but it is merely the muscular spasms of a corpse: it is as nothing to the wartime exodus when they went out in train loads to send back hated John Bull's lovely pounds by wire and money order and in hard cash. The spawning beds are empty in the hill homes of the small farms in the Moy valley and the men who once came home with the Winter spawning salmon and stayed to fertilize the land and their women come no more. No more are the women content with a two-month-of-the-year marriage and the loneliness of life without a husband and a father: if they marry and mate it is to have a marriage for real in London or Birmingham or Wigan.
>
> Today whole villages around Charlestown—for centuries the spawning stream of the people of Mayo and Sligo—are silted by depopulation and where in my memory there were shoals of children, more populous than the salmon parr in the town's rich river, no child plays and there is no promise of a child.*

As conditions at home deteriorate in comparison with the rest of Europe, young people find life dull and enervating. The revolution of rising expectations will continue to stimulate Irish emigration. Recently, the exodus has had a more alarming aspect. Many university students seem to be resigned to the prospect of emigration upon graduation. In 1967, a questionnaire answered by male students reading commerce, engineering, and science in the four Irish universities showed that 32 percent of commerce students, 59 percent of engineers, and 48 percent of science students intended to emigrate after graduation. That same year the report of the appointments board of Trinity College stated that of 193 graduates handled by the board, only 42 found jobs in the Republic. In 1968, the Eco-

---

* John Healy, *The Death of an Irish Town*. Cork, The Mercier Press, 1968.

nomic and Social Research Institute questioned male students at University College, Dublin, about their intention to emigrate temporarily. Only 5 percent answered "probably" or definitely "no," 14 percent were unsure, while 79 percent felt that they would definitely or probably emigrate.*

As an index of confidence by the most talented young people in the "new Ireland" described in so many books and articles published in the late sixties, these surveys are disturbing. The expansion of the university system, which has resulted in an increase in the number of full-time students from 8,676 in 1958 to about 22,000 in 1972, has apparently resulted in little benefit to Ireland but rather in a brain drain of catastrophic proportions. Whether intentionally or not, the universities are simply adding a growing proportion of their graduates to the thousands of unskilled workers who leave. In any other country this would be interpreted as a moment of crisis, the point where a complete re-evaluation of the worth of the system would be in order. Such a response goes against the Irish grain. Things could always be worse, they say.

* Richard Lynn, *The Irish Brain Drain*. Dublin, The Economic and Social Research Institute, 1968.

5

The Church and Its State

"If the majority of the Irish weren't Catholics," the Dublin Protestant politician Maurice Dockrell once wrote, "they would not be good little Protestants. They would be rip roaring anti-clerical Communists." It is probably true that the Irish have lived so long in their peculiarly antiquarian religious world that, given an unexpected whiff of real freedom, they might revert to a more familiar ideology of authoritarianism and dogmatism. The creaking administrative structure of the Irish Church, unchanged since four ecclesiastical provinces were created at the Synod of Kells in 1152, has the hierarchical skeleton of Communism. At the top, the cardinal's role parallels that of the Party Chairman, the bishops have their counterparts in the members of the Central Committee, while the priests are the institution's watchdogs of orthodoxy. Like the Communist Party, the Irish Church arrogates to itself the authority to set standards of morality, both public and private; it controls education; and its censorship system, even if it does not drive writers out of the country at the point of a gun, can send a reporter to jail for three months for interviewing an undesirable person, and in many cases has denied writers permission to publish material in their own country. There are times when the bishops and their flocks exhibit a superstitious bent that matches Communism's secular mystique, as on Sundays when the participants at a televised Mass pray for fair or wet weather, depending on the season. There are two national shrines in the West of Ireland, Knock and Croagh Patrick, where crowds of up to fifty thousand solemnly and patiently stand in line just as the faithful visit Lenin's tomb.

The Irish have lived for generations under the heavy hand of clerical authority, so long, in fact, that they feel everybody else in the world is out of step but themselves. After John Charles McQuaid, the Archbishop of Dublin, attended some sessions of the contentious Vatican Council, where he stood silent on such pressing matters as priestly celibacy, birth control, the role of women, and the infallibility of the Pope, he said soothingly on his return to Dublin, "There will be no change in the tranquillity of your Christian lives." For someone who helped create what is known to outsiders as the only theocratic state in the English-speaking world, and what many in Ireland believe is the last bastion of decency against the tide of sexuality and permissiveness, this regal tone was quite natural. Rome was wrong.

The belief that they have a corner on the real thing, as opposed to the *soi-disant* varieties of Catholicism practiced in Italy or the United States, helps to perpetuate clerical autocracy. McQuaid was quite certain that Popes John and Paul were on the wrong track, but at least he did not go so far as his craggy, cranky colleague from Cork, Bishop Cornelius Lucey, who in 1973, incensed at the dangerous degree of liberalism he detected in his small city, authorized publication of a children's catechism that rebuked the Vatican's position on ecumenism. A few of the revived orthodoxies in Lucey's version of the old-time religion went like this:

Q: Does the Church forbid marriages between certain persons?
A: Yes; the Church forbids marriages between certain persons such as near relatives, or a Catholic and a non-Catholic.

Q: What must I do to be a faithful follower of Christ?
A: To be a faithful follower of Christ, I must belong to the Catholic Church.

Unlike the bishops of some dioceses in the United States, the Irish clerics have not surrendered a pinch of power to their parishioners, nor do they contemplate any partnership with laymen in their administration of the Church's vast resources—land, churches, schools, hospitals, orphanages, and investment portfolios. The notoriously discriminatory clause in the Irish Constitution that read, "The State recognizes the special position of the Holy Catholic Apostolic and Roman Church as the guardian of the Faith professed by the majority of the citizens," was eliminated only in 1973, when William Cardinal Conway graciously said he would not "shed a tear" if the offensive clause was removed.

As I write, some lawyers representing various pressure groups have so warped a bill proposing the legalization of birth control in the Republic that it would take the combined talents of a busload of barristers to determine who is and who is not entitled to free sexual expression. To those growing numbers of young Catholics and non-Catholics in Ireland who resent living in an obscurantist state, and who are asserting their right to ask tough and often truculent questions about the power of the Church, the bishops and priests are unyielding. Some Irish Catholics would question that judgment, pointing to what they believe are signs of change: guitar music in the churches, the recognition by some priests that sexual problems and homosexuality do exist, sporadic debates about the Church's obligation to society. For every liberal who has surfaced, however, there are dozens of clerical and lay traditionalists who are outraged at what they often describe as heresy. After living again recently for a year in Ireland, I find it difficult to remember a single circumstance where important issues were at stake when the Church did not influence matters, from the murder of

law-abiding citizens in the North of Ireland to the breast feeding
of children.

This attempt to be all things to all men can lead to an
ambivalence that erodes moral authority. One such event took
place of an evening when Archbishop John Charles McQuaid
paid a friendly visit to Sean MacStiophain, the then leader of
the Provisional IRA, who was hospitalized because of his well-
publicized hunger strike. Precisely what the gunman and the
bishop had to say to each other has not been recorded for
posterity; what was recorded was a newspaper account of a mob
of IRA sympathizers outside the hospital addressed by a priest
who said he had a statement to make "in the name of Jesus
Christ and Sean MacStiophain." It had surprised me that the
Church had not excommunicated the killers by name long
before that night. The fact that the militant clerical spokesman
for God and the IRA was not at least disciplined by his supe-
riors left me with the depressing conclusion that the Church's
interpretation of morality made it perfectly correct for the
bishop to boost the prestige of the IRA but a sinful act for
anyone to read the gentle Dr. Spock's books, which are still
banned in the Republic.

As a sociological phenomenon, the Catholic Church in Ireland
is a classic example of a dynamic institution accruing larger and
larger shares of personnel, wealth, and power at the expense of
every government and private body. The Church has never cut
its cloth to fit the purses of the people, nor has it attempted, in a
managerial way, to coordinate the growth of its personnel to the
"market," or the number of people it serves. One of the intriguing mysteries is why the number of priests, nuns, and
brothers—the working personnel attached to the Irish Church—
doubled between 1900 and 1970, while the Catholic population
on the island it serves remained static. If documents and minutes exist to show who made the decisions leading to this

anomaly or why they were made, they are carefully sequestered by the Irish hierarchy.

The growth of both personnel and real estate has been inexorable. A great deal of time and talent must have been devoted to such matters as recruiting techniques, financial policies, and the management structure and philosophy of the guiding body. Even looked at in devotional terms, the ratio of one priest, nun, or brother to 147 communicants on the island (the Church has never recognized the partition of 1921 in its organizational structure) seems rather excessive. The best estimates available* show a total of 33,092 personnel attached to the Irish Church, with another 8,000 Irish-born attached to foreign orders. About 23,500 serve in Ireland; the remainder are scattered throughout the world, with a high concentration in North and South America and Africa. If looked at as a profession, therefore, the Church in Ireland is the largest employer, far surpassing the 10,000 people working for the Department of Posts and Telegraphs in the Republic. The greatest period of growth, it should be noted, took place after the achievement of independence in 1922, as the following figures show:

Year	1901	1926	1951	1970
Priests	3,454	3,836	5,135	6,204
Nuns	8,031	9,843	13,360	15,145
Brothers	1,159	1,111	1,625	2,198
Total	12,644	14,790	20,120	23,547

There is no religious or devotional reason to explain recruitment on such a scale for service in Ireland. As far back as 1903, Filson Young, a British writer, could say: "It is a fatal mistake to begin by underestimating the piety of the Irish, or by representing it as an unreal or insincere thing; nothing could be more absurd. It is thoroughly real and sincere. . . . No

---

* *Social Studies, the Irish Journal of Sociology,* March, 1972.

other country in the world, I believe, can boast of such piety as Ireland; they are, of all people, the most completely drilled and absorbed in the Christian religion." So it certainly was not the potential challenge of an irreligious population that made the sudden increase in Church personnel necessary. The editor of *Social Studies,* a journal edited and largely written by priests, offers an explanation of sorts for this remarkable growth: ". . . Irish nationalism and Irish Catholicism became the two great sources of ideals for Irishmen, inspiring them to live for God and die for Ireland. After the events of 1916 and the attainment of freedom in 1922, nationalism seemed to lose its vitality. In the 1930s and 1940s, Ireland as a nation became a closed introspective society out of the mainstream of modern life and modern politics. During that period, the Church was the only institution offering an ideal. The Church was looking out at the world and calling on young men and women to do something about the paganism and the poverty in which most of humanity lived."

If this idealism existed as a moving force in the recruiting process, it still does not explain the growth of Church personnel in Ireland. Clearly, one of the reasons must have been that because comparable job opportunities did not exist, being a priest, nun, or brother was a desirable profession in itself. Since the middle of the nineteenth century, the Irish Church has had a distinctly peasant cast; the majority of Church personnel have always come from relatively poor families.

It is, of course, a taboo in Ireland to discuss the financial standing of priests, but here, too, along with the promise of immediate attainment to higher social status, many recruits must have had financial security in mind. Just how wealthy a priest can become is largely a matter between himself and his conscience. An indication of the way matters stand can be seen in the published summaries of probated wills, such as this example, which appeared in a Dublin newspaper in the winter of 1973:

Canon James Murphy, P.P., of Ballymurrin, Enniscorthy, Co. Wexford, a Parish Priest, who died last year, left estate in England, Wales and Ireland valued at £15,157.92 [about $33,000], duty paid £1,220. He left £500 each for Masses to his executors, Very Rev. William Stafford and Very Rev. Michael Byrne, of Bree, Enniscorthy, £200 to the Clerical Sick Fund, Ferns Diocese, and the residue to the Jesuit Foreign Mission, Dublin.

The physical assets of the Church have grown so spectacularly that many believe it to be the nation's single largest private owner of property and wealth. The nineteenth-century face of the Church was more modest, the aim then being to place a church, a school, and a priest in every parish. By the early part of the twentieth century, when this goal had been achieved, the bishops set out on a vast construction program of schools, orphanages, colleges, churches, convents, monasteries, and novitiates. Every group participated, especially the nuns, who, according to a survey made by the Research and Development Unit of the Catholic Communications Institute of Ireland, had no fewer than 102 separate orders in 1971, most of them engaged in contemplative, nursing, teaching, and missionary work.

An accurate inventory of property holdings is hard to come by. Based on figures published by various sources in Ireland, a rough estimate is that the Church has 9,000 schools, 2,000 church halls, 3,000 churches, 1,000 religious communities, along with farms, residences, and choice parcels of urban real estate, especially in Dublin. Although most of this property is insured by the Irish Catholic Church Property Insurance Company, which was founded in 1902, the company's annual report is not helpful to anyone trying to assess Church wealth. Moreover, the Irish Church owns a good deal of property abroad; the insurance company opened its first offices in Britain in 1972, while Irish missionary orders presumably own property wherever they operate. (The clergy owns the insurance company, whose stock is shared by such people as the Archbishop of Dublin, the Bishops of Nara, Ferns, and Cork, along with religious orders like the Society of African Missions.) Based on the very low premiums charged, about $450 million worth of buildings are owned by the Church in Ireland alone, a highly conservative figure, because, as in all business organizations, property tends to be carried on the books at a figure far below its real market value.

Some of the churches I visited in Ireland held two and sometimes three collections every Sunday; if the faithful contributed on the very modest basis of fifty cents a week per head, the cash collections alone would amount to about $75 million a year. Modern methods of fund raising, however, have been introduced in Ireland by British companies, which charge a fee, sometimes up to 20 percent of the amount collected, for the management of the schemes. Professional fund raising in the home, on top of the constant solicitation of funds from the altar, leaves parishioners of modest means with a numbed feeling. In the winter of 1973, the faithful of the Dublin Diocese were asked to supply another $25 million for new parish churches and schools.

The Bishop of Tuam proposed a plan for a $1,850,000 edifice near the shrine village of Knock, which has a population of 140. The buildings are intended to accommodate pilgrims on weekends. No sooner had the bishop kicked off his fund-raising drive through a national advertising campaign (a brick in the new church costs $12.50) than a business group began lobbying for public funds to build an airport and a multilane highway leading to the sacred place. When it turned out that the archbishop's nephew was the project manager, this marriage between God and Mammon raised no eyebrows; a construction man simply said, "Fair play to him. Sure it would have created hell locally if he hadn't given the job to one of his own." Like the business community at Lourdes, which is not shy about using the hard sell on pilgrims, the Irish see no reason why prayer and profit should not go together. In the small town of Westport, population 3,500, near the other Irish shrine, Croagh

Patrick, the locals have provided seventy-four bars to slake the thirst of visitors.

Much of the choice unused land in Dublin, where real estate values have rocketed upward in value, is owned by the diocesan bishop or by the religious orders. The Dominican Order has been allowed to rezone seventy acres for use as "light industrial property," while the Jesuits have a plan to make fifty-four acres a few miles away into a commercial-residential development that would include 300,000 square feet of office space. The Congregation of the Sisters of Charity sold a hospital for $3.7 million; an office building will replace it. The Jesuits are attempting to build a shopping center on another suburban site. The Sisters of Mercy were offering 36.5 acres in 1973 "mainly for office development," and the Carmelite Order is involved in a complex deal with Allied Irish Banks for the construction of an office tower on their land. The land holdings of the Church in the Dublin area alone have been estimated at about four thousand acres; at a conservatively estimated $75,000 an acre, that land would fetch about $300 million.

Any incursion by a layman into the secret world of clerical finance is met with rebuff. The writer Honor Tracy was hauled into court by a priest simply for publishing details of the rather overluxurious house the priest was building with the parishioners' money. The clergy seems to believe that physical grandeur represents the growth of the Church. Poverty is an embarrassment. If the Archbishop of Dublin chose to get maximum use of his facilities by making the weekly obligatory Mass available on Saturdays, and if he ordered an end to the practice of separating schoolchildren by sex, which doubles the use of classrooms, the need for that $25 million worth of new churches and schools would disappear. By selling off valuable land, the Church could make $300 million available for investment.

What the Church needs most of all, of course, is some professional help in managing its affairs; a good deal of what passes for administration is nothing more than self-aggrandizement. The priests effectively resist any involvement in the day-to-day social problems of their parishioners; only a handful of the clergy have ever visited the festering slums of Dublin. The idea of living in those reeking flats as a means of pressuring the government to provide decent housing for the poor never seems to have occurred to them. A few liberal activists would like the Church to assume a more forceful social role, a proposal that risks further proliferation of power. Today the Church is just as elitist as ever, no more willing to hand over its parish properties to boards of lay trustees than it will allow lay control of the school system.

Of course, one of the obvious questions is: What do all the priests actually do, besides acting as pastors to their parishioners? Because there is no mandatory retirement age, a lot of them are too old to do much more than officiate at Mass. Of the twenty-eight Irish bishops, eleven are over sixty, five are seventy-five years or more. A tenth of all the priests are over seventy, while no less than seventy-three of the hardy souls are octogenarians, a quarter of the nuns are sixty or over, and 17 percent of the brothers will never see sixty again. Promotion in the crowded ranks is painfully slow; the average age for appointment as a parish priest is fifty-six, but in some dioceses, such as Waterford and Elphin, a man must reach the age of sixty-two before he gets his stripes.

A gathering of parish priests and bishops in Ireland has all the *brio* of a convention of geriatrics. The more active men busy themselves in a variety of endeavors—hunting, fishing, carpentry, getting themselves elected to local committees, raising cattle, operating ham radios, conducting choirs, operating lotteries and bingo games—for there is no restriction on the activity of a priest save running for political office, which is a tradition, not a law. Figures in clerical garb are as omnipresent as the legendary Bold Thady Quill, the subject of a lengthy ballad, at sporting events in Ireland—horse racing, rugby, soccer, hurling, sculling, golf, clay-pigeon shooting. At those events where gambling is available, priests are as active as lay punters; by personal observation, they also seem to have a larger proportion of winners. "Be strange and civil to the clergy," goes an Irish proverb. Social functions, whatever the sponsoring group or the occasion, are considered incomplete without a priest at the head table; there is a general belief that the presence of a priest reduces the amount of drinking and gives tone to the affair. The priest is supreme in his parish, while in the country at large the twenty-eight bishops and the cardinal stand alone.

In one of his encounters with a Church group in 1835, Tocqueville met with an archbishop, four bishops, and several priests. "They all appeared to be gentlemen," he wrote, ". . . clearly as much the leaders of a Party as the representatives of a church." In political affairs, the Church as an institution is supreme. For one thing, by sheer numbers of influential personnel, the Church outranks every other professional or union lobbying group. Most important is the clerical power to impose spiritual sanctions. At times it is difficult to determine from a public statement whether a bishop or priest is against a particular piece of legislation because he as an individual does not like it, or whether as a religious leader he considers it sinful. If the legislation bears on birth control or divorce, this leaves Catholic politicians between a stone and a hard place; the unchanged Church position in Ireland is that all methods of birth control and divorce are serious breaches of Church law, which means a Catholic member of Parliament can be placed in a position where he legislates sin, which is surely a sin in itself.

The ease with which a religious order can establish itself in Ireland creates intense competition for recruits among the thirty-four missionary societies established there, a bewildering array of organizations from a variety of countries with such exotic names as Pallotines, Rosminians, Mill Hillians, and

Canons Regular of the Lateran. The stated purpose of these orders is to train and dispatch people for proselytizing work abroad. Doubtless the fact that one out of every hundred priests alive today was trained in Ireland has come to the attention of missionary congregations, which feel a compulsion to grow by signing up people under their own particular banner.

One noteworthy case of an order that has been buffeted by the competitive climate is the Premonstratensian Order, a Belgian group which established a school and a seminary near the Northern Ireland border. I came to know the lord abbot of the establishment, a local man named Kevin Anthony Smith, who keeps in shape by taking rugged cross-country gallops on his hunter with the local horsemen. Perhaps because of complaints from more influential priests, the lord abbot's boarding school was closed, depriving him of a source of income from the students as well as potential recruits for his order. The lord abbot is a very resourceful man, as I discovered when he made a visit to New York, his initial stop on a round-the-world tour. On his first morning in Manhattan, I dropped him off at the Time-Life Building and watched him gingerly negotiate the traffic on his way to Saint Patrick's Cathedral. I had forgotten that a lord abbot ranks equally with a bishop, so I should not have been surprised when he recounted later in the day that he had had a nice chat with Terence Cardinal Cooke and had celebrated Mass in the Cathedral.

The universality of the Irish Church was demonstrated with telling effect, too, when the lord abbot decided to "Bless the House" after watching a New York Giants game on television. Perhaps he had been moved to action by the sight of Father Dudley, the chaplain of the Giants, who was visibly praying on the sideline, although with no effect on the score; in any event, the lord abbot blessed each room of my house, with liberal sprinklings of holy water added, an unexpected series of showers that sent my small West Highland terrier barking into the night. The unflappable resourcefulness of the lord abbot was

Sacred Heart of Jesus, Roche's Second Hand

Archbishop Dermot Ryan of Dublin, Ireland's largest diocese

Future bishops, Maynooth Seminary

Secular faiths: Tarot and hypnotism

Meditation in Dublin

Open-air market,
Moore Street, Dublin

Women factory workers, Tallaght

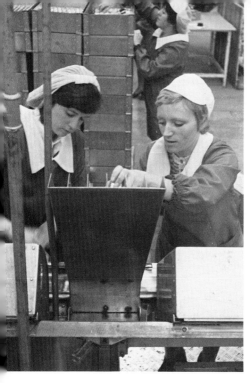

Supermarket, Stillorgan

Arts and crafts

clearly visible when I visited his establishment in Ireland. He had sold the school equipment and turned to raising pigs and cattle for income. Instead of schoolchildren with scholarships, his pride was now a heifer that had been awarded a blue ribbon at the local agricultural show.

Some ancient practices and superstitions have been incorporated into the Irish faith over the years. Only in 1973 did the practice of church "offerings" cease; members of a congregation were expected to contribute money for the burial of a deceased. The money was kept by the priest as an "offering." It is considered bad luck to pass a church without crossing oneself. For a Dubliner to walk three times around the Protestant Saint Mary's Chapel of Ease, known as the Black Church, is dangerous; the devil might appear. Fishing boats, factories, and aircraft are blessed by a clergyman in an annual ceremony. In country fields that bear crops like wheat and barley, unaccountable unsown hillocks are visible; they are fairy raths, which remain undisturbed because to interfere might bring bad luck. The common drinking toast of Ireland is not "Slainte," a myth perpetuated by Irish-American romantics, but the more traditional "Good luck." The country is dotted with "holy" places not sanctioned by the Church but enshrined in local tradition. The members of the Clare County Council spent some time in the winter of 1973 in serious debate about the condition of Saint Senan's Well, a local shrine that had been polluted by wandering cattle. One member suggested that the National Monuments Association might accept jurisdiction over the sacred place. There are wells with mysterious properties for curing illnesses in people and animals, not because of the mineral content of the water but because some saint stopped there.

As in India, Ireland has its "holy men," more often faith healers than mystics. The most famous of the Hibernian fakirs is

Finbarr Nolan, a miracle worker who has received such atten-
tion in the national media that he is usually referred to by his
first name, as in a recent newspaper headline: "Finbarr Takes
Britain by Storm." Making fun of Finbarr is just not done; the
Irish believe implicitly that he has what is called "the gift."
Finbarr is a star in his own right; he drives a supercharged
Jensen sports car, takes flying lessons, and is advised by Fred
Hift, a public-relations practitioner who numbers among his
other clients Julie Andrews, British Airways, and the Churchill
Centenary Trust. To offset his youthful vitality, Finbarr has
sprouted a wispy beard that makes him look like a chorus boy in
Jesus Christ Superstar. Finbarr's fame has traveled to the
United States; Joe Hyams, the Hollywood gossip columnist, says
he wants to write a solemn biography.

On an earlier visit to Ireland, I had watched Finbarr at work
in the center of Ireland's pig-producing country, a small village
called Gowna, in County Cavan. My first adviser on Finbarr was
Nial Plunkett, a general practitioner from London, who told
me, while we were discussing the incomes of healers, both
scientific and faith, "This fellow has the biggest practice you've
ever seen. I saw Finbarr on a television program on the BBC,
and he was calmly saying things like 'I'm going to Belfast to do
a cancer.' He had the flat Cavan accent, but he looks as confident as the biggest Cheyne-Stokes man on Harley Street.' " Hift
has since scrubbed up Finbarr's image. Plunkett, who happens
to be my brother-in-law, suggested that we journey to Gowna to
see Finbarr at work, and we did.

The road to Gowna is rough. "When a child is bad around
here," said Plunkett, "the mother threatens, 'Do you want to
spend a wet day in Gowna?' We'll just pop in and see what this
little gossoon is up to." On the way, Plunkett thought it
advisable to check with a local expert, Buddy McKiernan, who
was something of an authority. "Buddy has twelve children
now," explained Plunkett, "and his seventh one is a son. The

whole business about Finbarr's gift is based on the fact that he is the seventh son of a seventh son. So Buddy is hoping that if the fourteenth kid is a son he'll be able to skip a generation and maybe put the child into business, like Finbarr."

McKiernan had bad news when we met him in his farmyard. He explained that Finbarr's mother, hoping to head off false claimants to the "gift," had performed the "worm test" on Finbarr when he was a child. "The truth is this," said Mc-Kiernan. "The mother puts the worm in the child's hand, and if it shrivels up, he has the gift."

"Did you try it out on your son?" asked Plunkett.

" 'Deed I did. Not alone did the oul' worm not shrivel up, but it seemed to get a new lease on life."

"Does Finbarr have the gift?" asked Plunkett as we got back into the car to escape the pungent pig smell.

"He has something," said Buddy. "I heard he was off to a dance the other night with a load of women in the car."

As we headed for Gowna, I read about the scientific merits of the worm test in a clipping that Plunkett said he was going to present to the archivist of the Royal College of Surgeons. Brendan Nolan, the faith healer's brother, explained that because arthritis is really a worm in the spine, a touch from the hand of the master kills the disease.

About three miles from Gowna, the road became uncomfortably crowded. Buses, cars, bicycles, and an occasional pedestrian formed a long, slow, snaking line; people waved and greeted each other as if they were on the way to a race meeting on a bank holiday. "A man told me that Finbarr was doing a power of good for the local economy," said Plunkett. "He said that truckloads of fruit and booze were being shipped in from Dublin." The economic specialist proved correct. As we entered the village, a traffic jam of mighty proportions developed; Gowna consists of one long street, and Finbarr's father, a beaming ex-policeman, was selling parking space. The village pubs were crowded; throngs of men in blue suits spilled onto the narrow sidewalks, each carrying a glass with the satisfied look of one who is settling down for a long wake.

Finbarr was on duty in a low military-looking building of concrete bricks and corrugated metal. Outside sat the elderly patients, on one side a row of gnarled men leaning on their sticks, on the other a line of weary women. A few confined to wheelchairs sat mournfully, surrounded by relatives and friends praying the rosary. When we entered the dark building, we could see rows of old men sitting on benches in various stages of undress. Like communicants walking to the altar rail, the ailing filed one by one to a bench where a thin youngster with a pointy nose muttered incantations, followed by a liberal spray of water from a green plastic bucket. The youngster with the pointy nose turned out to be Finbarr, the liquid was holy water which he had borrowed from a church across the street. From out of the gloom stepped another youth guiding a figure stripped down to his shorts. Finbarr's incantation lengthened; we could hear a "God bless you," and the water was applied front and rear. "That poor man is in a terrible way," said Dr. Plunkett. This loudly announced medical judgment about a man who appeared to be in agony turned out to be a mistake. "You're not supposed to be in here," said a voice. We were escorted firmly to the door. "This is only for the patients."

Finbarr's bodyguard turned out to be his brother, Brendan, the authority on arthritis. An interview with Finbarr, he said, was impossible. "You'll have to make an appointment. And anyway we have to go to Mullingar this evening." The din from the knots of men along the street had reached a higher decibel level; a few unself-consciously had relieved themselves against a wall.

Our uncertainty, perhaps our unbelieving expressions, caused one of the blue suits to approach us on the street after our eviction. "Isn't it a shockin' thing altogether?" he said, as prescient as only the Irish countryman can be when he sees a stranger. "You'd think it was Lourdes, with the priest looking on from across the street." The big problem in the village, he told us, was that the county board of health was threatening to close the pubs because the ancient sewage system had buckled under the strain of all those visitors. However, an application had been made to the Tourist Board for emergency funds. "Do you know there's a Yank after writing to Finbarr offering him twenty thousand dollars to cure her arthritis? He'll be over there yet." That prediction seemed logical. A few months later a story appeared in the *National Enquirer,* a newspaper of sorts published in Florida, reporting that mail from around the world was pouring into Ireland, including a plea for help from India, which, although addressed to "His Holiness Finbarr Nolan," successfully reached its destination.

Perhaps in preparation for questions from *Scientific American,* Finbarr's brother, Brendan, had developed a new theory to explain the powerful secret. "It's a matter of cells," he was quoted as saying. "If cells in any area of the body lose their power, then a hundred and one ailments afflict the body. The cells can be recharged or regenerated, but only by an emissive power, similar to the cell power contained by some rare species of the human race, like the seventh son of a seventh son." He was careful to add for the traditionalists, "Of course, the power that Finbarr has comes in the first place from God."

In matters of morality, the Irish hierarchy has always been puritanical. Of the pantheon of twentieth-century clerics, none was more influential in governing private morality than John Charles McQuaid, the Archbishop of Dublin. During his thirty-one-year reign, which ended providentially in 1973, McQuaid presided grimly over the sexual life of the city. The son of a dispensary doctor, McQuaid was born in the nineteenth century in the small country town of Cootehill, where sexual behavior was set with the rigidity of a contemporary cadre of Maoists in

China. To live in Dublin during his regime was to experience the intimidation of the block-surveillance system perfected by the commissars. No aspect of sexual life escaped him; in his career, one builder was prevented from offering two-bedroom houses because McQuaid felt that a properly procreating family needed at least three. He banned the participation of schoolgirls in international athletic events because he felt that it might be "an occasion of sin" for Catholics and Protestants to shower together. A squad of ambulatory censors under his direction patrolled the streets to ensure that displays of ladies' underwear conformed to some mysterious clerical standard. The display of what seemed to be a condom in Tennessee Williams' *The Rose Tattoo* brought the full might of the constabulary down on the tiny theatre, culminating in a full-dress trial, complete with wigs, barristers, and production of the evidence, which turned out to be nothing but a small empty envelope. It was, of course, the thought that mattered. McQuaid's thin, mournful, asymmetrical body (he had a lung removed, which gave him a lopsided gait) was seldom seen in public. He detested crowds but managed to keep an eye on things by surprise patrols in his limousine; a priest who appeared in public without a hat could be banished to some rural wilderness.

When McQuaid took hold of the symbol of power, his bishop's crosier, he allowed one of the priests under his command to publish parts of the infamous anti-Semitic forgery *The Protocols of Zion*. He was stirred to censor personally the press, casting an eye on lonely-hearts advertisements, editorials, fashion illustrations, and especially movie publicity manufactured in the evil pits of Hollywood. The solicitous newspaper management of the *Irish Independent,* a national daily, sent most of its editorials to the palace for proofreading. Although the staff was well aware of His Grace's odd requests, occasionally an error occurred that brought down bolts of messianic thunder. Such was the case when the Otto Preminger movie *Carmen Jones* was screened. The movie had been scissored to McQuaid's taste, but somehow the Saul Bass advertisements were published without his review. A crash project ensued, with a house artist airbrushing the cleavage and thighs of Dorothy Dandridge, the star of the movie, so that she ended up looking like Harry Belafonte in drag.

When he died in 1973, McQuaid had added sixty new parishes to his diocese. In his funeral cortege marched like acolytes the President, the Prime Minister, two cardinals, twenty-eight bishops, the entire Cabinet, the governor of the Bank of Ireland, a handful of mayors, the head of the Knights of Columbus, the chief of police, with the head of the armed forces bringing up the rear. It seemed appropriate that in the week of his death a newspaper reporter in Dublin received notice that a book on pregnancy by a British gynecologist had been seized by the book section of the Customs and Excise Department under the Censorship of Publications Act.

The puritanical Jansenist tradition of McQuaid and his peers is a powerful one. One could speculate, as many do, that the Irish carry with them a great weight of sexual guilt, imposed in public by harsh denunciation and in private through the ritual of confession. The blight of sexual puritanism afflicts thought and behavior; it unbalances any debate on books, films, freedom of the press, censorship, entertainment, education, public morality, marriage, health services, and even Northern Ireland, precisely the subjects that Paul Blanshard, the American civil libertarian, dealt with more than twenty years ago in his book *The Irish and Catholic Power*. The Red menace, which was part of the obsession in those days, has almost disappeared, but the tangled knot of infantile sexual taboos is as strong as ever. When Mary Robinson, a cool young lawyer, introduced in the Senate in 1973 a private member's bill which would partially legalize the sale and use of birth-control devices, the eruption was painful and produced the kind of melodramatic debate and eventually the kind of comic conclusion that the Irish cherish. Mrs. Robinson introduced her bill in the form of a question:

"Whether it is tolerable, in terms of life in the Republic, that the laws of the state should taint with criminality, describe as criminal offenses, matters which a minority of citizens—not necessarily a religious minority—regard as morally justified and their own personal concern?" This attempt to distinguish between public and private morality stirred the clergy, and not a few traditionalist laymen, to a frothing rage.

It seemed entirely appropriate that the civilian leader of the battle against birth control should be one Desmond Broadberry, a humorless fellow with an angry face that looks like a frost-bitten chestnut, whose qualification is the number of children he has fathered. Broadberry had sired seventeen little ones when he entered the fray, and he triumphantly announced that Mrs. Broadberry had brought forth an eighteenth just after he had come to grips with the enemy on a television debate, in the course of which his only articulate words were "Mary Robinson's bill will never become law and that is all I will say on that." A Broadberry follower, James Barry, got off one of the best lines of the year when he described pills and condoms as "satanic devices which are degrading the human race to its lowest level since creation's dawn."

At the beginning, the clergy had little to say, although they organized a national letter-writing campaign of abstruse theological and constitutional arguments and roundhouse denunciations of Mary Robinson. Two unprecedented events brought the clergy on the scene. First, the Supreme Court of the Republic declared the prohibition of birth control unconstitutional. That news was soon followed by the arrival of some mail-order mechanics from Britain who advertised delivery of condoms to the home "under plain cover." The arrival of the devils from London gave the battle an international flavor, like the annual rugby encounters between Ireland and England at Twickenham, described by a participant as "awful physical."

The level of the debate in the Dail on such matters can be measured by a strange definition of marriage offered by plump, stately Erskine Childers, who has since been elevated to the Presidency of the Republic. "I once read in a book," said Childers, "that a marriage could be compared to one partner holding a violin and the other partner holding the bow and being able to play a tune well together." Fortunately, the imagery stopped with the dinner bell; otherwise Mr. Childers might have been tempted to go into the mysteries of stroking, applying resin, or the best way to master difficult pizzicato techniques.

The response of the hierarchy to the Robinson bill placed Catholic politicians in the Republic in an embarrassing posture. A section of the lengthy document, signed by the Most Reverend Dr. McCormack, the secretary to the hierarchy, revealed the old insuperable obstacle to the reunification of Ireland:

> The question at issue is not whether artificial contraception is morally right or wrong. The clear teaching of the Catholic Church is that it is morally wrong. No change in state law can make the use of contraceptives morally right since what is wrong in itself remains wrong, regardless of what state law says. . . . The real question facing the legislators is: what effect would the increased availability of contraceptives have on the quality of life in the Republic of Ireland? This is a question of public, not private morality. What the legislators have to decide is whether a change in the law would on balance do more harm than good by damaging the character of the society for which they are responsible.

Not alone did this interpretation of "the quality of life" vindicate the charges by Protestants in the North that the Catholic Church would try to enforce its standards of morality on everybody in the event of reunification, but it proved conclusively, if proof was needed, that the bishops were as boldly political as ever. One curious question raised by the statement concerns the status of Catholics in the North, who are free to avail themselves of contraceptive devices and abortions under the British nationalized health service. If they are really living in a land of sin, as the bishops suggest, should they come across the border into the Catholic Republic? And did the bishops' statement imply that the Church preferred the maintenance of partition and the continuation of the four-year sectarian war rather than toleration of the creation of a single sectarian state?

To Conor Cruise O'Brien, who has been attempting to assuage Protestant fears, the stand of the bishops meant that Protestants would interpret the vote on Mrs. Robinson's bill not as a division on the merits of contraception but a straight test of whether the Republic was under home rule or Rome rule. "It may be said that the question of contraception and the question of peace are not really related issues," said O'Brien. "They are in fact very closely related. Whether we acknowledge it or not, the fear of being incorporated into the Republic, with standards, values and practices which are felt to be alien, is most acutely alive in the minds of many Northern Protestants. The contraceptive issue has become a symbol of what is feared. It is a potent symbol, because it is a deeply emotional one and because the emotions it stirs up in both communities are antagonistic." Northern Ireland Protestants cannot be faulted if their interpretation of Rome rule is something other than the definition advanced by Pope Paul at the Second Vatican Council when he concluded proceedings by saying that the Church was "entirely on the side of man and in his service." Catholic priests in the North have a rigidly sectarian and nationalist outlook, their language quite as sulphurous as the outbursts of the fundamentalist Protestant leader Ian Paisley.

It is worth quoting at length from a statement published in a Dublin newspaper by Father Denis Fall, the nationalist priest I had met in New York, in order to appreciate the fears of Protestants when they are asked to become a minority in a unified Catholic state. Father Fall lives in Northern Ireland, teaches at Saint Patrick's Academy, and spends a good deal of time visiting internment camps where Catholics who are suspected of shooting and bombing are detained.

The people of the Irish Republic is [sic] faced with a fundamental choice in the question of legalizing the sale of contraceptives and allowing literature advocating and advertising them—not to speak of undoing the damage already done by the Supreme Court decision permitting importation of contraceptives.

A lot of silly nonsense has been talked in the Senate and elsewhere about new laws and schemes to provide contraceptives for married people only. Note well: (1) Once the blanket prohibition is removed it will prove impossible to restrict contraceptives to married couples. Married women could act as agents for them and pass them to their single friends—for a fee. Wedding rings are cheap; doctors and chemists might be avaricious.

(2) But let's face it—it is a more serious matter for married people to have contraceptives available than for single people who are intent on fornication. It is a blasphemy against the nature of marriage as it is understood by the majority of the people in the Republic—and it is contrary to the understanding of marriage in the Irish constitution, Article 41. Daily more and more my wonder grows that the Supreme Court could have given such a decision. Contraceptives in marriage do more harm than to single people.

(3) Northern Ireland has contraception and Therapeutic Abortion. Is family life corrupted there? To some extent, yes. But you have a split community; the Catholics have contempt for contraceptives as Unionist things. But if a native Irish government, following a Supreme Court misinterpreting a Christian Constitution for the country, gives its approval to contraceptives, a vast change will speedily be brought about in the moral ideals of the people, a great corruption will take place—and right speedily will the same government and Court bring in abortion to follow the Abortifacients. This would destroy the ideal of the family as outlined in Article 41 of the Irish constitution.

(4) We hear much about wives putting up with drunk husbands, husbands with delicate wives. Will it increase the marital happiness of these wives to know that their husbands are walking around

Dublin with a pocketful of government approved contraceptives in their pockets—*deanta in Eireann le ceadunas an Aire Cirt agus Dli?** Is it the Irish ideal for the bridegroom to fly out to Majorca with new wife and a pocketful of contraceptives, removing all the romance out of marriage? Think of the dreadful effects on family life, on what Article 41.1 calls "a moral institution." The Common Good cannot be achieved by such a sordid environment.

It is the state's duty to promote Chastity by not bringing in any legislation that would damage family life and corrupt young people.

This revealing epistle adequately disposes of the idea commonly held by Irish-Americans that the conflict in the North of Ireland is just a struggle against colonial domination by Britain. By carefully omitting the section of the Constitution on which he bases his case, Father Fall gives the game away. The Irish Constitution is a document drafted under the supervision of, and with the full approval of, the Irish hierarchy in 1937, an attempt to define the Catholic version of the Christian state. It is a constitution written in such amorphous language that one can only assume that the draftees, Eamon de Valera among them, either had great difficulty in defining a Catholic state, or did such a sloppy job that those who are living might justifiably be brought up on charges of inciting barratry. Article 41, on which Father Fall relies so heavily, attempts to define sexual behavior. It recognizes the family as "the natural primary and fundamental unit group of Society, and as a moral institution possessing inalienable and imprescriptible rights, antecedent and superior to all positive law," prohibits divorce, and says that mothers "shall not be obliged by economic necessity to engage in labour to the neglect of their duties in the home." The Catholic Church interprets this to mean that marriage consists of an endless series of pregnancies, the absence of which Father Fall suggests, would eliminate romance. (If "labour" were otherwise interpreted, it would be a valid argument *for* birth control.) What Father Fall forgot to say was that the laws

* "Made in Ireland by permission of the Minister of Justice."

prohibiting contraception are tied inextricably to the censorship laws. If birth control is legalized, the business of book banning will also disappear.

The legal barriers against contraception have a curious history. In 1929, the Censorship of Publications Act made it illegal to advocate the use of contraception. This was not satisfactory to the Church; in 1931, it contested the appointment of a Protestant, a Letitia Dunbar-Harrison as county librarian of Mayo. The argument advanced by the Dean of Tuam might seem strange to Americans, but it underlines the continuity of Catholic views. The Dean argued: "We are not appointing a washwoman or a mechanic, but an educated girl who ought to know what books to put into the hands of the Catholic boys and girls of this country. The views of Catholics and Protestants, especially of late years, on such subjects as birth control and divorce are at variance. At the Lambeth conference we had an episcopal blessing pronounced on birth control, and one of the most distinguished clergymen in England is going in for trial marriages. Supposing there were books attacking these fundamental truths of Catholicity, is it safe to entrust a girl who is not a Catholic, and is not in sympathy with Catholic views, with their handling?" When the government attempted to install Miss Dunbar-Harrison, the Mayo County Council sided with the Dean and organized a boycott of all library services. Eventually the government backed down, agreed to the appointment of a Catholic, and offered the young Protestant woman a job at the Military Library in Dublin.

The Censorship Act was not enough in the eyes of the Church; people could order contraceptives by mail from England. A Criminal Law Amendment Act, passed in 1935, prohibited the sale and importation of contraceptives. The act did not forbid the *use* of contraceptives, so that if a supply of condoms is dropped by parachute, or an anonymous donor leaves a package of birth-control pills under a Christmas tree, the finder is entitled to use them without fear of a jail sentence.

In 1967, the Censorship Act was amended, not so much because of pressure by the local population but because of embarrassment suffered by government ministers who were baited when traveling abroad about the similarity of the censorship provisions in Ireland and those in the Soviet Union. The amended act removed the ban on books after twelve years of prohibition, thus making available about five thousand previously unavailable titles. However, the censorship board was authorized to reimpose the ban if it desired; among the books rebanned was *The Ginger Man,* whose author, J. P. Donleavy, lives in Ireland.

Nor was this the only farcical aspect of the whole business. In its desperate search for foreign investors, the Irish government had invited Syntex, the company that had grown prosperous through marketing the birth-control pill, to locate a plant in the South of Ireland. Unlike the Dean of Tuam in the librarian controversy, no priests opposed the entry of the godless Syntex enterprise. Nor did anyone raise the interesting point that because Syntex was granted tax-free status, the government was, in effect, subsidizing the contraceptive business.

The law, as now interpreted, means Irish Catholic girls can *make* contraceptives but not use them. The hierarchy wisely backed away from any theological threshings of this paradox. To add to all the confusion, the provision of the Censorship Act forbidding advocacy of "the unnatural prevention of conception" was retained. Thus, if a novel contains a line of dialogue such as "I hope you took the pill today" (presumably "*a* pill" would pass), if a newspaper or magazine contains an advertisement offering information on birth control, it is, under the most strict interpretation, subject to the ban. In the full spirit of the law, the five-man censorship board could prevent people from watching any programs or debates on British television that presented contraception in a favorable light, but short of confiscating all the TV sets in the Republic, most of which are wired to receive signals from England and Northern Ireland, the censors are helpless in this matter.

The capricious nature of Irish censorship might seem amusing to outsiders; to the artist it imposes barriers that restrict both his audience and his income. The part-time five-man book censorship board met nine times in 1970, examined 314 books, and banned 160 of them. Officially, 158 books were declared "indecent or obscene," two violated the statutes against advocacy of contraception or abortion. Nobody in Dublin believes that the censorship board actually reads all the books submitted. Rather, there is a strong impression that groups of self-appointed legionnaires of decency underline certain passages, which are offered as evidence of "immorality" to the censors. An extraordinary form of economic censorship also prevails. Philip Roth's *Portnoy's Complaint* can be sold in the hard-cover edition, not in paperback.

No author has been able to challenge the obvious illegality of this kind of censorship. Lee Dunne, a young Dublin writer, believes that his book *Paddy Maguire Is Dead* was banned in 1972 because it was distributed as a paperback. When Dunne invited arrest by giving away copies of the book in a Dublin street, the police refused to intervene. John Broderick, another novelist, some of whose books are available in hard-cover editions but not in paperback, complains that the lack of access to the considerable Irish market can cut in half the sales of a novel published in England. "You cannot carry out moral sanitation any more than physical sanitation, without indecent exposure," wrote George Bernard Shaw. The Irish prefer to do without the exposure. Trials of persons charged with sexual crimes are either held *in camera* or censored by protective newspaper editors. Foreign magazines are mysteriously seized by the Irish Post Office, by the hand of some prurient employee, or by upholders of an unwritten law that proscribes certain publications. While Irish viewers can enjoy frontal nudity on British television, such publications as *Playboy, Penthouse,* and *Oui* are banned. A Dublin editor considered that he had achieved a publishing breakthrough in 1973 when he reprinted a photograph of a rubber-clad model from a Pirelli calendar.

The birth-control controversy is the most visible sign that a sexual revolution of sorts is taking place. Most of the restlessness centers on the imposition of puritan standards in marriage. (A lot of sociologists believe that the low marriage rate may reflect a singularly Irish system of birth control.) In order to enforce its view that the sole purpose of marriage is procreation, the Church, helped by a willing state, has constructed a maze of legal barriers surrounding such matters as divorce, legal separation, legitimacy, desertion, financial support for deserted wives, and adoption. Those who seek legal redress find themselves confronted with a massive Catch-22. Divorce, of course, is forbidden by law, and although the Church has the power to nullify a marriage, the chances of receiving such relief through an ecclesiastical court are almost nil, besides being prohibitively expensive. If an applicant *is* granted a decree of nullification, the game becomes even more complex. Under Church law, either of the partners can remarry, but such a marriage is not recognized by the state until the civil courts grant a similar decree. In desperation, people resort to what is euphemistically called the "Irish divorce," a business of husband deserting wife by moving to England. When that happens, the wife has no legal rights. She can neither sue her husband for maintenance nor seek nullification of the marriage. The last census shows that some eleven thousand husbands had abandoned their wives, presumably because of the complexities of Church and civil law surrounding the dissolution of marriage.

This interpretation of canon law is not universal by any means. In the United States, a Catholic marriage is no longer considered an immutable contract for life. Before the Vatican Council of 1965, an annulment could be granted only because of such defects as sexual impotency, an intent on the part of one of the partners not to have children, coercion, insanity, or because of a prior valid marriage. Things have eased considerably since then, however. In 1972, the tribunal of the Diocese of Brooklyn granted 356 annulments compared to about 33 in 1969. The average cost to the applicants is about a hundred dollars, and the court, which consists of five full-time and twelve part-time justices, can give a decision, once the evidence is assembled, on the same day as the trial. Using a system of psychological testing, which is interpreted by psychiatrists, the court seeks to uncover the neuroses and personality disorders that lead to the breakdown of a marriage. One of the justices, Monsignor Marion J. Reinhardt, explained the grounds for nullification. "Usually, both partners are sick. One-third are schizophrenic and about two-thirds have serious personality disorders, which affect their judgment and ability to relate in an interpersonal relationship, even though they may function normally in other situations." The Canon Law Society of America estimates that in some dioceses sixteen times as many marriages are being officially set aside as were annulled fifteen years ago.

In 1967, an all-party committee of the Dail recommended easing the ban against divorce on two grounds: that it ignored the wishes "of a certain minority of the population who would wish to have divorce facilities" and that the absence of divorce was a source of embarrassment to those seeking to bring about better relations between North and South. In serial order, the bishops rejected the suggestion with such vehemence that the matter was never put to a referendum, a constitutional requirement that was imposed in 1937. Typical was William Cardinal Conway's comment. "The proposal would involve the setting up of divorce courts in the Republic," he said. "In the beginning they would be limited in scope, but inevitably this would only be the first step. Everyone knows how these things spread once the gates are opened." The cardinal may have had a shrewd notion that the institution of divorce courts would have brought to light the enormous hidden tensions of Irish family life. Experts estimate that grounds exist in one out of every four Irish marriages for separation or divorce.

The writ of the Church is not absolute in sexual behavior. Prostitution has always been a feature of Dublin life, but until recent years it was confined to the gloomy dock area and to the slums of the north city, the "Monto" area in *Ulysses,* places unlikely to be visited at night by tourists. In recent years, however, the ladies of the evening have appeared in force on the more fashionable South Side, where they parade at night along a route that extends from the American Embassy to the big convention-style Burlington Hotel. On occasion, P. V. Doyle, the neat mustachioed owner of that hotel, who is also the present chairman of the Irish Tourist Board, has expressed anger and embarrassment at the numbers of whores that circle his establishment. Despite sudden raids on the street by squads of plain-clothes police, the traffic goes on; customers traverse the area in cars and signal whenever they spot a likely partner. There is a touch of *la dolce vita* in some of the older, more solemn hotels, and the small smoky night clubs that cater to the more adventurous have a distinctly raffish, erotic atmosphere. Even in the small stuffy city of Cork, prostitution is a topic for public debate; a local priest brought matters there into the open when he began a rehabilitation campaign for teenage prostitutes.

The increase in prostitution is one measure of the change in morality; another is the increase in the number of abortions. Although abortion is illegal in Ireland, an agency in Dublin provides transport to Britain for such emergencies, charging about $400 for the round trip and for medical services. British government figures show that the number of abortions performed on women from the Republic has increased from 64 in 1968 to 577 in 1971. The number of babies born to unmarried mothers is also increasing; in 1969, there were 1,600 so-called "illegitimate births" in the Republic, a figure that could possibly be doubled if the number of births to mothers from the

Republic that took place in the North of Ireland and in Britain were included. About 90 percent of the babies are placed for adoption, almost three times the rate of other European countries, for the birth of a baby to an unmarried Catholic mother is punished in most cases by social ostracism.

Nobody could reject the evidence that modern Irish family life is as distant from the bucolic ideal as is possible to imagine. Consider the structure of the Irish family. Because of emigration, male celibacy, and the unavailability of family-planning services, the characteristics of the Irish family are unmatched anywhere. Census returns for 1961 show that among families who had a child born that year, 3.54 percent already had one child, 8.4 percent had two, 39.9 percent three, 35.8 percent had between six and nine children, and no less than 12.5 percent of the families were trying to care for ten or more children. The same pattern was repeated in 1966, when the head count showed that about 60 percent of all children belonged to families with four or more children. Since the number of such families is only eighty thousand, it is clear that, involuntarily, a small part of the population has assumed nothing less than the heroic burden of perpetuating the native Irish Catholic race. Just 7 percent of the population over fifteen years of age is responsible for the upbringing of 60 percent of the future generation.

Any clergyman who deviates from the traditional Victorian view that "abnormal" sexual behavior should be severely punished is treated as a dangerous eccentric. When Dr. James Good, professor of theology at Cork University, called the publication of the papal encyclical *Humanae Vitae*, which reiterated the Church's opposition to birth control, "a major tragedy for the Church," his superior, Bishop Cornelius Lucey, had him removed from the faculty. Dr. Good is a most unlikely candidate for rebel of the year. A bony self-effacing scholastic who gives the impression that he never speaks without going through agonizing appraisals of his private conscience as a man and his public conscience as a dissident theologian, he is nonetheless worried about what he calls the "creeping infallibility" of the Church. This state of affairs, he suggests, is born of a clerical system of education that is as irrelevant as a burnt-out satellite in the outer atmosphere. The Irish hierarchy is a product of an arid philosophical system of Catholic apologetics which allows a bad system to be defended by good arguments and vice versa. As Dr. Good put it at a press conference: "Moral theology, in particular, became a lazy thinkers' paradise in which discussion rarely got beyond the simple statement that 'X is contrary to the Natural Law and is intrinsically wrong'—where X stood for anything that the moral theologian did not approve, like divorce, contraception, abortion, masturbation and the like."

Dr. Good seems to have a genius for exposing the eccentric ways of the Irish hierarchy. At a seminar in 1973, he scandalized the traditionalists by stating that, in the course of counseling more than a thousand unmarried mothers, he was unable to find one "decent" mortal sin among the lot. A mortal sin, he explained, like some solemn outcast priest in a Graham Greene novel, is such a frightful crime it is almost impossible to commit one, and even if someone succeeded, there is little chance of repentance. This was the last straw for the masters of apologetics. Not alone were there venial and mortal sins, they rebutted, but there was another peculiar variety of "reserved" sin, absolution of which can only be granted by a bishop. A reserved sin, it turned out after much learned correspondence, is recidivist in character, as when an IRA gunman persists in inflicting damage on the property of a Protestant neighbor. Not murder, it should be noted by theological students, but a crime against property.

In a pluralist society the issue could be boiled down to this: Is the quality of life affected favorably or adversely by the power of the Church?

In a Catholic nation with Catholic laws, the question is seldom put so bluntly. Fully 95 percent of the population is officially classified as Catholic, an unchallengeable majority living by laws on marriage, censorship, divorce, adoption, birth control, abortion, and so on that clearly violate the rights of other religious sects. The Church of Ireland (known as Anglican elsewhere) has about 100,000 adherents, the Presbyterians 19,000, the Methodists 7,000, other tiny groups, including the Society of Friends and Unitarians (known in the North as Nonsubscribing Presbyterians), about 12,000. The Jewish community numbers about 3,000.

With such an overpowering presence, Catholics can afford to be generous, even patronizing, to tiny religious minorities. The election of Erskine Childers, a Protestant, to the ceremonial office of President was trumpeted loudly as an example of equality. In fact, his selection as a candidate by the Fianna Fail Party was a reward for long, unquestioning service. A pervasive but carefully hidden prejudice against Protestants exists. For example, a Protestant has little chance of buying a farm previously owned by a Catholic. In the border counties of Cavan and Monaghan, the reverse rule applies. In business, firms are known as Catholic or Protestant depending on the makeup of the board of directors. (The use of the token outsider or two was adopted early in the existence of the state.)

For most Americans, the belief that the Republic is more than even-handed in its treatment of minorities was reinforced by the annual presence in New York of Robert Briscoe, the Jewish Lord Mayor of Dublin, who usually took advantage of his visit to promote Irish whiskey and light a menorah on the steps of City Hall. The Dublin mayoralty is not an elective office. By agreement, the representatives of the various political parties on the City Council circulated the job among themselves; Briscoe happened to be the Fianna Fail councilor at the time and an old political comrade of Eamon de Valera. Jewish businessmen who were not protégés of de Valera have a different tale to tell, only in private. A merchant, who shall be known here as Edward Black, recalls the glee of Dubliners during World War II when a few stray German bombs dropped near the Temple on the South Side of the city. "My own customers were needling me that Hitler was going to blast the Jews out of Dublin," he told me. "Now it's a little more subtle. If I need a customs clearance on goods from abroad, it takes me twice as long to get it as it does for a Catholic." Black, like many other Jews and Protestants, from time to time feels subtle prods of vengeful superiority. He does not complain.

In Ireland, where the residents have never known the right of free speech, dissidents, with the exception of a handful of pioneers, seldom challenge the system head on. Debate on questions that ruffle national pride or disturb Church leadership are conducted in a circuitous, unconnected fashion. Journalists who criticize the censorship system usually end up with the caveat "I'm not completely against censorship; I wouldn't want my kids to read that filth you have in America." Still, the rumblings of dissent, if muted, can clearly be heard. Parents are alarmed at the style and quality of Church-controlled education; intellectuals attribute the state of the arts to the preservation of an environment that is hostile to freedom of expression; social workers chafe at the plight of poor families who seem to be permanently trapped at the bottom of the ladder; businessmen are suddenly conscious of the lamentable lack of a scientific tradition, which makes their competitive position in Europe untenable; some students are behaving as students do, unhappy with everything.

To a hierarchy that is a prisoner of its past, these uneasy stirrings are viewed with great suspicion. The Church sees itself as the repository of the true faith, protector of the family, guardian of a distinctive Irish Catholic way of life. Countless organizations and institutions of the modern Irish state were fashioned to preserve this distinctly Catholic culture, such as the Catholic Boy Scouts, the Catholic Girl Scouts, the Catholic

Youth Crusade, the Legion of Mary (an attempt to restore the cult of the Virgin), the Pioneer Total Abstinence Association, the Irish Christian Community Movement, and even the Gaelic Athletic Association, which gives to Irish athletic and sporting events a uniquely Catholic flavor.

To elderly Church leaders who hold to the simple theology that poverty is ineradicable and that being poor has a certain dignity, any talk of materialism is the antithesis of the Gaelic, nationalist, Catholic tradition. This austere view of life is not at variance with the professed philosophy of some political leaders. As recently as 1943, the then Prime Minister Eamon de Valera articulated a religious life style. "The Ireland which we have dreamed of," he said, "would be the home of a people who valued material wealth only as a basis of a right living, of a people who were satisfied with frugal comfort and devoted their leisure to things of the spirit; a land whose countryside would be bright with cosy homestead, whose fields and villages would be joyous with sounds of industry, with the romping of sturdy children, the contests of athletic youth, the laughter of comely maidens; whose firesides would be forums for the wisdom of old age. It would, in a word, be the home of a people living the life that God desires men should live."

Outdated and iconoclastic as this rustic vision may be, it is shared, with just slight amendments, by a surprising number of people, including Erskine Childers, de Valera's Protestant successor as President. Writing for the English Catholic weekly *The Tablet* in 1972, Childers told why he loved Ireland.

. . . I love living in a country where, without excessive, maddening inefficiency, the rat race is only beginning in some areas of living.

I love being able to send my child to almost any school, knowing as I prepare the child to face adolescence the child will not be corrupted by foul influences.

I find the near proximity, the pervasive influence of clergy and nuns of all denominations absolutely essential if we are to escape the virtual obliteration of individual and collective responsibility for the state of society. I recognize that all the churches have the difficult task of relating their liturgies and their teaching to the challenge of the 'seventies. . . . I revel in the moderate, rainy climate, which, please God, will keep away the jet set and the hordes of packaged trippers basking on sun soaked beaches.

Childers does no service to his country by perpetuating the idealized myth that the Irish family lives decently, is reasonably happy, lives remote from the strains of modern industrialized society. That may be true of some families. It is equally true that more than a quarter of Irish families depend on a weekly cash payment from the government to sustain themselves. A more realistic picture of Irish life was presented by a social worker at a conference on poverty held in November, 1971. This conference, it should be noted, raised no great outcry in the press; apparently such conditions are not unusual.

Mrs. B. is 34, had ten children and fifteen pregnancies. She was married at sixteen and thought it was great. A week later the ring was pawned. Her husband was unemployed at the time and has never worked since. She thinks he may be in bad health. In any case, he doesn't feel fit to work.

Mr. B. has had five prison terms—all for breaking into pubs. "He would take porter from the Pope." Each time he is found stupid on the floor and has never gotten away with anything. When he sobers up, he tells his wife not to worry and cries like a child. She wonders if he has no brains, does he not care or know how impossible it is for her to manage. . . .

The eldest child is 16 and was reared by Mrs. B.'s sister. She doesn't live at home and would be ashamed of the address. The next child is fifteen and was taken from school before her time to help her mother. Even if the child was not actually mildly retarded she would have to believe that she was from the number of times she is addressed as a "dummy" or a "brainless fool." She can neither read, write nor tell the time but is quite normal, if immature in conversation. A few attempts to get light housekeeping jobs failed when she was found blowing her nose in the tea towel while she dried the dishes, unable to make a bed and generally clueless. Moreover she frequently had to miss a day if her mother was sick or had to take a child to the doctor and was finally sacked for irregular attendance. The remainder of the children range from 14 years to six months. The seven-year-old is also mildly retarded and attending a special school.

Perhaps the real extent of their poverty can be seen in little incidents like running out of washing powder and having to leave the clothes soaking until she gets a few bob; being without even a newspaper to cover the floor after it is washed; keeping a child from school because the jumper washed the previous night isn't dry; being covered only with a few coats in the middle of winter because the child who shares the bed with them gets diarrhea and everything has to be washed and takes days to dry—she wouldn't have the price of the laundrette.

It is the bleakness of the future which upsets Mrs. B. most. She can see no end to the struggle and sometimes just wants to run away. She will scream and beat the children and regret it afterwards.*

In many ways, the Church-controlled system of education, which excludes any form of sex instruction not approved by the hierarchy, contributes to the formation and perpetuation of this style of living. "The entire educational structure of Irish life is a privileged and protected form of ecclesiastical culture, endowed by the state," wrote Paul Blanshard in 1953.† Very little of the educational system has changed in the intervening years, the most contentious debate swirling about the compulsory teaching of the Irish language.

The structure of the system reflects ancient class distinction. At the bottom, about four thousand primary schools, almost all of them owned, managed, and staffed by a parish priest, educate

---

* *Social Studies, the Irish Journal of Sociology,* August, 1972.
† Paul Blanshard, *The Irish and Catholic Power.* Boston, Beacon Press, 1953.

some 500,000 youngsters. The quality of teaching may be judged by the fact that primary school teachers are not required to have a university degree; the size of the average class in Dublin is about fifty. The second, smaller tier consists of about nine hundred secondary, vocational, comprehensive, and community schools that house about 180,000 pupils between the ages of twelve and eighteen. Again the majority of these schools are owned, managed, and staffed by the Church. At the apex is the elite university system, formally nondenominational, but divided into the Catholic-controlled National University of Ireland, with its three constituent colleges in Dublin, Cork, and Galway, and the University of Dublin (Trinity College). Trinity, founded in 1591, has always been looked on by the hierarchy as an alien Protestant-controlled institution. In 1958, the Church forbade Catholics to attend, except by special dispensation, under pain of mortal sin. When the two universities applied for government funds in 1967 to build competing engineering schools, the government proposed a merger. Even though the hierarchy went so far as to petition the Vatican for a relaxation on the ban against Catholic attendance at Trinity, the merger never took place.

No Irish government has ever questioned the right of the Church to control education, and thereby perpetuate a structure that clearly discriminates against the poor and the middle-class student. Rather, successive governments have assured the Church that its philosophy will remain unchallenged. This duty was performed for the present administration in January, 1974, by Richard Ryan, the rather prim, humorless Minister for Finance at a reunion dinner of his alma mater, a Cistercian college. "The religious owners and managers of schools are trustees of the rights of parents and children," said Ryan. "Their schools represent the generosity and sacrifices of generations of religious authorities and parents alike. An educational system leavened with such loyalty is not to be lightly discarded. The government, of which I have the honor to be a member, will not lack respect for the vital part which religion plays in education."

One indication of the value placed on learning is that the government spends a smaller proportion of the national budget on education today than it did forty-five years ago. In the 1929–30 fiscal year, 20 percent of total state expenditure was devoted to education. By 1949–50, this share had dropped to 10.4 percent, and although the amount has increased by about 4 percent since then, it is clearly too little to do anything more than fulfill the requirement that every child attend school. Despite much talk of reform, each of the educational institutions still operates as a discrete entity; there is no coordination between the lower and middle levels, little attempt at job counseling, and, most surprising of all, there are no incentives for university students to choose areas of study leading to anything other than the traditional overcrowded professional occupations. A lot of college graduates are competing just for the jobs of those who retire or die.

The birth-control controversy ended in a farcical scene acted out in the Dail in the summer of 1974. Under the pressure of public opinion—a number of polls showed that a majority of voters favored the legalization of contraception—the government introduced a bill which would have allowed married couples to buy a pill or condom. The influence of the twenty-eight bishops, however, counted for a great deal more than the will of the majority. When it came time to vote, Prime Minister Liam Cosgrave and some of his colleagues voted against their own bill. As usual, Cosgrave found it unnecessary to explain this devious deed. Everybody understood that he could not breach that old stone wall, the Catholic Church.

6

Politics by Divine Revelation

Half a century of independence has done little to change the tone and texture of Irish politics. Like those new Americans observed by Tocqueville on his nineteenth-century travels, the Irish are full of irritable patriotism. The constant search into the grab bag of history for selected proofs of national greatness, as if the country was as newborn as an African nation suddenly released from colonial bondage, suggests that the Irish are not quite certain that they are a nation. I suspect that one of the reasons for this obsession with the glories of the past is that Ireland really has no modern history, apart from the running quarrel with the British over Northern Ireland. Until quite recently, it would have been possible to write the history of Ireland in the twentieth century without any reference to nuclear power, the computer, the pill, World War II, the welfare state, the ecumenical movement, higher education, the rights of women, or any other of the attitudes, life styles, artifacts, and inventions that have changed the Western World. Ireland stood aloof, as if the country felt quite superior to such ephemera.

"Ireland is an unusual place," said President John F. Kennedy on his departure in 1963. "What happened five hundred or a thousand years ago is as yesterday." I like to think that

Kennedy had in mind the greeting of Eamon de Valera, the old blind President, who reached back to the Battle of Clontarf, fought in 1014, to establish the political credentials of the distinguished visitor. After a few Gaelic flourishes, de Valera said, "Mr. President, I thought it fitting that my first words of welcome to you should be in our native language, the language of your ancestors, the language that was spoken by the great Cinneide clans of the Dal gChais who, under the mighty King Brian, nine and a half centuries ago, not far from the spot on which we are standing, smashed the invader and broke the Norse power forever." During Kennedy's visit, I was told, de Valera's conversation never went further, politically speaking, than the double-dealings of Lloyd George.

"Lest We Forget" might be the heading for the endless refresher courses in history that Irish newspapers provide their readers on the attitudes of British leaders to Ireland. One list, published in the *Sunday Press* in September, 1973, said that Gladstone was ahead of his time, Balfour was "Bloody Balfour," Asquith executed the 1916 leaders, Bonar Law's behavior was correct, Ramsay MacDonald had no wish to become ensnared in Irish affairs, Baldwin found the Irish tiresome, Neville Chamberlain was acceptable because de Valera had sent his widow a telegram, Winston Churchill was an early supporter of Home Rule but later changed his tune, Clement Attlee attended Terence MacSwiney's funeral, Anthony Eden showed an intelligent grasp of the position, Harold Macmillan had no wish to become involved, and the Earl of Rosebery was fed up to the teeth with the "fly blown phylacteries of the past." That analysis took two columns on a busy Sunday.

Despite the patriotic fervor, the Irish are cynical toward their politicians. A priest in Saint Patrick's College tells the story of a visit by Parnell to the nearby village of Kilnaleck, where the great man was to speak after a torchlight procession. The parish priest, who was elsewhere during the meeting, asked on his return what Parnell had spoken on. "Begob, Father," replied a villager, "I was far back in the crowd, but I think he spoke on a door." Local historians place Parnell on a barrel. Kennedy, who cut his teeth on the ward-heeling politics of South Boston, would have recognized that dry disinterest.

Another unchanging element like patriotism in Irish politics is patronage. When I worked in Ireland in the fifties, my father-in-law, a country doctor, was wakened late one night by the sound of gravel thrown against his bedroom window. The following conversation took place when he recognized the figure standing in the driveway.

"Well, Ned, this is a nice time of night to wake up the household. What's wrong?"

"It's the wife, Dr. Plunkett. She's poorly, and she wants to know if you'll come right away."

"I saw her yesterday, man, and she was fine. Is she in labor?"

"Not at all, Doctor. She's always voted like I told her, for the de Valera crowd."

The caller believed that even emergency medical care is part of the political system, and, in most cases, although not in this particular one, he would have been correct in his assumption. Jobbery, a more accurate word for patronage, is tucked away, as it were, in the armpit of the Irish body politic, invisible, often unpleasant, but an indispensable appendage. When I read descriptions of the patronage system in New York politics under the Tammany bosses Croker, Tweed, and Murphy, the machine seems like an unreliable Model T compared to the Rolls-Royce smoothness of the Irish vehicle. The Tammany model occasionally faltered, especially during the cold season when investigators came around. The Irish system covers the nation, extending from the 144 members of the Dail and the sixty Senators, through twenty-seven county councils, seven borough corporations, four county boroughs, nine district councils, twenty-eight boards of town commissioners, fifty-six judges, forty-three state corporations, five regional medical boards, ten government ministerial offices, the national radio and television system, each calibrated to function smoothly and tightly as a unit. The only sound heard at sixty miles an hour is the rustle of ten-pound notes in the back seat.

Businessmen are expected to contribute to the political parties in return for favors. When he was Prime Minister in 1972, Jack Lynch asked, "Is there anything wrong or to be ashamed of in people who can afford it subscribing to the political party or regime they think best fitted for the administration of the country's affairs?" Obviously not, for in 1967 Mr. Lynch's party had formed a fund-raising corporation called TACA, which expected a minimum contribution of a hundred pounds apiece from businessmen who attended private meetings with the political leaders. (The average wage for an industrial worker then was £1,200 a year.) Only a few eyebrows were raised when Mr. Lynch and his wife took a trip to Japan as guests of the Gulf Oil Corporation, which operates an oil refinery near the Prime Minister's home town of Cork. No law exists to force the publication of gifts to either political parties or individual politicians.

Examples of political corruption are legion. In the sixties, a Cabinet minister increased his net worth by millions through real estate speculation. This was rather excessive, even for Irish tastes, though in the absence of any conflict-of-interest legislation, perfectly legal. For the Cabinet minister it was a simple matter of knowing in advance the zoning restrictions the government would place on public and private construction in the greater Dublin area. Fortuitously, the land he bought at low prices always seemed to be located in the most desirable areas. The same political leader used his tax-free profits in the Republic for further real estate speculation in the North of Ireland, where land values dropped sharply after the bombings began a few years ago. This might seem to raise a conflict of interest, because the politician has been called on from time to time to give his expert opinion on events in the North. One wonders what the attitude would be in Dublin if, say, a member of the British Cabinet was known to have bought options on land and buildings in Belfast while at the same time advising the British Prime Minister on Northern Ireland policy. No doubt the Englishman would have been added to that list of devilish, devious empire builders.

Socialism is a nasty word in Ireland, yet it is difficult to think of a nonsocialist economic structure where the government's presence is so pervasive. From the foundation of the state, the government has been the employer of first resort. Electric power, ground transportation, shipping, airlines, steel, sugar, chemicals, harbor development, radio and television, even the care and feeding of the Irish greyhound are managed by more than forty state-controlled corporations. It may sound like Yugoslavia. The Irish say it is not a love of socialism, however, that moved them in this leftward direction but the lack of private capital. To test this assertion, an American offered to buy the state-owned telephone company, lock, stock, and hand-cranked instruments. He was, of course, turned down. Modernization would mean fewer jobs, and there is hardly a family in the country which does not receive a government paycheck.

The state provides subsidies for almost everything, from the construction of luxury hotels to the financing of programs to eradicate the disease of brucellosis in cattle. A wide world of opportunity exists between the penthouse of a hotel in Dublin and a small farmyard 250 miles away in Kerry for the knowledgeable. The clique-ridden universe includes doctors, lawyers, engineers, planners, advertising and public-relations men, building contractors, bankers, veterinarians, architects, travel agents, government inspectors, and a lot of other people who handle applications for subsidies, who approve, finance, and execute the programs. And many of the subsidies seem misdirected, if generous. Why does one individual get most of the subsidies for new hotel construction? Or why is a farmer allowed to pollute an entire lake so badly that ecologists feel it is beyond reclamation? Why does a government-financed housing program result in the construction of uninhabitable houses

Memorial to Eamon de Valera,
National Museum, Dublin

Kilmainham Jail,
museum of heroes

President Erskine Childers and his leader, de Valera,
Aras an Uachtarain, Dublin

Prime Minister Liam Cosgrave in the shadow of Michael Collins,
Government Buildings, Dublin

Gerry Fitt, M.P., leader of Northern Ireland's Social Democratic and Labour Party

Senator Brendan Halligan, General Secretary of the Irish Labour Party, Senate Chamber

Brendan Corish, leader of the Irish Labour Party

Conor Cruise O'Brien, writer, diplomat, politician, with his adopted children

Garret FitzGerald, Minister
for Foreign Affairs

Justin Keating, Minister for
Industry and Commerce

Senator Mary Robinson, constitutional lawyer

with improperly designed heating and ventilating systems? The answer to all these questions is that pretty nearly everyone condones corruption, favoritism, and influence peddling, from the chairman of a bank to the local tax collector. One of the longest government debates during my stay in Dublin was a vituperative battle as to who would control the appointment of tax collectors.

If a doctor seeks an appointment, political influence is not amiss. "Pull," as the Irish call it, is a requisite at the lowest economic levels as well, because government agencies apply what is called a "means test" to applicants seeking old age pensions, medical care, hospitalization, and other social services. If an unemployed man has trouble collecting his weekly pittance, and very often one does, a letter from a politician quickly solves the problem.

The tax structure is loaded in favor of the relatively few rich; much of the revenue comes from high sales taxes. One can only assume the weight of political influence has been applied. It is a mystery why the elected representatives of the poor and the lower middle class, who number the great majority of voters, have failed to impose a capital gains tax. Selected foreign artists receive tax-free status from the government (the list of those who receive this favor is secret). The Irish worker, with an average income of less than $3,000 a year, meekly pays for the civic services used by these writers and film directors.

Necessity nourishes influence peddling in a society where work is scarce. From road menders to barristers, competition exists for every available job, openings usually created by death or retirement. All too often this competition is settled by the weight of political influence. The culture of corruption hits hardest at the young, who are quickly disabused of illusions. When the underpaid employee in a factory or hotel discovers that the owner has large unreported subsidies from the government, his enthusiasm for work is replaced by idle cynicism. Government statistics prove that the worker in the Republic is less industrious than his Northern Ireland counterpart. And the North, as everybody knows, has its own system of Orange patronage.

Foreigners who fail to fall in line with the custom of the country can find themselves entangled in the mysterious rules of local bureaucracy. When one Irish-American spent $5 million on a new hotel in the West of Ireland, he found it impossible to open because, unluckily, the builder had violated an obscure safety regulation that was not applied to neighboring hotels. Enraged, the Irish-American left his hotel standing empty as a protest against what he considered double-dealing. A routine example of newspaper comment on the political scene ran in the *Connacht Tribune,* a Galway newspaper, in August, 1973: "Party politics, with the bitterness and vicious discrimination inherent in them, have been the damnation of Ireland. The lust for power and party and personal gain has been such that Irish politics becomes synonymous with graft, corruption and rottenness of every description."

The law in Ireland is a very serious and, financially, big business. The incomes of solicitors and barristers benefit greatly from the astonishingly large number of civil actions that are taken to court. The Irish have always been a litigious people—"I'll bring the law on you" is usually the final word in a squabble over some minor matter—and the legal profession encourages the use of the courtroom to resolve such disputes. Civil suits over such trivia as the trespass of a cow into a neighboring field are common. When the circuit comes to town, local newspapers print columns of summaries and transcripts, with each headline specifying the amount of money the plaintiff won in a civil case.

Beneath the tranquil surface, there are simmering pools of hidden animosities between individuals, between families, between villages, and between classes. And by the use of the courts to resolve quarrels, the hatred is perpetuated. During a trial, a man's character can be irredeemably damaged when he is cross-examined over some inconsequential quarrel. Perhaps the chances of his daughter marrying a neighbor's son are destroyed. Litigation almost always leads to bad feeling, and the loser will sometimes resort to burning his neighbor's barn or haystack in revenge. Without litigation country life would be savage indeed, for the Irishman gets his pound of flesh one way or another, if not in a courtroom, then by physical means. Tinkers, who are by convention and choice outside the legal system, settle intrafamily disputes such as an insult to one of their women by fighting in a curiously formal ritual in which the rival males strip to the waist, arm themselves with sticks, or sometimes more lethal weapons, and fight it out until one combatant lies unconscious in a pool of blood. Unlike more respectable folk, the tinkers sink their differences later over a pint or two of potcheen.

Irish-American lawyers, especially the criminal trial specialists, may rely on histrionic appeals to juries, but Irish barristers, who plead from the books, cite precedent after precedent before the lay jury. The contrast in courtroom styles reflects the class system in Ireland. A typical American defendant looks on his lawyer as an employee; the Irish defendant sees his barrister as a man of knowledge, influence, superior education, and mysterious powers. An American lawyer has a drink with his client outside the courtroom when the trial ends. An Irish barrister, priestlike in black silken robes and headgear, retires to chambers for a glass of port with his colleagues. No mingling with the masses. No judge in Ireland has ever been convicted for bribery or corruption, so, in a sense, they seem to be above the law.

Class differences are most apparent in the lower courts, where judges treat the poor, the mendicants, deserted mothers, alcoholics, and unemployed as common nuisances. In one case I recall, a young man who was summoned to appear in court for selling literature without a peddler's license acted as his own attorney. The fact that the literature happened to include the *Communist Manifesto* sent the judge into a paroxysm of rage. The young man was sentenced to jail before he could present his defense. He was dragged from the courtroom to the holding cell. The offense itself was trivial, for as visitors to Dublin are well aware, Dublin is a city of peddlers selling everything from books to blankets. What mattered was that someone appeared without a lawyer, challenged the judge, and in so doing, challenged the system. No lawyer came to his defense either, although many of them were taking their ease within hearing range of the incident. For years, a Dublin journalist, Nell McCafferty, has been documenting such cases in an effort to stir up public opinion for court reform. Few people seem to care.

A half-crown barrister is a euphemism for one at the bottom of his trade, a lawyer who might be competent enough in a case involving a trespassing cow or the sale of a defective secondhand car. More complicated and important cases are given to men who have the reputation of being winning advocates in their field of specialization, for successful barristers tend to specialize in narrow aspects of law, whether it be personal damage suits, company litigation, or the defense of IRA members, which is handled by a very small select group.

In Dublin, the gowned and bewigged judges and barristers are housed in the Four Courts building, named after the judicial system which has four courts, ranging from the district level to the Supreme Court. Destroyed in 1922 during the Civil War, whether by an unhappy litigant is unknown, the Four Courts has long since been restored to its old Victorian splendor. There is a touch of Victoriana, too, in the solemn demeanor of the participants. A solicitor hands a foolscap brief to a junior counsel, who in turn reads it and explains the case to his senior counsel, a majestic figure who actually pleads the case. "Taking silk" is the term for the solemn ceremony that takes place when a junior counsel is elevated to senior status. Only then is the senior counsel, garbed in silk, allowed to wear his full-bottomed wig, a piece of headgear like a sheep's fleece, which extends to the shoulders.

Great prestige is attached to the profession. Apart from its lucrative aspects, most of the prominent politicians are lawyers. The tradition is an old one, for the eighteenth-century Irish Parliament consisted mostly of lawyers; even today, the legislative calendar of the Dail, which conducts most of its business in the winter and spring, is said to be a reflection of the needs of the eighteenth-century barristers, who wanted time to ride the various legal circuits. Daniel O'Connell, the most effective political leader in the nineteenth century, was a rambunctious lawyer who boasted that he could drive a coach and four through any English law. Very often he did. Jack Lynch, the former Prime Minister and leader of the Fianna Fail Party, rode the circuit in Munster before he settled down to a full-time career as a politician. Unlike O'Connell, who used colorful language in court as if he were addressing a political meeting, Lynch sounds like a lawyer even when he talks informally in places as far away from Ireland as the Plaza Hotel in New York. There is a practical reason for choosing law as a profession; a defeated lawyer can return to his practice if he loses his parliamentary seat.

Some politicians who are not lawyers claim that the present Irish Constitution benefits only the legal profession, and one can sympathize with such a view when a seemingly simple case involving parental rights over children has to be tried in the Supreme Court because of constitutional ambiguities. The Constitution is faulted by a diversity of people and organizations. Successive governments have claimed that constitutional articles dealing with the rights of property made them impotent to control land speculation. Labor experts say that the proliferation of trade unions—more than one hundred—is due, in part, to the constitutional interpretation of the rights of freedom of association. Deserted wives, children of broken families, the few Catholics who get an expensive annulment from the Church and remarry, are among the victims of the ambiguous Constitution.

The great and essential difference between the Irish and the British legal systems is the powerful role of the Catholic Church and Catholic lawyers in Ireland. While the Irish legal system was never formally merged with that of Britain, even under conquest, Irish courts usually relied on British precedents in deciding cases. When Ireland became independent, the legal system took a distinctive Catholic coloring. Laws pertaining to censorship, birth control, and such matters were passed with the approval of various Catholic attorneys general. The courts were "packed," in the sense that judges were known to approve of these peculiarly Irish laws; otherwise, lawyers would surely have challenged the constitutionality of such invasions of freedom and privacy. In effect, if one law had been declared unconstitutional, the legal edifice would have collapsed.

English common law was injected by Catholics in Ireland with a liberal dose of dogma from various papal encyclicals. After the passage of the 1937 Constitution, which was drafted, some say, by ecclesiastical hands, there emerged what can only be called a new body of Irish Catholic law. In the book *Church and State in Modern Ireland*,* a case is cited in which a priest was fined for contempt because he refused to reveal confidential information in court. Under English law, this was perfectly correct procedure. There, even the secrets of the confessional are not privileged. A militant Catholic judge, George Gavan Duffy, who was a member of the High Court from 1936 to 1951, and the court's president for five of those years, heard the priest's appeal. His decision made it clear that from this point on the law would distinguish between the rights of Irish Catholics and English Catholics.

The strange, sectarian landmark decision read in part:

* J. H. Whyte, *Church and State in Modern Ireland*. Dublin, Gill and Macmillan, 1971.

While common law in Ireland and England may generally co-
incide, it is now recognized that they are not necessarily the same;
in particular the customs and public opinion of the two countries
diverge on matters touching religion, and the common law in force
must harmonise with the constitution. . . . That constitution in
express terms recognises the special position among us of the Holy
Catholic Apostolic and Roman Church as the guardian of the Faith
professed by the great majority of the citizens; and that special
recognition is sole and deliberate. The same constitution affirms
the indefeasible right of the Irish people to develop its life in ac-
cordance with its own genius and traditions. In a state where nine
out of every ten citizens today are Catholics and on a matter closely
touching the religious outlook of the people, it would be intolerable that the common law, as expounded after the Reformation in
a Protestant land, should be taken to bind a nation which persist-
ently repudiated the Reformation as heresy.

Needless to say, the genius and tradition of the Irish, then
and now, are reflected mainly in literary works, written in
English, which the Censorship Board has banned. Although the
"special position" article has since disappeared, and some elements of censorship have been relaxed, the Republic still lives
under the ultramontane provisions of the Constitution. Even
some lawyers are saying that the 1937 document should be
scrapped and replaced by a shorter, more concise constitution.
This is no easy task in a country with no clear-cut division
between the roles of the Church and state. For two years a
committee composed of representatives of the three political
parties has been meeting in secret to discuss changes in the
Constitution. So far nothing has emerged. The aspect of secrecy
may seem a mystery to those who are not Irish. The reason, of
course, is that the hierarchy must signal its approval of any
changes before they are put to the people in a referendum.
Open discussion about the Constitution seldom takes place in
the Dail. Politicians who criticize the Church in private cannot
bring themselves to challenge the influence of the bishops in

public. If a question is asked about some controversial aspect of the Constitution, the ministerial reply usually is "There is a stone wall there." Nobody needs to be told the meaning of that euphemism. There was a time, not very long ago, when the church hierarchy would have handled matters in a decisive if heavy-handed fashion. The views of the bishops would be made known to the politicians, the politicians would assent, the citizens would get the news in a pastoral letter read from every pulpit in the land during Sunday Mass.

The most misunderstood part of the political process is the role of the Catholic Church. Some writers have contended that the influence of the hierarchy is on the wane. It is true that a certain feline cautiousness has replaced the bacon-and-cabbage authoritarianism of the fifties. Church spokesmen are given formal training in the arts of public relations. As an example of this new-found egalitarianism, I saw the Reverend Bishop of Kerry sing a song on Irish television. Nonetheless, the Church's continuing opposition to any changes in the laws on censorship, birth control, divorce, and adoption is a matter of recent record. The hierarchy still intervenes directly as it did in 1949, when clerical disapproval forced the government to back down on a proposal for free medical care. Proof of the Church veto became known only when the then Minister for Health, Dr. Noel Browne, chose to make public some correspondence between the bishops and the government.

Irish politicians tend to consult bishops before introducing controversial legislation, a practice which in itself imputes veto power to the bishops. Fear of public condemnation from the pulpit outweighs all other considerations. A politician's every utterance on matters that the bishops considered controversial is contained, a politician of high rank told me, in a dossier. He had read his own with great enjoyment. And because most politicians are practicing Catholics, this knowledge doubtless acts as a restraint on public statements and on the introduction of controversial legislation, such as a bill permitting divorce.

What makes the matter even more intriguing is that my informant asserts that the Vatican keeps its own file on the actions of the Irish bishops, apparently because some of them have not been as vocal in their condemnation of the IRA as Rome thinks they should be. One report by a Vatican investigator started off with this provocative sentence: "The Irish Bishops are small men and, as such, are apt to panic in moments of crisis." Which way they ran when the panic set in, my informant was not about to say.

The formal structure of government in the Republic is roughly similar to England's. The President, elected by popular vote for a seven-year term, is, like the British monarch, a purely ceremonial figure who receives visitors at his residence in the Phoenix Park, presides at garden parties, and attends state functions. After a general election, the dominant party, or coalition of parties, names a government. The legislature consists of an upper and a lower house, although the Irish Senate, like the House of Lords in England, can only delay or comment on bills that are sent along by the Dail. Leinster House, the seat of the Dail and the Senate, is an imposing structure in the busiest part of Dublin, a monument of the Anglo-Irish aristocracy built in 1748.

The Prime Minister is called *Taoiseach* ("T-shock"), the members of the Dail, "TD's," a contraction of the Gaelic *Teachta Dala*. Members are supposed to address each other as "Deputy." In times of stress, however, more colorful names are used. A deputy is immune from arrest, except for treason, felony, or breach of the peace, not only in the precincts of the Dail but outside while traveling to and from the august place. The Dail once had a reputation for fistfights on the floor of the house. Deputies still invite each other out on the lawn for a few rounds of bare-fisted fighting, rather like the pinking duelists of Buck Whaley's day, but by the time they have reached the fresh air the ardor of battle has usually cooled. The Gaelic flavor of the Dail is illusory. Most of the deputies neither understand nor speak the native language with precision; about 1 percent of the time is taken up with business in Gaelic, most of that devoted to a brief debate on the financial grants to the rapidly shrinking Gaelic-speaking districts. An official translator sits at the ready; seldom called upon, he rests as if in prayerful contemplation.

Of the sixty members in the Senate, eleven are nominated by the Taoiseach, six are elected by the graduates of the universities, and forty-three are chosen from five panels representing Culture and Education, Agriculture, Labor, Industry, and Public Administration. This highly undemocratic method of selection is another bow to the wishes of the Catholic hierarchy, who wanted vocational representation in politics, a sort of elite that would represent the various cultural and economic interests. Except for the university electors, who choose their candidates carefully, senators tend to represent the views of the political parties who nominate them, such as Senator Desmond Hanifin, an oil salesman who does trojan work for the de Valera crowd as an organizer and fund raiser. Among those appointed to the Senate by the Prime Minister after the 1972 election were the two wealthiest businessmen in Ireland, Patrick McGrath of the Irish Sweepstakes and Lord Iveagh, the beloved chairman of Guinness. No one is quite sure which vocational panel they represent, because neither distinguished senator has spoken since his appointment.

The deputies generally talk a great deal when the Dail is in session, usually about ninety days a year, and, from the perspective of a visitor used to the meanderings of House and Senate sessions in Washington, the talk is often highly stimulating, not to say abusive. One deputy, infuriated by the activity of another during question time, shouted, "Will you sit down! You're up and down like a whore's knickers." This was topped by a voice from the back bench: "And you're in and out like a customer." On a typical day in May, 1973, a lot of time was spent on such topics as increases in welfare benefits, the smuggling of Argentine beef, the backlog of telephone installations, commercial banking, and the salaries of the top executives in state corporations.

Oliver J. Flanagan can usually be depended on for comic relief during these rather boring proceedings. Oliver is known as the politicians' politician, unbeatable in elections, impervious to insult, gracious to everyone. His ideology is based on the social-credit ideas that were fashionable in the prairie provinces of Canada during the thirties. In his first campaign, more than thirty years ago, he rode through his district on a bicycle wearing a sandwich board that read "Here Comes Oliver" in front and "There Goes Flanagan" in the rear. His name has been a household word ever since. Oliver's best-remembered line is "We had no sex in Ireland until television came." He is solicitous of the convent sisters in his district. And, when I was in Dublin, he was campaigning vigorously for the installation of toilets for tourists at Clonmacnoise, the site of an eighth-century monastery.

Some other original suggestions have been made from time to time by deputies, especially memorable a proposal by Fintan Coogan from Galway that public seating in the city square be electrically wired so that tinkers using the seats at night would receive a "light shock." The air of the Dail proceedings is casual, as befits the part-time post it is for most deputies. Not that they underestimate the value of an elective post. A new member, Anthony Healy from Cork, when asked why he was in politics, answered, "The last generation died for politics; now some people should live for it."

As the English translation of their names suggests, the two major political parties, Fianna Fail (Soldiers of Destiny) and Fine Gael (the Irish Tribes) are, in the poet Patrick Kavanagh's memorable line, sailing in "puddles of the past." Their doctrinal differences rest not on economic issues but on the cleavage that took place after the 1916 rising when the Soldiers of Destiny, led by Eamon de Valera, resisted partition, and the Irish Tribes reluctantly accepted the island's division. People of my generation find the continuation of this feud incomprehensible, since neither party had the military means to drive both the British and the Northern Protestants from Ireland. And an independent undivided island would have entailed just that; the Protestants were not inclined to accept dominion by a Catholic majority. This sour tradition of nationalist politics is perpetuated because the present generation of party leaders might be called the post-1916 class. Like the sons of elderly farmers in the West of Ireland, they had to wait a long time before stepping into their fathers' shoes, which seem in many cases to be several sizes too large. Some of the names are undoubtedly familiar. All are products of a gerontocratic, politically introverted society.

This small group of O'Montagues and McCapulets have treated the two parties as their own private fiefdoms. Liam Cosgrave, the Prime Minister of the present coalition government, is a son of William Cosgrave, who headed the first Free State government. Garret FitzGerald, Minister for Foreign Affairs, is a son of Desmond FitzGerald, who held that same post under Cosgrave the first. John A. Costello, the Fine Gael Prime Minister of a coalition government in the forties, is the father of Declan Costello, Attorney General in the present government. Thomas O'Higgins, the unsuccessful Fine Gael candidate in the 1973 presidential elections, is a nephew of Kevin O'Higgins, also a member of the first Cosgrave Cabinet.

On the other side of the aisle, the Fianna Fail Party has its ranking members of the founding fathers' families. Eamon de Valera's son Vivion is a busy politician, and he is also chairman of the company that publishes the party's three newspapers. President Erskine Childers' father was a de Valera supporter who was shot by the Fine Gael faction in the Civil War. The late Robert Briscoe, another de Valera crony, has a son, Ben, in the back benches. Charles Haughey, who has served in various Cabinet posts, is a son-in-law of Sean Lemass, who succeeded de Valera as Prime Minister in 1959. The bloodlines in the political stud book have been preserved as jealously as those of treasured thoroughbreds.

The Irish Labour Party, a minority partner in the coalition government, has influence far beyond its representation in the Dail. For one thing, its policies generally approximate the moderate socialism of Britain and Germany, which brings a whiff of fresh air into the Dail and makes the party appear more relevant and realistic when it comes to talk about the Common Market. More important, the Labour Party long ago sailed out of the nationalist doldrums. For the eighteen-year-olds who recently got the vote, and to whom 1916 is as distant as the Battle of Clontarf, a party that looks out at Europe is infinitely preferable to two tribes threshing the chaff of ancient history. The presence of such concerned and talented people as Conor Cruise O'Brien and the lesser-known but equally talented Justin Keating and Dr. Noel Browne lifts the party out of parochialism onto the European stage. Unfortunately, Labour has been unable to hack through the thickets of patronage and nationalism that choke rational discourse. The tall, melancholy figure of Eamon de Valera throws a shadow over contemporary events, not least the machinations of the IRA. To understand the often puzzling actions of contemporary political leaders, one must start with the Chief.

When de Valera retired from public life in 1973, the *Sunday Press,* the official organ of the Fianna Fail, carried an article headed "Greatest Statesman I Have Known." The author, Lord Longford, recalled that Lloyd George had called de Valera "a white man," presumably a term of the highest nobility in the dim days of the British Raj. Whether the Welsh wizard called Gandhi a "brown man," the noble Lord has not recorded. "It is true that on the whole he has performed on a small stage, that of Ireland," wrote Longford. "But he has at critical moments, and at a great material disadvantage been called on to fight his corner against men like Churchill and Roosevelt, to whom the world has not unjustly imputed enormous stature. And he has more than held his own." Acres of such hagiography were published in newspapers throughout the country. It is certainly true that de Valera dominated Irish politics for almost half a century, and his deeds, or lack of them, are endlessly debated. And the English and American families who lost sons in World War II will never forget his visit to the German Embassy in Dublin to offer condolences on the death of Hitler.

Slightly contemptuous of his fellow Irishmen, vicious enough to have executed some IRA leaders during World War II when he could have imprisoned them, so vain that he cooperated with the authors of volume after volume of carefully constructed biographies, de Valera made his last appearance abroad at the funeral of John Kennedy in Washington, where, along with Haile Selassie, he looked like a ghost from the League of Nations. During his last days as President he occasionally granted an interview to a foreign journalist, from which we can get a glimpse of the old man's last days. Staring blindly at the chestnut trees outside his mansion in the Phoenix Park, he scrawled on a large pad with a crayon, rather like James Joyce. He visited an old friend in the hospital for whom he prescribed brandy. His only recreation appeared to be solving mathematical puzzles read to him by a secretary. He left a country dangerously near bankruptcy and a population that was psychologically damaged by decades of decay. Yet he personally never lost an election; people still shouted "Up de Valera" as their sons and daughters left for England.

In practical matters, such as getting elected, he was cute as a mongrel fox. Peadar O'Donnell, the writer and radical politician, provides an enlightening vignette of the statesman as Tammany boss. "I sat beside him once on a platform in the West," O'Donnell told me in the course of explaining the philistine ways of Irish politicians. "Some local yob was going on for what seemed hours, about calves and milk and a lot of things he knew nothing about. The fellow on de Valera's right said, 'Will this eejit ever shut up?' Dev turned to him with his long old face and said, 'That's why I am where I am today and you're nothing. You'll get up and give a brilliant analysis of the English policy on cheap food and how it affects the livelihood of the Irish farmer. But nobody will be listening to you except yourself. This fellow that's talking all the *raimeas* [nonsense] now is far more important, because he's talking for thirty thousand other farmers like himself.' "

De Valera may have been the only European leader, with the obvious exceptions of Franco and Salazar, who survived in spite of failure. He achieved this partly because he always seemed to be above the common man. We are told that he hated dancing, gambling, drinking, foul language, and obscene literature—the public and secret vices of the Irish masses. They admired him for his ascetic personality, as if they could not trust themselves to elect a leader in their own image. If we are to judge by his last political statement, written for a memorial volume on the fiftieth anniversary of the 1916 rising,* he wanted to be judged not as a politician, but as a statesman-saint.

"Political freedom alone was not the ultimate goal," wrote the reformed revolutionary.

It was to be, rather, the enabling condition for the gradual building up of a community in which an ever increasing number of its members, relieved from the pressure of exacting economic demands, would be free to devote themselves more and more to the mind and spirit, and so, able to have the happiness of a full life. Our nation could then become again, as it was for centuries in the past, a great intellectual and missionary center from which would go forth the satisfying saving truths of Divine Revelation, as well as the fruits of the ripest secular knowledge.

* *The Irish Uprising.* New York, CBS, 1966.

De Valera set a political style of indecision, vagueness, vacillation, caprice, and cajolery that others adopted. We can safely speculate that the Chief's last picture of Ireland as a sort of monastic settlement of intellectual missionaries was colored by his own egotism; he could not bring himself to talk about such earthly failures as unemployment, emigration, and education. All this would be rather harmless if the studied ambivalence had not contained a lethal time bomb. De Valera was, of course, a man of violence who precipitated the Irish Civil War of 1921. He never renounced Ireland's dream to annex Northern Ireland. In theory, if not in fact, the Catholic Constitution applied to the entire island. Textbooks in Catholic schools perpetuated the nationalist ideals, a sort of blood-and-soil image of a Gaelic Ireland. At times he scorned the rule of the majority; the people have no right to do wrong, he once said in his schoolmasterish style. The IRA seems to have taken that line to heart.

In Irish family life the father imposes his will with a blithe indifference to the preferences of others. He holds the purse strings, carves the roast, and sets a time when each child should be at home in the evening. Children are chattels in the family economy, often used to supplement the family income, never allowed to spend their small earnings, which they must hand up to Father. So it is in politics. De Valera's successor as Prime Minister, Sean Lemass, is often portrayed as the first of a new, more realistic school of politicians. This judgment is based mainly on the fact that he allowed foreign capital to invest in Ireland without any strings attached, an inevitable consequence of de Valera's ruinous self-sufficient economic policy. Whenever I interviewed Lemass, he went on at length about the necessity of creating a growing economy, always looking and sounding like a worldly croupier at the end of a busy night. Unfortunately, he had copied the "Father knows best" style of the Chief when it came to such important matters as national planning. He refused to allow debate in the Dail on such vital measures, preferring to draft programs in closed-door sessions with civil servants.

Father Lemass did not just carve the roast. He decided what the family should see on television every night. Control of broadcasting by the state is now an accepted practice. The government appoints a supposedly independent governing body with a directive to monitor broad matters of policy, such as the amount of time devoted to news, political party broadcasts, Irish language, and the like. Lemass considered himself something of an expert on television, a subject he talked about with British Prime Minister Harold Wilson. And he had nothing to learn of the art of political patronage. One can feel the hand of government in the studios of Montrose, the television center in Dublin. Program producers are, of course, conscious of the Church's censorship of all matter with a sexual content. They trim their offerings to suit. Criticism of practices that bring the supposedly high moral standards of the country into disrepute is not tolerated. Political corruption is an unmentionable topic.

Restless newsmen, who felt neutered by the restrictions, once tried a lesser target. In the sixties, reporters from the television news service put together a documentary showing the activities of illegal moneylenders in Dublin. Although the practice is as familiar to the Dublin poor as their weekly visits to the city's numerous pawnshops, the government was so angry about this public proof of usury, supposedly unknown in Catholic countries, that it instituted a long expensive inquiry into the matter. The upshot was that the messengers who had delivered the familiar bad news were shot by the king. Well, not quite; the reporting crew were put out to pasture, as it were, making documentaries on the care and feeding of Charolais cattle and such wonders.

As for political news, the Irish must depend on the British broadcasting and print media for an objective account of affairs in their own country. In 1972, Kevin O'Kelly, a radio reporter, was jailed for three months after he broadcast an interview with an IRA leader; later his interview notes and tapes were used to convict that man of violence. When the governing body of RTE, the television and radio system, protested, they were fired by Jack Lynch, the deceptively benign-appearing Fianna Fail leader who succeeded Lemass as Prime Minister.

John Mary Lynch, whose middle name suggests the pious nature of his parents, was an athlete of some renown before he took to the law as a profession. Law led to politics, and in 1965 Lynch was named Prime Minister, much to the surprise of local experts. He has a reputation of being lazy about details and forgetful about important matters discussed in Cabinet. On one occasion he acknowledged that he had failed to follow through when the British tipped him off about the presence in Ireland of espionage agents. His soft Cork accent, soulful expression, and a habit of appearing in public with priests and sisters earned him the title "The Darling of the Convents" in the English press. In the sixties, Lynch made Communism an issue in Irish politics by suggesting that somehow the members of the Labour Party were more loyal to Moscow than to the Church. The smear tactics worked, as several members of the Labour Party told me.

When it came to controlling the IRA, however, Lynch was out of his depth. As a lawyer, he was quite familiar with statutes that gave the government the necessary tools to arrest the members of that organization, who were easily recognized in the bars and hotels of the Republic. For some reason known only to himself, the Prime Minister insisted that he needed draconian measures to deal with the gunmen, nothing less than a sweeping mandate to arrest any citizen suspected of being a member of that organization. In 1972, he dusted off the Offenses Against the State Act, passed as a security measure during World War II. He proposed an extraordinary amendment that reversed the traditional procedures of justice. The amended act permits the arrest of any citizen suspected of being a member of an illegal organization. Those arrested are presumed to be guilty solely on the word of a police officer. The defendant must prove his innocence in court, an impossible task because it would require the presence of a known IRA leader to swear that the defendant was not a member.

This notorious bill, more reminiscent of the police controls used in dictatorships and Communist countries, was opposed vigorously by the Labour Party in the Republic, by some members of Fine Gael, and by Catholics in the North, who were being harassed by similar legislation enacted by the gerrymandered Protestant-controlled legislature in Belfast. Bernadette Devlin arrived in Dublin to address a tumultuous mass meeting in Liberty Hall. "If this bill is passed through the Dail," shouted Miss Devlin, shaking with passion, "may the hand of the President who signs it wither as he signs it, and may every one of his dead comrades who fought and died for this country appear before his dim eyes and curse his beating heart." A preliminary head count showed that the bill would have been defeated in the Dail. On the night of the crucial vote, however, two bombs providentially exploded in Dublin, killing two people and injuring hundreds. Some members of the main opposition party switched their votes upon hearing the news. The new Offenses Against the State Act became law under these rather provident circumstances.

Without the assistance of Liam Cosgrave, the leader of Fine Gael who is now Prime Minister, the anti-IRA law could not have passed. Like his father, who was the first Prime Minister, Cosgrave believes that a touch of harsh discipline is necessary now and then. And in the past, Fine Gael leaders have been noted for taking extreme measures. In the thirties, elements of the party leaned toward fascism. General Eoin O'Duffy led an Irish contingent to fight on the side of Franco. In Dublin, members donned blue shirts, beat up political opponents, and strutted the streets to marching songs. Yeats supplied the words:

What's equality?—Muck in the yard:
Historic Nations grow
From above to below.

As I watched him on television that night of the fateful
Dublin bombings, Liam Cosgrave did not look like a man who
would be comfortable in the blue shirt of an Irish Falange.
With his starched collar, clipped mustache, and diffident manner, he looked a little like Neville Chamberlain bringing home
the good news from Munich. Like Chamberlain, he was wrong
in his prediction of subsequent events. The IRA continue to
operate, predatory fish swimming among harmless minnows.
Cosgrave is said to be an efficient chairman at Cabinet meetings
but decidedly lacking in the single-mindedness of a de Valera. A
remark of Lord Iveagh, when the Guinness chairman was appointed to the Senate, places the Prime Minister in his best-
known public role. "I've met Liam Cosgrave, of course, but I
don't know him all that well. Our common interests would be
on the racecourse rather than in party politics." Just in case
anyone might get the idea that he was consorting only with the
gentry, Cosgrave also appointed a shop steward from the
brewery to the upper house.

While Cosgrave is at the races, or riding to hounds, Garret
FitzGerald, the Minister for Foreign Affairs, is likely to be
drafting instructions for the Irish Ambassador to Moscow or
polishing a speech on the plight of the underdeveloped regions
of the Common Market. FitzGerald is an economist, lawyer,
lecturer, journalist, and politician, a Sean of all trades yet a
master of at least one, for he is said to be one of the few
politicians in Europe who understands the devilishly complex
workings of the Common Market Commission in Brussels.
While staking his claim for party leadership—and on merit he
deserves it—the bushy-haired earnest son of the first Irish Foreign Minister is planting the Irish flag in strange territories.

Small nations must make their presence known in a world of

great military powers by symbolic means, usually through the creation of a national airline and the exchange of diplomats with as many countries as possible. The Irish ambassadors and consuls are scattered almost as widely as the sellers of Irish Sweepstakes tickets. Twenty-four full-fledged ambassadors are assigned to places like Washington, London, Ankara, and the Vatican. Lesser posts for honorary consuls include Thailand, Zambia, El Salvador, Kansas City, Guyana, and the British protectorate of Hong Kong, where a Mr. Nolan flies the green, white, and orange flag at the Hong Kong and Kowloon Wharf and Godown Company. Doubtless he hosts the obligatory party after the coolies hang up their longshoremen's hooks on St. Patrick's Day.

In 1974, Ireland agreed to exchange ambassadors with the Soviet Union. This was something of a coup for Garret Fitz-Gerald; he had to override the vocal opposition of virulent anti-Communists and no doubt the predictable private objections of the Catholic hierarchy. Some Irish journalists traveled to Moscow for an on-the-spot look, seeking some Russian-Irish connection, however febrile. A story that Marshal Timoshenko, the great hero of World War II, was really Irish, a descendant of a saddle maker who had set up shop in Leningrad under the business title of Tim O'Shea and Co., turned out to be false. The correspondents did manage to mention in dispatches John Field, an eighteenth-century composer and pianist from Dublin who played for the czars. Despite the parochial flatulence of the Dublin press, the event is of some note in a country where the Archbishop of Dublin attempted to prevent the Irish national soccer team from playing exhibition games against Communist opponents. The exchange of ambassadors should squelch the sly suggestion of Jack Lynch and the Soldiers of Destiny that only members of the Irish Labour Party are capable of getting into bed, figuratively speaking, of course, with seductive Godless Atheistic Communists.

FitzGerald is very much a Couéist, who has taken it upon

himself to tell his countrymen that every day in every way Irish life is getting better and better. At times, he makes such claims on very shaky grounds. The Moscow connection, while it will hardly lead to a great increase in trade, is a very positive step, a wider window on the modern world. I somehow like the idea of an Irish theatre group mesmerizing the workers of a collective farm on the steppes of Central Asia with a performance of Sean O'Casey's play *The Star Turns Red*.

On my first visit to Labour Party headquarters in Dublin, I felt that I had inadvertently stepped into an American Democratic party branch office. A few pictures hung on the wall, mementos of meetings with foreign and domestic dignitaries. The floor was bare. Serious politicians never spend money on such frippery. Filing cabinets bulged with the names of present and prospective voters. Some copies of the party manifesto were stacked on a bare wooden table. In an inner office sat the serious, shrewd general secretary of the party, Brendan Halligan, whose pragmatism helped save the party from a suicidal obsession with nationalization. Halligan wants to win elections first, and it is largely because of his strategy that the party now holds some important Cabinet posts in the coalition government.

The leader of the Labour Party, Brendan Corish, is Minister for Health, a delicate post that draws fire from both the Catholic Church and the Irish Medical Association. In opposition, Corish has harped on the injustices of the medical care system, which is the antithesis of the socialized system introduced by the British Labour Party in 1948, and which, of course, was adopted in Northern Ireland. Gradually Corish is attempting to provide some basic free medical services for all. That will take a lot of time and money. While time is a plentiful commodity in Ireland, money for social services is not. A good argument can be made that improvement in education deserves first priority; at the very least, the university system should accommodate far more than three out of every hundred students in the land.

This is a job for an unemotional mediator, which is Brendan Corish's thankless task. In the meantime, he is also a mediator of sorts at party councils, where a tug of war continues between the right- and left-wing factions of the party. The presence of Conor Cruise O'Brien, diplomat, literary man, and now politician, at Cabinet meetings is disconcerting. Knowledgeable people say that conversation is muted because O'Brien might write a book, the definitive insider's book which will explain the aimless tackings of the Irish ship of state as the crew tries to sail out of the puddles of the past. While in the Irish diplomatic corps, O'Brien wrote *Maria Cross,* under the pseudonym of Donat O'Donnell, a collection of essays on Catholic writers. Dag Hammarskjöld, the Secretary General of the United Nations, an eclectic reader, happened to choose O'Brien as head of the UN mission in the Congo in 1960 because of an appealing quality he detected in that volume. O'Brien resigned from the mission in a blaze of publicity because nations like Britain were covertly assisting the secessionist regime in Katanga while paying lip service to the United Nations' policy of unity in that new African country. For a time, he was vice chancellor of the University of Ghana. Then he arrived on the New York scene, where he was appointed to an Albert Schweitzer Chair of the Humanities at New York University. In 1969, he returned to Dublin, where he was elected to the Dail. Irish politics has not been quite the same since his arrival.

The Ministry of Posts and Telegraphs is at the low level in Cabinet rankings. At question time in the Dail, O'Brien shows impatience when the Soldiers of Destiny ask him endless questions about the installation of public telephones at some country crossroads. Outside the Dail, he has a national forum. Hardly a day goes by without O'Brien reminding his countrymen that they are not gifted by God with a correct, irrefutable understanding of all the great issues of the day—not the question of partition, or "Irish culture," or racial superiority, or education, or broadcasting. Men of moderation in the North of

Ireland talk to O'Brien, which maddens the single-track Catholic mind. "The fact that Northern Protestants tend to like me," he once wrote, "is regarded in some quarters as a highly suspicious circumstance. 'The Prods like ye, so there must be something wrong with ye' is a reaction I occasionally encounter even from one or two of our own kind." O'Brien shrugs off such mindless flayings. The Irish have been tossing off such inanities for so long that they glide off his shoulders like drops of a soft spring shower. What must have surprised him is that some Dubliners feel his accent is not Irish enough for their taste. I doubt he will take time out for elocution lessons, nor will he preface his sentences with "Musha" to please the loyal sons of self-conscious nationalist Ireland.

The realism of the Labour Party makes even Irish sophisticates grind their teeth in fury. That peripatetic president of Heinz, Tony O'Reilly, remarked with great intensity when we were discussing political personalities, "Justin Keating is a Marxist." This absolutist judgment came when Keating, the Minister for Industry and Commerce, announced that he was about to tax a foreign-owned mining company in which O'Reilly had an interest. Keating's policy is no different from that of an exemplary Christian Democrat, Eduardo Frei, former President of Chile, who imposed taxes on American mining companies like Anaconda and Kennecott.

Irish businessmen have lived so long in their tax-free haven that the idea of paying *any* taxes seems to them like confiscation. In his youth, Keating had a brief flirtation with left-wing politics just about the time that O'Reilly was identifying his ideological leanings by his friendship with the leaders of the Fianna Fail Party. The two men are roughly of equal age, but their ideological differences could not be wider. Keating is an intense and practical man who opposed Ireland's entry into the Common Market. Nobody could deny the realism of his remarks then: "The whole of Ireland is still a colony of Britain, while at the same time the Irish ruling class is involved with

British imperialism. In the domination of the economy, in the distortion of agriculture, in the domination of the Republic's financial institutions there is a demonstration of all that socialists mean by imperialism." Keating accepts the Irish decision to join the European Community with some reluctance. As a Cabinet minister and a leader of the Labour Party, he makes businessmen like O'Reilly extremely nervous. They fear that the day may come when multinational corporations with subsidiaries in Ireland will actually pay some taxes.

Men of splendid passion are usually shunted aside in politics by those who consider themselves more practical. Something of the kind has happened to Dr. Noel Browne, another Labour Party member, who now sits on the political sidelines in the Senate. Browne's accomplishments as Minister for Health have had a more lasting and beneficial effect on the lives of Irish people than any other governmental action since the country became independent. In 1948, he launched successful attacks on tuberculosis and infant mortality, the twin plagues of Irish society. When he tried to extend proper medical care to pregnant women, irrespective of their marital status, income, or husband's political affiliation, he ran into the old stone wall—the Catholic hierarchy. The whole sordid business is well documented. Still awaiting publication is the bishops' theological reasoning of why it is sinful for Catholics in Ireland to have free government-administered medical services and not sinful for English Catholics.

Dr. Browne likes to call himself a practicing politician; the Irish, including most of the Labour Party, think him quite impractical. He is an unabashed extreme socialist who believes that government control of the economy is necessary before any substantial change takes place in the quality of life. When he says things like "I don't believe that parliamentary democracy is ever going to lead, I'm sorry to say, to a serious redistribution of wealth in the way that I would like to see it happen," he is only expressing a conviction held by many Irish people, especially the young. The belief is held by many that some powerful cliques, including the Church, have prevented the reorganization of society.

As a psychiatrist, Dr. Browne expresses some interesting opinions on subjects the Irish prefer not to talk about. He has compared the partners in unsuccessful marriages to victims who are forced, because of the absence of divorce, to live in a cockpit of mutual hatred. "Even when there is a good marriage," he once wrote, "because of our defective educational system, very few of our Irish parents know how to rear a child simply because they have not the slightest idea about the great delicacy and complexity of the psycho-sexual process of evolution towards a mature personality. The authoritarian didactic punitive Irish parent is world famous, as is his frequently neurotic deceitful and anxious child." Educated himself under the rigid discipline of religious teaching brothers, he attributes a good deal of the violence in everyday life to the educational system, where savage corporal punishment is inflicted on children. Politics intrudes here. If the government took control of the schools from the Church and if divorce was permitted, life would be infinitely more tolerable.

With the single exception of the irrepressible Senator Mary Robinson, women have had no influence in Irish politics. Legal restrictions and religious traditions impose second-class citizenship on women from birth. Until quite recently, women who married were dismissed from the Civil Service. Pregnancy is rewarded by the government through income subsidies, so-called children's allowances that encourage mostly poor families to have more and more children. In 1965, a considerable proportion of married women over forty were still bearing children. That same year, more than 19 percent of women who gave birth already had five or more children. The quality of life in large families can be imagined from the details in a news story, given here in condensed form, which appeared in the *Irish Times* in July, 1973:

Mrs. Redmond is typical. Aged 26, she lives with her husband—one of the fortunate few in Benburb Street who has a steady job—and eight children under 10 years old, in two small rooms. Twenty-three people share the lavatory. At times, she says, the smell is so bad that she must run out.

The buildings are filthy, rat infested and clearly unfit for habitation by any living creature. Anyone who kept a beast in such a place would, rightly, be prosecuted by the Society for the Prevention of Cruelty to Animals.

There is nowhere for the children to play. Mrs. Redmond must keep one toddler in a go-car all the time because there is nowhere he can learn to creep. . . .

The chairman [of the street committee] led me through a noisome hallway to inspect the backyard which was littered with human feces. The children could not get into the lavatory, he explained. Then we stumbled through a dungeon like corridor in total darkness to Mr. and Mrs. Redmond's "flat." They showed me their bedroom, a bed for the parents, another for five boys and a girl, a cot, a pram. The baby, I was told, sleeps in a cot on top of a wardrobe. There was also a gas stove in the bedroom where the cooking is done.

Mr. Redmond said if one of the children is sick he put him on his own bed and slept on the sofa. Mr. Redmond is a normal sized man, the sofa three feet long. The children often suffer from diarrhoea. Mr. Redmond works in the Gas Company. "When I am working I dread coming home."

The Redmonds were married when she was sixteen, he was 17½, and they have been seeking a house ever since. "We went to the corporation," said Mr. Redmond. "They always say, 'Have an extra child.' Now we have eight and we are still here."

The absence of contraception has had some other noticeable effects, such as the extraordinary number of late marriages. This social phenomenon is commonly referred to as the Irish method of birth control. Many young women who seek marriage without large numbers of unwanted children are forced to emigrate; the statistics in census reports lead one to this inescapable conclusion. In 1966, the last year for which statistics on this important subject are available, women accounted for half the population and only a quarter of the labor force, a proportion lower than in any other of the member countries of the OECD. In that year, an astonishingly tiny number of only 25,800 married women were at work. Needless to say, married women are hardly represented at all in the three centers of lay power: banking, business, and politics. In Ireland's male-dominated society, the woman's place is either in the kitchen or in a pregnancy ward. Women's liberation is certainly talked about, and the comprehensive list of women's grievances can be read in newspapers or magazines.

Unfortunately for women, the Irish place first things last in their list of national political priorities. Politicians are still obsessed with the old thorn in the festering Irish side—Northern Ireland. A revisionist school of historians and political experts, including some members of the Irish Communist Party who have become quite vocal of late, recently advanced what they call a "two-nation" theory. In essence, their proposition is that Ireland is not one country but two: Protestants in the North, Catholics in the South, each with different political, cultural, and racial backgrounds. However, this sterile approach is not much of an improvement on the present realities.

It is, of course, a welcome sign of realism that a few Catholics admit that Protestants in the North have a right to live there and a legitimate right to resist inclusion by force in a Catholic state with a Catholic Constitution. The proponents of this two-nation theory have not said that all the Catholics in the North should move South, and vice versa, but they imply as much. An endless succession of squabbles would result if this proposition were taken seriously. One can envision the left-wing Marxist IRA setting up, as an example of nonsectarian working-class solidarity, a Workers' Republic that would straddle the border between North and South. The right-wing Provisional Catholic IRA could settle down in a small enclave in the West of

Ireland, speaking Gaelic, wearing kilts, the women spinning soft tweeds at the peat fire, and the men oiling their automatic rifles for one more invasion of the Protestant North. Of course, Ian Paisley's right-wing Presbyterians, who disagree with moderate Protestants on just about everything, from inclusion in the Common Market to Biblical interpretations, could form their own little government.

One comes away from contemporary Ireland with the feeling that debate about nationalism has not changed a great deal since the afternoon when Leopold Bloom and the bibulous blathering mourners of poor little Paddy Dignam stood at the counter of Barney Kiernan's pub:

Bloom was talking and talking with John Wyse and he quite excited with his dunducketymudcoloured mug on him and his old plumeyes rolling about

—Persecution, says he, all the history of the world is full of it. Perpetuating national hatred among nations.

—But do you know what a nation means? says John Wyse.

—Yes, says Bloom.

—What is it? says John Wyse.

—A nation? says Bloom. A nation is the same people living in the same place.

—By God, then, says Ned, laughing, if that's so I'm a nation for I'm living in the same place for the past five years.

So of course everyone had a laugh at Bloom and says he, trying to muck out of it:

—Or also living in different places.

7

Northern Ireland and the Origin of Violence

"If in the North there are people
who spiritually want to be English
rather than Irish, they can go and we
will see that they get the right
adequate compensation for their property."

EAMON DE VALERA, 1962
(quoted by C. L. Sulzberger, in
The Last of the Giants)

"If Guns are made for shooting,
Then skulls are made to crack.
You've never seen a better Taig
Than with a bullet in his back."

Contemporary Protestant
bully-boy ballad

Most tragic of all the sights on the streets of Belfast is the presence of children, both Protestant and Catholic, who have become apprentice murderers. Day begins in a violent home where guns are casually displayed on the kitchen table. The children walk to school in an atmosphere of intimidation, Catholics harassed by Protestants and vice versa. Classes are disrupted by bomb threats, explosions, and gunfire. These children are the potential recruits of the IRA and its Protestant counterparts, the Ulster Volunteers. They become full-fledged members of their respective illegal organizations when they can prove their first "kill."

The sight of these hard-eyed young psychopaths has a particular personal relevance for me. Long before the present
guerrilla warfare began, Northern Ireland was a very familiar
place. It was not home, but very close to home. In the early
fifties, my sister, who is a Catholic, had married a young man
from the region, an estimable good-humored Protestant who
wanted to do nothing more than raise a family and live a
normal life in a civilized community. But which community?
Life in Belfast would have meant social ostracism, and the
distinct possibility of job discrimination. If the children were
raised as Catholics, life would be intolerable; no Protestant
employer would allow a friend of popery on his premises. What
about Dublin, presented then, as now, as a city of tolerance? A
job application presented to a Catholic employer would show
that this man was a dyed-in-the-sash Orangeman; at least such
an inference would be drawn, because he had attended a
Masonic school in Dublin. And of course in Dublin, as in
Belfast, the question of which schools, Catholic or Protestant,
the children might attend, would be vital in the eyes of the
Catholic neighbors. Mixed marriages in Ireland, North or
South, are messy affairs.

A sensible couple, they went abroad, working in Brussels,
London, Geneva, Detroit, and Istanbul. Nobody asked questions about their religious persuasion or the schools their four
handsome children were attending. On their regular visits to
Ireland, the atmosphere among relatives on both sides of the
border was distinctly chilly. It was a small price to pay. In 1973,
two friends of theirs, another Catholic-Protestant couple who
had chosen to risk living in the North of Ireland, had their
small hotel burned down. They were lucky to escape to England with their lives. I thought of all this when I saw deranged
children—there is no other description possible—throwing
stones and Molotov cocktails at the armored cars on the streets
of Belfast.

Every summer in the sixties, I drove into Northern Ireland

with my wife in a car loaded with children, to see friends, play golf, and write. One had the sense of entering a foreign country. The children loved the idea of crossing through customs posts; they thought an English candy called Quality Street, which was available in little towns like Enniskillen and Newcastle, infinitely preferable to the stuff in Dublin. They were highly amused at the "Fuck the Pope" style of graffiti on the gable ends of houses in Protestant communities. The amusement facilities for children at beaches like Portrush and Portstewart were better than anything available in Southern resort towns like Bray and Galway.

As for me, I felt uneasy, uncomfortable, sometimes angry. As we drove through the "Catholic" towns like Newry, Strabane, and Derry, I could not help but identify with the unemployed Catholic men lounged outside the bars and bookie shops, bored, indifferent, hopeless. To sign my name, identifiably Catholic, in the register of a hotel owned by Protestants, or of a golf club whose members were Orangemen, was to invite a look of hatred, derision, and contempt. I was "one of those." Even in the mid-sixties, when ministers of the Dublin and Belfast governments were talking to each other for the first time since partition in 1922, I can remember one chilling moment at night when the armed "B Specials," the paramilitary force of the ruling Unionist party, stopped my car and searched it, sending the children into a temporary state of shock. Violence was never very far beneath the surface.

To cross the border in 1972 and 1973 was to enter a war zone. On the road from Dublin, Irish police searched cars thoroughly, especially if the IRA had carried out one of their bank robberies in the Republic. In a small town where I stayed overnight with friends, the IRA took control at night; police disappeared while the men of violence loaded up Volkswagen vans with explosives and machine guns. Their assignment was to crater border roads with explosives so that patrolling British army units would be halted and perhaps ambushed. Nobody in the village talked about it, nor did anyone criticize the IRA. The local doctor who ministered to the IRA wounded, who signed death certificates if one or two died on the mission, was a pillar of the community, churchgoer, sportsman, a member of a respectable bourgeois political party, a contributor to good causes. "A decent man," as the Irish say.

For decades this town has been the center of a lucrative smuggling business, created by the artificial border lines finally drawn in 1925. In pre-border days, the town served as a market center for a wide area. The local newspaper still carries news of court cases, local elections, deaths, births, marriages, and auctions on both sides of the border. Smuggling became a necessity in World War II, when the Republic desperately needed the kind of industrial hardware being turned out by Belfast factories. The local shopkeepers, farmers, and delivery men were only too happy to oblige. Prods and Taigs buried their differences in the interests of commerce. Occasionally they even allowed a "dipper" to share the loot. Dippers are fundamentalist Baptists who undergo the strange baptismal rite of total immersion. The tariff barriers cradling the tiny businesses in the Republic enhanced the profit potential of smuggling in the fifties. Machine tools, razor blades, tires, automobile engines, electronic goods, records, books, clothing, and especially condoms commanded premium prices in the Republic. Just about any artifact that was either too expensive or, as in the case of condoms, unavailable in the South came across on the hundreds of tiny unpaved roads that linked the two regions.

If either government placed a bounty on the destruction of cattle with diseases such as tuberculosis or brucellosis, the infected animals were smuggled to the nearest agricultural station. Traffic in pigs was especially profitable because of different price levels posted by bacon factories in the two regions. Southern smugglers did their banking in the North. A large accumulation of cash might create embarrassment, especially if the man's only visible means of support was a small farm. Such extralegal business has survived through all the turmoil. In 1973, the number of cheap transistor radios smuggled into the South reached such proportions that four manufacturers threatened to close down unless the government halted the traffic. Recently, a truckload of Israeli vegetables was confiscated by officers of the Republic's customs service. The border, despite the British patrols, is a sieve. Money talks, bribery between some Prods and Taigs is still acceptable. People in Dublin and Belfast wonder how arms get through to Belfast and Derry. A fair-sized load can be moved in the back of a bread delivery truck while police and customs officials on both sides turn their backs.

Despite the extralegal camaraderie of smuggling, relations between Protestants and Catholics were never normal in the region around this town. If a Catholic attempted to buy a contiguous farm on the Northern side of the border, which made perfect economic sense, he was outbid by a coalition organized by the Orange Lodge. Similarly, if a Protestant attempted to add some land previously in Catholic hands, he was frozen out by a group of Catholics. The cold sectarian war formerly conducted with checkbooks is now fought with guns and bombs.

In the early morning hours while I was there, a small Anglican (Church of Ireland) Church had been set ablaze. The pastor of the Anglican Church is seventy-two, his congregation is tiny, he is the unofficial historian of the area. He has always been one of the moving forces for good, ameliorating sectarian differences by visiting with the local priest. Those who caused this fire bombing are known, but the leader has been spirited to Chicago, where he is treated as a hero in the war against the British. The Anglican pastor is no more British than I am, but it makes no difference now. "We'll drive them all out" is the cry.

In Belfast, Derry, and Strabane now, the groups of indolent unemployed Catholics outside the bars and bookie offices are gone. Men have a spring in their step; perhaps it is the abnormal excitement of being in a battle zone, the catharsis of violent action, the prospect that they are, after fifty years of overt and covert discrimination, on a mission of sweet revenge. The news that a ten-year-old boy has been found in the River Lagan, dismembered, mutilated, and burned, causes no concern. The young soldiers of the British Army—some of them seem to me teenagers—are terrified and trigger-happy, flopping on their bellies at the sound of a car backfiring. It is said that the Provisional IRA pays a bounty of a hundred pounds for every British soldier shot; occasionally an errant sniper blows the head off an innocent passerby. On Saturday night, Belfast floats on a comforting soporific cushion of drugs and alcohol. The new Catholic ballad "The Men Behind the Wire" is a song of defiance heard everywhere; the song commemorates Monday, August 9, 1971, when the Unionist government, with the approval of the British, instituted internment without trial for Catholics suspected of being members of the IRA.

> Armored cars and tanks and guns,
> Came to take away our sons,
> But every man will stand behind
> The Men Behind the Wire.
>
> Through the little streets of Belfast,
> In the dark of early morn,
> British soldiers came marauding,
> Wrecking little homes with scorn;
>
> Heedless of the crying children,
> Dragging fathers from their beds;
> Beating sons while helpless Mothers
> Watch the blood pour from their heads.
>
> But for them no judge and jury
> Nor indeed a crime at all.
> Being Irish means they're guilty,
> So we're guilty one and all.

> Round the world the truth will echo,
> Cromwell's men are here again.
> England's name again is sullied
> In the eyes of honest men.
>
> Proudly march behind our banner
> Firmly stand behind our men.
> We will have them free to help us,
> Build a nation once again.
>
> On the people step together,
> Proudly, firmly on your way.
> Never fear and never falter,
> Till the boys come home to stay.

Surrounded by death, destruction, and torture, children in the North of Ireland are growing up with the idea that violence is justifiable and, indeed, a normal part of their everyday lives. In the first two years of the fighting, suicide rates in the North of Ireland took a sharp drop; for some despairing people, violence that is outer-directed makes life worth living. Much publicity is given to a statement by Father Michael Connolly, a pro-IRA priest in the Republic who sees the guerrilla warfare as a "holy war against pagans and people who have no respect for human dignity." This kind of talk is common, the irrationality reciprocated at the weekly meetings of the Orange Lodges. Dr. S. J. Knox, a superintendent of Ulster's largest mental institution and consultant psychiatrist at a Belfast jail, has said, "If the present stress was suddenly lifted, many people in Ulster would become profoundly depressed."

A group of Catholic children from Derry, sent across the border to the tranquil surroundings of Kilnacrott Abbey, refused to take part in conventional games like track and field and football. Instead, they constructed their own version of a British Saracen armored car, an omnipresent vehicle in the streets of Derry, which they pelted with rocks. "They are not normal children," a priest at the abbey told me. "I'm a little afraid of them myself."

In 1973, the winning poem in a contest for schoolchildren in the North, written by Sarah Barbour, entitled "Ten Little Soldier Men," was a poignant exercise in youthful irony. The poem reads:

> Ten little soldier men standing in a line,
> A sniper came and shot one and then there were nine.
>
> Nine would-be statesmen working very late,
> One had his car blown up and then there were eight.
>
> Eight youthful choristers singing songs to Heaven,
> One was hit by flying glass and then there were seven.
>
> Seven "with-it" schoolgirls looking round for kicks,
> One got a big surprise and then there were six.
>
> Six loyal policemen hoping to survive,
> A bullet hit one in the back and then there were five.
>
> Five busy housewives shopping in a store,
> One picked a parcel up and then there were four.
>
> Four Long Kesh prisoners longing to be free,
> One made his getaway and then there were three.
>
> Three old age pensioners with nothing much to do,
> One went to Coleraine and then there were two.
>
> Two happy "pub-crawlers" having lots of fun,
> Bombs went off behind the bar and then there was one.
>
> One worker wondering when the war would cease,
> A booby-trap exploded and then there was peace.*

The roots of violence in Ireland can be traced back to re- liance on the gun as the ultimate political weapon. Catholics

* *Irish Times,* December 19, 1973.

and Protestants formed armed illegal secret societies in the seventeenth and eighteenth centuries; both the modern IRA and the armed Protestant factions fighting in Belfast can trace their genealogy back to the days of the Whiteboys, the Hearts of Steel, the Fenians, and the Irish Republican Brotherhood. Men of violence are glorified. Sir Edward Carson, leader of the gunmen who created the separate loyalist region now known as Northern Ireland, is venerated by Orangemen. They placed his statue on the commanding heights of Stormont, the headquarters of regional government in Belfast. Eamon de Valera and the revolutionaries of 1916 are portrayed as heroic freedom fighters by militant Catholics, North and South.

The story of the Irish fight for freedom, as related in the history books of Catholic schools throughout Ireland, recites the atrocities of the British, from the sack of Drogheda in 1649 to the bestialities of the Black and Tans in the 1920s. Protestant children are taught to revere the heroic defenders of Derry, who ate rats and vermin rather than surrender to the papist thugs. This old and tattered history is repeated by Orangemen every twelfth of July, when they congregate 100,000 strong to enjoy sulphurous speeches which, for racial and religious incitement to violence, equal in ferocity any language recorded during the blood and soil days of Nazi Germany. Catholics solemnly participate in their own atavistic rites: orations over the graves of nationalist leaders, Easter Week prayers at the formal Garden of Remembrance in Parnell Square, in Dublin for the executed leaders of the 1916 rebellion, ceremonial volleys by IRA men over the graves of their martyred comrades in arms. In the minds of many Irishmen, Orange and Green, there is an acceptance of violence as a legitimate expression of political power. Nothing exemplifies that better than the lines from the contemporary street ballads I have quoted. On the Orange side: "You've never seen a better Taig than with a bullet in his back." On the Catholic, Republican side: "We will have them free to help us, build a nation once again." What they are really saying is this: If violence was justified in the past, why not now?

A perverted form of nationalism ("Kill the other fellow") is shared by both sides. If one looks closely, however, if one has lived in both societies, one sees some other shared characteristics. Protestants and Catholics attend churches which claim to be the founts of the one true religion; fire and brimstone–style preaching is much enjoyed by the congregations. Protestants and Catholics display insecurity by advancing dubious claims to assert their cultural superiority. Illegal armed societies are tolerated, sheltered, and financed by people on both sides. Both the Dublin and Belfast governments from time to time use "Special Powers" laws to incarcerate political dissidents without trial. (It is not generally known that the Dublin government threatened to imprison protesting farmers in the 1960s.)

Political leaders who try to break out of this lockstep of absolutism are accused of selling out the national heritage. Brian Faulkner, the present leader of the rational Protestants in the North, is called a "Lundyite," after the Protestant leader who tried to make an accommodation with Catholic forces during the siege of Derry. Gerry Fitt, the leader of the moderate Social Democratic and Labour Party, with a membership almost entirely Catholic, is called a lot of unprintable names; in the jargon of Catholic nationalists he is known as a "West Briton," a euphemism for someone who acknowledges British supremacy in all things. Moderates in Dublin like Prime Minister Liam Cosgrave and Conor Cruise O'Brien share the "West Briton" classification because they have suggested that a million Protestants cannot be bombed into a United Ireland.

The seeds of irrational violence can be traced to the Irish home, where in too many cases the use of physical force is as normal as bacon and cabbage. By the time the smallest Irish child reaches the classroom, he is already conditioned to brutality. The upbringing of children in Ireland, Taigs and Prods, is fraught with beatings of wife by husband, of children by the distressed and tense mother. Anybody who lives in Ireland can testify to the absence of love in the average home; there is little physical affection, especially in large families. Arguments are seldom talked through to a resolution. More often than not disputes are resolved by beatings. Violence reaches a criminal level in hundreds, perhaps thousands of cases. Mrs. Erin Pizzy, founder of the Chiswick Women's Aid Center in London, receives dozens of phone calls every week on behalf of battered wives who have been forced to leave Ireland with their children. Recently, one woman from the Republic, disfigured by a facial attack that entailed taking thirty-eight stitches, arrived at the Chiswick center with her sixteen children. Another arrived blinded in one eye. Women's Aid, an Irish group, brought Mrs. Pizzy to Dublin in order to dramatize the appalling extent of wife beatings. A Catholic woman, identified only as Jean, said that every third or fourth wife in Ballymun, the enormous new high-rise apartment complex in suburban Dublin, was constantly beaten. With typical British understatement, Mrs. Pizzy said, "It is pretty disgraceful that these women have to leave Ireland and come to us for help."

The average Irish family is, in effect, a one-parent family; the father is usually absent, either at work or drinking with his friends. The idea of a childless marriage is beyond the comprehension of most young Irish people, who are conditioned by the Church's teaching against birth control. Those who can't have children of their own adopt children, carefully screened for possible defect. Children that are the result of liaisons with black seamen find no adoptive homes, as in South Vietnam. Society carefully stacks the cards against conscientious poor and middle-class parents who desire smaller families by making the acquisition of acceptable housing dependent on a large family. As Dr. Noel Browne puts it: "The unwanted child becomes an unhappy and anxious child of anxious, angry and frustrated parents, of which the appalling battered babies statistics is an extreme example."

If the North of Ireland is floating on a cloud of drugs and alcohol, a lot of people across the border also rely on these soporifics. In one Dublin suburb, Portmarnock, populated almost entirely by young people raising families, the adults seem to be on a perpetual drug-induced "happy jag"; children crave attention, but the parents, whether at home or in cars (for this is not a poor area by Irish standards) or in supermarkets or cocktail lounges, glide through life with unreal, almost beatific smiles of contentment. As for the extraordinary consumption of alcohol, the government of the Republic is reluctant to launch a full-scale campaign against excessive drinking; about half of the £200 million spent on hard liquor and beer (the amount of wine consumed is infinitesimal) returns to the government in the form of taxes. In 1970, economists were dismayed that a million work days had been lost through strikes; but in every year, 16 million days are lost through illness, a good deal of that absenteeism presumably a consequence of alcoholism.

One can only surmise that the outbreak of violence in Ireland is a cathartic relief for part of an unstable, frustrated population which cannot be lulled by drugs. We know something about the alarming incidence of mental illness in the Republic. One out of every three persons consulting his family doctor has a psychiatric problem. More than 60 percent of all admissions to psychiatric hospitals are readmissions. Experts say that one person in five surviving to seventy years of age will be admitted to a psychiatric hospital.

The picture in the North is not so clear. How does one classify the man who shoots a British soldier, the Orange militant who bombs a Catholic pub, the Catholic women who tar and feather a young girl because she has been keeping company with a British soldier? Are they patriots or psychopaths? Of the thousand-odd people who have been killed in the past five years, a few seem to have been the victims of bestial sexual crimes.

What we do know, from studies made by Anthony Spencer, a lecturer in the Social Studies Department of Queen's University, is that in Ballymurphy, a working-class Catholic area of Belfast, the incidence of mental illness is three times greater than the Northern Ireland average. Obviously, a regional study cannot be made while the men of violence are in control. I suspect, however, that the general pattern would be quite similar to that of the Republic. I was intrigued by a suggestion put forward at a meeting of the Northern Ireland Association of Mental Health in 1973 that unemployed men, often the descendants of several generations of unemployed, be given a special status which would eliminate them entirely from the potential working population. The reason: full-time employment, with its demand for regular hours and consistent productivity, would increase their chances of having a mental breakdown.

The suggestion that some Provisional IRA gunmen are unthinking robots, the products of a rigid, authoritarian society, has been put forward by Dr. Noel Browne. He draws from his own experience, having been educated first in Ireland by the Marist Christian Brothers, with their emphasis on corporal punishment, glorification of violent leaders, and Gaelic cultural supremacy, then later studying at an English Jesuit College. Browne says, "I have experience of the whole lot of them and therefore I speak with some authority when I say that I was educated to hate the British. . . . In fact, I left Marist Brothers in Ballinrobe and went to England, Windsor, in the early thirties, and when I was away all my class ended up in Mountjoy Jail because of their Republican sympathies."

For those who might find this view a little jarring, the opinions of Dr. Browne should be carefully weighed. He is not given to careless or flippant judgments, and his stature is high among his peers, especially outside Ireland. He is hated by many Catholic nationalists for presenting a picture of the ardent Catholic as a sectarian murderer, and that is the paradox of the quintessential IRA member. One of the national stereotypes is that of the feckless stage Irishman, slightly tipsy, always good for a song and a joke, a little bit of a liar, still, all in all a decent fellow. Far more damaging is the portrayal of the IRA man as James Cagney, the selfless patriot in a trenchcoat—"I'm doing it for Ireland, Mother"—with the predictable paraphernalia: revolver, rosary beads, and a picture of his virginal girl friend. In the course of a long article which appeared in the *Sunday Press* in December, 1973, Dr. Browne reflected on why the land of saints and scholars produces this Christian gunman. It is significant that Dr. Browne chose a national newspaper read by the most Green of Irish nationalists to present his views; he is one of the few in Ireland who retain faith in rational discourse.

The unusually high Irish mental hospital bed occupancy figures, very high alcoholism and rapidly increasing dangerous drug abuse figures, including heavy cigarette smoking, are all "anxiety" indicators, and are their own tribute to the clearly high stress nature of our lives in Ireland. . . . These high Irish anxiety rate figures are also a tribute to the failure of our profession, over the years, to educate or initiate or carry through any serious study designed to find out the reasons for this unique and disturbing position which Ireland holds in the civilized world for our insanity rate. The Irish psychiatrist has, over the years, been content to act as the benevolent jailer in his usually sordid though benevolent jails called mental hospitals. This pattern of care happily is now changing in many parts of the Republic, and psychiatrists and psychologists are learning to become more involved in social issues with all the authority of their special knowledge and experience. . . .

The truth is that there is practically no part of the lifestyle of a citizen in the Republic, from the cradle to the grave, which has not had already built into it serious and obvious causative stress factors which lead to anxiety of varying degrees of intensity. . . .

Anxiety or fear, stemming from deprivation of love, and punishment, are the dynamics which are predominant in virtually all our human relationships in Ireland. Our religion, which is ostensibly the Christian religion of love, compassion and tolerance, first teaches us to fear a punishing God and to fear a punitive, retributive hell, and fear the devil. In the home and in our family life, our infant, "child," adolescent relationships are based on fear, we are disciplined under either pain, withdrawal of love or both.

We are made to fear and what is called "respect" our parents— when it must be obvious that love cannot coexist with fear. Fear simply leads to a practice of deceit by the child on the parents, to other adults, and especially to the teacher. In manner the child pretends to conform while the threat of punishment exists, or else he simply learns to deceive and lie to avoid the distress of punishment.

In education the fear of physical punishment, sarcasm or ridicule is the disciplinary nexus between child and teacher. So, where many of our teachers are members of religious orders, we have the anomalous position of being made afraid of these followers of Christ, instead of learning to love them and one another.

How familiar those words are for me, and, I suspect, thousands of my generation. Anxiety, fear, punishment, and the longing for revenge were the steppingstones of my formative years. My household was indeed a cockpit of hatred, with simmering silences between frustrated parents erupting into violent physical clashes of terrifying intensity. Even as a young child, it was quite apparent to me that here were two totally incompatible people locked in a nest of common contempt and hatred. It was quite natural that they should turn on their children as the cause of their pain, and natural, too, that they should dole out physical punishment as an outlet for their seething frustrations. Life in an Irish-language school finished off my kindergarten experience, as it were, in physical education. Corporal punishment was not merely accepted; parents felt it necessary to temper the high spirits and mild rebelliousness of children. It is still a national pastime, as it was when I attended school in Ireland, for teachers to obtain a touch of sexual satisfaction from beating children, on the face with their fists, on bare legs with canes, and by twisting their arms. This educational technique is much admired by parents as the essence of discipline, which is what Irish education seems to be all about.

When I lived in Dublin researching this book, I was not at all surprised that an Eileen Moore, described as a mother of four, had begun a national campaign to legalize the use of birching as a punishment for juvenile offenders. She was encouraged to present her case in the national press because her branch of the Irish Countrywomen's Association had approved the idea of birching by seventy-four votes to ten. Need one speculate on the manner in which the mothers of Ireland discipline their own children?

Perhaps four out of every ten marriages in Ireland are failures; in the absence of divorce one cannot be certain. What is certain is that a substantial number of children are brought up in an atmosphere without love, respect, affection, charity, or dignity. The bestial standards of behavior behind all those lace curtains in Ireland are hidden to outsiders; even if a mother is beaten to a pulp, children have been conditioned not to call on neighborly assistance. Father is king, Mother is a chattel. In my own case, my brother and sister and I attempted to get the Catholic Church to grant an annulment to our parents, but the idea was dismissed out of hand by our parish priest; although a sum of money more substantial than we possessed, I learned afterward, would have worked theological miracles. The family eventually split—my mother institutionalized permanently, my father left with three children. It is the norm in an abnormal society. Whenever I see the face of an IRA bomber or interview the innumerable chiefs of staff which that organization seems to possess, I say to myself, "There, but for the grace of common sense, go I." As with Dr. Browne, who is a generation older than myself, with me also some of the IRA names that grace the pages of the daily newspapers are men who were school companions. They chose a road of revenge, and there are times when I can hardly blame them.

The holy war in the North has been helped along by the perpetuation of separate and equally poisonous systems of sectarian education. At the primary-school level Protestant and Catholic children are divided about equally between the sectarian schools. This polarization continues through life, in jobs, recreation, sports, and politics. It is nurtured weekly by types like the Reverend Ian Paisley, the fundamentalist preacher who rattles the roofs of Belfast every Sunday morning with his antipopery sermons. On the Catholic side are leaders like William J. Philbin, the Bishop of Down and Connor, who recently refused to grant the sacrament of confirmation to Catholic schoolchildren who attended non-Catholic schools. The sectarian division is recognized even in the Church of Ireland's Book of Common Prayer, which contains separate prayers for state ceremonies in the Republic of Ireland and in the North.

The bishops have, of course, condemned violence. The Catholic hierarchy's stern view of IRA membership expressed in the fifties still stands: "Acting then in virtue of the authority conferred on us by our sacred office, we declare that it is a mortal sin for a Catholic to become or remain a member of an organization or society which arrogates to itself the right to bear arms or to use them against its own or another state; that it is also sinful for a Catholic to co-operate with, express approval of, or otherwise assist any such organization or society, and that, if the co-operation or assistance be notable, the sin committed be mortal." And Cardinal Conway has consistently spoken out against IRA outrages.

Unfortunately, the cardinal's views are not shared by a number of clerics in his jurisdiction. Borrowing from the teachings of Don Hélder Câmara, a Brazilian bishop, some Irish clerics have made a case for what they call "institutionalized violence."

In essence, they say that a powerless, politically neutralized, poor society has a right to rebel against authority. The comparison of the lot of the Indian in Brazil with that of the Catholic in Northern Ireland is, of course, ludicrous. As Conor Cruise O'Brien pointed out, if a poor Catholic in the North has the right to take arms against the establishment, the poor Catholic in the Republic has twice as much right to resort to the bomb, because he is that much poorer.

The gallows humor on the streets of Belfast is perhaps a better indicator of the Catholic layman's view of violence and his belief, rightly or wrongly, that the strictures of the bishops are exercises in public relations. An elderly lady goes to confession in Belfast.

Old lady: "Father, forgive me. You remember that bomb that exploded last night?"

Priest: "Yes, my child."

Old lady: "I might have had something to do with it."

Priest: "Tell me about it, my child."

Old lady: "A man put something in my shopping bag and told me to leave it in a pub."

Priest: "Was any damage caused?"

Old lady: "Five British soldiers were killed, Father, and—"

Priest: "Oh, that's political stuff. Have you sinned against the flesh, woman? Anything serious like that?"

The final word on the bigotry of Catholics and Protestants should be given to Dr. Richard Hanson, an Anglican bishop who left Northern Ireland in disgust in May, 1973, with this sorrowful epitaph: "Each of them is using Christianity against the other. They are using Christianity to power their politics. Each of them identifies their version of Christianity with a particular ideology, indeed they subordinate it to a political ideology. This becomes a fire to stoke their hatred. Christianity is not something they feel they have in common. This is what I find so appalling about Northern Ireland. And that is why in a certain sense I feel I cannot be associated officially with Christianity in the North any longer." Christians in England who witness the indiscriminate bombings every night on their television sets no longer look upon the Irish as coreligionists but as strange, amoral sects not far removed from savagery.

By the time the British government assumed direct rule in Northern Ireland, in March, 1972, in contrast with the more independent local government that had existed under the British monarchy for fifty years, the place was a charnel house of hatred. For half a century, Catholics had presented their grievances. They had claimed, rightly, that the controlling Unionist Party had maintained an apartheid state, complete with police force, political gerrymandering, discrimination in jobs, housing, education, government appointments, even the location of new industries. Nobody listened, at least nobody listened where it mattered, in Westminster. The British government has always been reluctant to intervene in Northern Ireland, preferring to look on as the warring factions fight among themselves. It was clear in 1969, when Prime Minister Terence O'Neill, a well-meaning but rather bumbling leader, was ousted by the Unionist Party because he had granted some minimal demands to Catholics, that serious trouble was on the way. Brian Faulkner, who took over the party after a short and disastrous spell of non-leadership by O'Neill's cousin, James Chichester-Clark, was initially viewed by Catholics as a hard-line Orange bigot. Subsequently, the bowler-hatted Orangemen looked on Faulkner, when he agreed to a division of political power between Catholics and Protestants, as being soft on Catholics. Like the Irish weather, Northern Ireland's political friendships and hatreds are unpredictable; they change by the hour. The only constant is forthright bigotry. Although a British government commission has authenticated every charge of Unionist discrimination, the cry from the intransigent Protestants is still "No surrender."

For the Protestant oligarchy, direct British rule meant the end of a strangely unnatural alliance. The Unionist Party, composed of wealthy landlords, small businessmen, farmers, poor workers, and the riffraff of the Orange Order and the paramilitary forces, was cemented together only by hatred of Catholics. British recognition of Catholic claims to power-sharing split the Protestant coalition. Unconcealed contempt by British politicians who visited Orange leaders left the super-loyalists uncertain about the continuity of their English connection. Protestant forces are now split among half a dozen factions, with every leader of an Orange Lodge a potential little Duce. One faction waves the Union Jack and swears unending loyalty to the Crown. Others sport the Red Hand, Ulster's armorial crest, and refer to Northern Ireland as "our country." From time to time militant Protestants meet with the IRA, doleful companions in misery. Protestant terrorist groups, such as the Ulster Volunteers and Ulster Defense Association, operate with the aid and financial assistance of ostensibly respectable Protestant organizations. These underground terrorists specialize in assassinations, bombings, sabotage, and such bestialities as carving the initials of their organizations on the bodies of wives of Catholic politicians. The UDA occasionally undertakes raids across the border into the Republic. Most political experts credit them with the terrorist bombings in Dublin and other Southern towns. Unlike the IRA, Protestant terrorists have no safe havens in the Republic. They must resort to fast hit-and-run tactics.

As for the half-million Catholics in the North, they are divided, as the popular song goes, into forty shades of green. Even the Catholic men of violence are split into two groups (in the North as in the South) : the Provisional IRA ("Provos") , a nationalist organization with one simple aim, to drive the British out; and the Official IRA ("Officials") , left-wingers with a program to form a nonsectarian Workers Republic of Ireland. The IRA, which can trace its lineage back to the 1850s, when the Fenians banded together in the United States for an invasion of Canada ("Think Big," might be the gunmen's motto), had its single moment of glory during the week-long rising in Dublin back in 1916. For almost half a century the organization limped along, led mostly by malcontents, drifters, and dreamers. Such alumni as Sean McBride, who is now prominent in Amnesty International, and Eamon de Valera were eminently respectable citizens when the IRA voted itself out of existence in 1962 after an abortive attempt to reclaim the North by force. For a time, the gunmen settled down to what must have been a dull routine of regular employment.

The "Officials" appeared in the mid-sixties, about the time young radicals like Bernadette Devlin were rediscovering socialism at Queen's University. They read Marx instead of Patrick Pearse. They sang a hopeful "We Shall Overcome" rather than the lugubrious "Wrap the Green Flag Round Me, Boys." The heroes of this little band of radicals, products of the superior British university system, were not the men of 1916, who were shot with a prayer on their lips and rosary beads wrapped around their fingers; the Belfast students much admired Fidel Castro and identified themselves with the radicals of Havana University, who had turned Cuba from an American economic dependency into a client state of Russia. Communist doctrine allied with emotional nationalism can be a powerful force in a poor country, especially a place living on the nerve endings of religious fanaticism. Conservative politicians, North and South, looked on the presence of this un-Irish ideology with equal distaste and uneasiness.

This IRA successfully infiltrated the Northern Ireland Civil Rights Association. They acted as stewards in protest marches; they talked the language of the poor, the unemployed, the victims of discrimination. Initially, the civil rights movement in the North had been the preserve of middle-class Catholics whose demands were minimal: one man, one vote; an end to gerrymandering, job discrimination, and the allocation of houses. When socialist, Trotskyites, Communists, Maoists, IRA members, and other radicals joined up, the alliance changed complexion, from a pale green to a deep red. For a short period, Bernadette Devlin McAliskey was the darling of this movement. Middle-class nationalists and radical agitators alike saw in her an Irish Joan of Arc, ready to immolate herself at the stake of Irish Catholic unity. Bernadette Devlin McAliskey was too much of a realist to compare herself with anyone, but very soon she, too, began to behave and sound like an Irish La Pasionaria. On her first visit to the United States, she alienated Irish-Americans by comparing the plight of the Irish to that of the American Negro. She refused to accept the keys of the City of New York from Mayor John Lindsay; the implication was that she would not play an expected role with any member of the establishment, Irish or true-blue WASP. When she ran across the floor of the House of Commons to deliver a right cross to the jaw of pompous Reginald Maudling, the Home Secretary, who was waffling about the murder of thirteen Catholics in Derry, she offended the sensibilities of proper citizens everywhere. Her decision to have a child without benefit of clergy was the last straw for many, a symbolic act which showed that she had severed all ties with conventional Catholic teaching.

Like so many young Catholics educated in Queen's University, Belfast, Bernadette McAliskey could not care less about the religious differences that divide the island. She believes Britain will eventually leave Ireland because public opinion in England will not tolerate the enormous financial demands made by the intransigence of the Protestant separatists in Northern Ireland. To her, a United Ireland means the evolution of a political system with clear-cut ideological differences, the proletariat against the capitalists. She is a little ahead of her time. She lost her seat in the House of Commons in 1974 because Catholics in her district are not quite ready for the Workers Republic of a United Ireland she advocates. And a Communist candidate in Belfast received only a handful of votes in a recent local election.

The appearance of the radical Northern coalition, with connections among radical groups in Dublin, was a new departure in Irish politics. The ruling Fianna Fail Party had long since shed its cloth-cap image. Some of its leaders were very wealthy individuals; most of the party's financial support came from businessmen who, in turn, were the beneficiaries of government contracts and favorable tax laws. It must have dawned on Prime Minister Jack Lynch and his Cabinet that the eruption in the North could easily spill across the border. Powerless as the Northern Ireland Catholics were, their standard of living was measurably higher than that of the average worker in the South. An alliance between the working class on both sides of the border might unify the country, but it would also mean the end of the hegemony enjoyed for so long by Fianna Fail. Even more threatening to the business establishment was the specter of a left-wing party that might nationalize every decent-sized business in the land. In fact, the Northern radicals, for all their bluster, could not have achieved such a program. Most of the voters on both sides of the border are middle of the roaders, anti-Communist, religious, and very suspicious of change. Still, the threat was enough to move the Fianna Fail Party into action.

During all the violence in the North of Ireland, the government of the Republic, however much it wanted to intervene, was impotent. The Republic's army numbered less than the staff of the telephone and telegraph system. The air force had a few obsolete trainer jets. The Irish navy was a couple of mahogany-bottomed boats used to chase foreign fishing trawlers away from Irish territorial waters. Pressure on the Dublin government to intervene became intense as Catholic areas came under attack in 1969. At one point, the Cabinet actually debated whether to fight a war in Northern Ireland; the most realistic action for the tiny army was considered too expensive. The Cabinet was split between those who wished to arm the Catholics in the North and the more conservative who looked for outside help, such as intervention by the United Nations. But the UN could not act, because Northern Ireland is considered an integral part of Great Britain. The Westminster government was not about to have contingents of Indian, Canadian, and Yugoslav troops keeping peace among the warring Irish tribes.

One way to fight this ideological and financial threat, more than one politician must have thought, would be to recreate a purely Catholic, nationalist, non-Marxist IRA, which would defend Catholics in the North while offering no threat to the government in Dublin. Pure green gunmen, without a trace of red, fortuitously appeared in Belfast and Derry, well armed, not a copy of *Das Kapital* nor a picture of Fidel Castro in their knapsacks, complete with the essential appendage of modern warfare, a public relations staff. The Provos had the blessings of some Dublin businessmen and politicians who contributed substantial sums. In the United States a dormant organization was revived to glorify the green gunmen. Nothing in Ireland is quite as transparently simple as it appears to an outsider. Behind the naïve Provos were wealthy businessmen who either bought or took options on land and property in Northern Ireland. Real estate values dropped as the war continued, and commercial insurance coverage was suspended. When the war is over, no history of the event will be complete without an inventory of the transfer of property which took place in the most bearish of all markets.

It was a little ironic that the leader of the Provisionals was an Englishman, John Stephenson, who joined the IRA in England in the fifties and was imprisoned for his part in an arms raid on a military camp. In jail, he was transformed into the quintessential Gael. He learned Irish and all the nationalist lore of his Irish friends. He changed his name to Sean MacStiophain and reappeared as the military leader of the Provisional IRA, in the guise of a very orthodox Catholic. When the Provisionals were experimenting with chemical-filled condoms as possible bomb fuses, Stephenson refused to carry the outlawed artifact across the border from Northern Ireland. He elected to go on a hunger strike when the Dublin government jailed him. After a few weeks, he accepted nourishment, and his stature as a leader was diminished. The IRA likes to create martyrs. By choosing life rather than death, Stephenson found himself deposed when he was released from jail.

Stephenson, a small pudgy fellow who was a nonentity before joining the IRA, is anything but an imposing figure. When he took to wearing a black eye-patch after receiving a letter bomb in the mail, he looked like a provincial music-hall artist playing Long John Silver. Rumor had it in Dublin that while on hunger strike he ate toothpaste and drank his shower water. The satirical English magazine *Private Eye* found in Stephenson ripe material for a ballad suggesting that the chief gunman was either a consummate faker or a sacrificial lamb.

> I sing of Ireland's heroes,
> Of Pearse and Connolly
> Of Michael Collins brave and true
> And Leon O'Trotsky.
>
> A holy son was Sean Stiofain
> And night and day he prayed
> Until at last to his dying bed
> Came Archbishop McQuaid.
>
> They waited by his dying bed to hear
> What his last wish should be
> In a dying whisper came the words
> "Give us a cup of tea."

Had the IRA received that kind of satirical treatment, which the respectable Irish reserve for each other in the Dublin media, the men of violence would never have attained the mystique they now possess. A tiny minority movement of adventurers—and the IRA had but a few hundred active members in 1969—could not have survived a strong dose of such ridicule. The Dublin government, unfortunately, helped preserve the fiction that the IRA is a band of gallant Gaels by preventing appearances by IRA leaders on Irish television. I can think of no better way of exposing the bombastic bloody-minded nonsense of the gunmen than to have people like Stephenson recite their belief in the virtues of violence and their contempt for democracy constantly on television. Censorship helped create the mystique of martyrdom.

Without a constant supply of money and arms from the United States, the IRA would be crippled. Hardly a day goes by in New York without some kind of function in honor of the Provisionals. Never is heard a discouraging word about violence at these affairs where collections are taken up in the name of the "men behind the wire." Most of the money, of course, is channeled to the Provisionals. The cause is helped by journalists who present the IRA in a sympathetic way, either through ignorance or as friendly propagandists. On one occasion in New York, I was invited, along with a number of other editors and writers, to a meeting where we were asked to serve, in effect, as propagandists for the cause. Most declined, yet a few zealots, driven by some atavistic demons, were happy to offer their services. Selective editorial judgment helps. Skilled hands were at work in the spring of 1974, when the national press ignored the conviction of four Irishmen in Baltimore on charges of gun-running.

The Provisional IRA created its martyr in June, 1974, when Michael Gaughan, a convicted bank robber, died in a London jail after a sixty-five-day hunger strike. Gaughan was instantly elevated to the status of Terence MacSwiney, the Lord Mayor of Cork, who died in another British prison in 1920 after a lengthy hunger strike. Not alone did the IRA parade Gaughan's coffin, draped with the Irish tricolor, through the streets of London and Dublin, but the Catholic clergy helped by giving the dead man a Requiem Mass and by refusing to declare Gaughan a suicide, which, of course, he was. When Gaughan died, a number of other young hunger strikers were ordered to cease their fast.

The right-wing Provisionals are now the dominant IRA organization, in money and numbers. Among their members are armed thugs and criminals who raid banks and snatch payrolls. While I was in Ireland, one such group sat in a hotel lounge in Dundalk, a border town in the Republic, brandishing their guns. Apparently they had wagered money stolen in a bank raid on a horse race in England. When their horse failed to win, they shot the television set. One member of the gang was pointed out to me in Dublin, a tough, foul-mouthed individual in his late twenties who frequented one of the city's numerous singing pubs. He was at large because few citizens will testify against an IRA man. And with good reason. An editorial writer for a provincial newspaper was savagely beaten for criticizing the Provisional IRA.

Foreign journalists have no difficulty finding Provisional spokesmen in Dublin. Like many front men for illegal organizations, they have developed a veneer of sophistication when dealing with the press. I spent several evenings with one Provisional noncombatant, a small shabbily dressed elderly man with a *Fainne* ("fawn-ya"), a gold ring, on his lapel, the insignia of a Gaelic speaker. He regularly visited IRA men interned in Northern Ireland. Among other duties, he was responsible for production and delivery of a Provisional news sheet with graphic accounts of British atrocities. He handed me a document which, he claimed, was among the indoctrination materials given to British soldiers upon their arrival in Northern Ireland. I have checked with others who are knowledgeable on such matters, and they insist that, indeed, this inflammatory material—alleged to be the IRA oath—was administered to the first contingents of British soldiers. (The authors of a Penguin book, *Ulster*, have included the "oath" in their text.) Precisely who gave this propaganda gift to the British is a mystery:

I swear by Almighty God . . . by the Blessed Virgin Mary . . . by her tears and wailings . . . by the Blessed Rosary and Holy

Beads . . . to fight until we die, wading in the fields of Red Gore of the Saxon Tyrants and Murderers of the Glorious Cause of Nationality, and if spared, to fight until there is not a single vestige and a space for a footpath left to tell that the Holy Soil of Ireland was trodden on by the Saxon Tyrants and the murderers, and moreover, when the English Protestant Robbers and Beasts in Ireland shall be driven into the sea like the Swine that Jesus Christ caused to be drowned, we shall embark for, and take, England, root out every vestige of the accursed Blood of the Heretics, Adulterers and Murderers of Henry VIII and possess ourselves of the treasures of the Beasts that have so long kept our Beloved Isle of Saints . . . in bondage . . . and we shall not give up the conquest until we have our Holy Father complete ruler of the British Isles . . . so help me God.

Many of those who joined the Provisional IRA seemed to have been afflicted by frustration and boredom. Maria McGuire, a young Dublin woman who joined the Provisionals, became a great and good friend of its top leaders. She left after a year, disenchanted with the murder of civilians. In her biography,* McGuire says she joined the IRA because "All Ireland had were symbols of freedom: our own flag, our own stamps, and our own sterling currency, which cannot be used in Britain, even though British sterling can be used in Ireland." Her life, until she began carrying a gun for her friends, was typical of that of a girl growing up in Dublin. Her father was a clerk in the Civil Service; she became disenchanted with the Catholic Church, took courses in English, tried acting, attempted suicide (decidedly atypical, I thought, but perhaps not), fled to Spain, married ("disastrous and consequently short lived"), and in 1971 returned to Dublin to join the Provisional IRA, where she was told to hide her religious apostasy. She apparently knew nothing of politics and for a time got a thrill out of being an insider.

* Maria McGuire, *To Take Arms, My Year with the IRA Provisionals*. New York, Viking Press, 1973.

What is interesting in McGuire's story is that her revolt seems to be part of a world-wide phenomenon. A number of bored college-educated young adults seem to find an almost sexual excitement in getting close to, or being involved in, violence and murder. Conventional life seems to be unbearably predictable. In McGuire's case, she associated herself with the cause of Irish nationalism, and she parrots the clichés of the Provisional IRA ad nauseam. After a United Ireland, what? She never says, nor do any of the Provisional leaders.

The Provisional IRA could exist only with the assistance of powerful allies. In 1970, British intelligence officers discovered a plot to smuggle arms illegally into Northern Ireland. The information was passed along through various channels until it reached the desk of Prime Minister Jack Lynch in the form of an anonymous note which read as follows:

A plot to bring in arms from Germany worth £80,000 for the North under the guise of the Dept. of Defense has been discovered. Those involved are: Captain James Kelly I.O., Col. Heffernon Director of Intelligence (both held over the week end in the Bridwell), Gibbons, Haughey, Blayney and the Jones Brothers of Rathmines Road and Rosapena Hotel in Donegal.

See that this scandal is not hushed up.

Garda

The Gibbons and Blayney referred to were ministers in the Fianna Fail government. Blayney, a nationalist from the northwest county of Donegal, was insistent that the government should provide aid to Catholics in the North. His influence was minimal, for he was on occasion a figure of fun at Cabinet meetings. During discussions on Northern Ireland, his rapid-fire, almost incomprehensible speeches earned him the name Black and Decker, because, as a listener told me, everything he said sounded like "blackanddeckerblackanddeckerblackanddecker."

Haughey is a far more interesting and complex personality,

usually referred to by Dubliners as "a cute fellow," not exactly a term of endearment. He came to prominence in the Fianna Fail Party when he married the daughter of Prime Minister Sean Lemass. An accounting firm which he founded with another party member thrived. He helped to organize TACA, the fundraising arm of the party. Elected to the Dail from a Dublin constituency, he served in various ministerial posts. By Irish standards, he became very wealthy, mainly through the standard business of real estate dealings. Some people thought he should have been Prime Minister; he had the reputation of being an able, if ruthless, administrator. Arrogance may have made him a few enemies in the Cabinet. He is a facile, clever poor boy who suddenly became rich and powerful. He never lets anyone forget it.

As a Haughey watcher over the years, for he often arrived to represent the Irish government at ceremonial functions in New York, I began to think of him as the Blazes Boylan of contemporary Dublin. He is everything that Richard Nixon would like to be. Whether riding to hounds, watching his few steeplechasers, eying the ladies, buying an island off the Kerry coast, or making a political speech, Haughey always appears to be enjoying himself hugely. His notoriety earned him an invitation to lecture at Harvard. He also attempts to write the impenetrable jargon of art criticism, as this sample from a 1973 issue of *Arts in Ireland* shows:

> Habitation and cultivation are the primordial concerns of man and there is no doubt that the paintings do say something about these things. Yet, they are not, in my opinion, at all literary.

One cannot expect a past pupil of the Irish Christian Brothers to have attained perfection in all things.

Lynch dismissed Haughey from his Cabinet post upon reading the anonymous note from "Garda." In the curious ways of Irish politics, this fall from grace did not end Haughey's political career, for he remained as a member of the Dail. Indeed, his

popularity among nationalists increased; the gun-running alle-
gation, true or not, made him something of a hero. Naturally,
there was a criminal charge to face before Haughey could regain
his standing in the party; after two trials, a jury found him
not guilty. Later, during a Dail inquiry, a senior police official
testified that Haughey had met with a leader of the IRA and
had promised him fifty thousand pounds. Foreigners thought
there were still a few loose ends to be cleared up. The Irish,
who enjoy intrigue, seem to prefer this inconclusive ending to a
mysterious episode.

Strutting the Dublin scene, Haughey seems omnipresent,
talking in the Dail, lunching with officials of Irish Airlines,
making speeches at the openings of art exhibitions, and, of
course, appearing at the race meetings. He agreed to meet with
me, called it off, then said maybe, and finally said no. He
walked into my hotel one evening and stood a couple of feet
away from me. We said nothing. It is a tactic that Haughey has
used before, when he kept Max Ophuls, the French film director, hanging around Dublin. Ophuls had the satisfaction of
inserting a borrowed film clip into his documentary *A Sense of
Loss,* which shows Haughey ranting about the specter of socialism in Ireland, like a very junior Senator Joe McCarthy. I
prefer to think of Haughey as a perfect product of his society.
He may very well be a future Prime Minister of Ireland. His
constituents elected him in 1973 with an enormous majority. If
Ireland was a monarchy, his friends would undoubtedly crown
him king.

Only a few Irishmen, not including Haughey, have acknowledged that without the presence of the British army a full-scale
savage civil war would erupt throughout the entire island of
Ireland. It goes against the Irish nature to admit that the
English are good for anything; when it comes to events in his

own country, the average Irishman has an inherent tribal belief that the English presence is malevolent. It was not the English army that started the sectarian violence, but God-fearing Catholics and Protestants who do not subscribe to the basic processes of democratic rule. Now the pornography of violence has affected everyone—politicians, clergymen, civilians, and soldiers. More than a thousand lives have been senselessly lost since the conflict began five years ago. The violence has spread outside the borders of the six-county region, to Great Britain and the Republic of Ireland, where many innocent people have been killed or maimed by bombs. Russian and American arms have appeared in the hands of the combatants.

"Why is it," George Orwell once wrote, "that the worst extremes of jingoism and racialism have to be tolerated when they come from an Irishman? Why is a statement like 'My country right or wrong' reprehensible when applied to England and worthy of respect if applied to Ireland?" Part of the answer, of course, is that the underdog, as in a boxing ring, always has the sympathy of the crowd. And the English have a guilt complex about their treatment, or rather mistreatment, of the Irish over the centuries. Then there is the matter of emotion, the English psyche crippled from the lack of it (witness the coal miners' strike in 1974, when a national election was called because the Tory government thought that sixty-five dollars a week was just about right for those grubby fellows), the Irish so full of passion that a sentimental ballad brings tears to their eyes.

The trouble is that the border problem has been flooded by too much Hibernian emotion. One has to begin by asking if there is a mandate for unification, either in the North or throughout the island of Ireland. In a unified country, would the Republic's laws governing birth control, family planning, censorship, abortion, adoption, and divorce prevail? Fortunately, some people are beginning to ask these thorny questions, and there are some answers available to get the debate back on rational terrain.

The majority of the people in the North want Britain to stay. In March, 1973, voters were offered two propositions—to remain part of the United Kingdom or to be joined with the Republic of Ireland. The result was 591,820 in favor of the link with Britain, 6,463 for amalgamation with the Republic. A great number of Catholic voters abstained, or were prevented from voting by intimidation. Had all the Catholics voted, the majority would still have preferred the link with Britain. And for good economic reasons. However poor Northern Ireland is—and the average worker there earns 15 percent less than his counterpart in Britain—he is more affluent than the average worker in the Republic. No sensible person is going to vote himself into the poorhouse.

As for the claim that Britain gains some colonial dividend from its presence in the North, that assertion is absurd. Northern Ireland has no valuable natural resources. Its population represents 2.5 percent of all the people living in the British Isles. The two main industries, shipbuilding and aircraft, have been kept afloat by subsidies from Westminster. Since the end of World War II, unemployment has been chronic, on occasion five times higher than in Great Britain. The agricultural sector is now reduced to sixty thousand farms averaging fifty acres. The story is familiar: an economy marked by emigration, poverty, high unemployment, just like that of the Republic of Ireland. Britain must prop up this ailing, anguished little statelet that cannot support itself. No less an authority than William Whitelaw, the former Secretary of State for Northern Ireland, who spent two years trying to mediate a settlement of the sectarian guerrilla war, has said that Britain's presence will be necessary for years to come—perhaps decades. If that is so, the taxpayers of Great Britain will see £3 billion of their money disappear in the next decade. Whether they are prepared to see so much of their treasure and so many of their troops expended in the protection of a foreign country (the English do not look upon the Northern Irish as fellow countrymen) is doubtful. The English economy has been hovering on the edge of disaster since World War II; now, some eminent economists are predicting bankruptcy and depression. It is small wonder that the expensive, insoluble conflict on another island has infuriated the English. When Protestant terrorists and Paisleyites staged a two-week strike in May, 1974, in protest against the pragmatic British approach to partition, an exasperated Harold Wilson called them "spongers." Economic realities seldom intrude on the consciousness of fanatics. After Wilson's attack, Ian Paisley and his followers sported pieces of orange sponge on their lapels.

For years the claim has been made that a referendum of *all* the voters in Ireland would result in a unified country. When Catholics were driven out of their homes in Belfast—tens of thousands were forced to leave because their houses were destroyed or because they lived in Protestant neighborhoods—quite a few fled across the border to the Republic. They did not remain. Welfare benefits in the Republic were too low to support these families who could find neither jobs nor adequate housing. For many of these nationalists it was the first visit South. And the last. They moved back to Northern Ireland at the first opportunity.

In the fiscal year 1971–72, per capita public expenditure on social services in the North was 91 percent higher than in the Republic. In Belfast, a man with a wife and two children receives unemployment and sickness benefits 65 percent higher than he would under the Republic's system. A family with five children in Derry can count on children's allowances 77 percent over those paid in Dublin. Northern families receive supplementary payments if income drops below a specified level. Unemployed parents get rent subsidies from the local government. Everyone in the North is entitled to the free medical benefits of the British welfare state, including contraceptives and advice on family planning.

Politicians in the Republic have always been vague on the cost of unifying—and therefore matching—social security systems with those of the North. In an interview in 1971 with *Der Spiegel*, a German news magazine, Prime Minister Jack Lynch casually said that the disparity between the economies was no barrier to unification. Barry Desmond, a member of the Republic's Labour Party, produced some revealing calculations; the British government was subsidizing social welfare in the North to the tune of £100 million a year. Desmond thinks the cost of providing social services on the British model for everyone in a United Ireland would be £150 million more than the present cost of services in the North. When he tried to pin down the government, the following dialogue ensued:

MR. DESMOND: Surely the Minister for Social Welfare has some idea of the dimensions of the cost. All I am asking is whether the Minister accepts that the figure would not be less than 150 million . . . I will not argue further.

MR. J. BRENNAN: I always refrain from giving a figure when it may be a wrong one.

MR. DESMOND: I challenge the Minister to dispute the 150 million figure.

MR. TREACY: Is the Minister not prepared to give an estimate?

MR. J. BRENNAN: I am not.

MR. DESMOND: The cost of unity my eye.*

Lay a ruler on the map of Ireland; that half which lies to the west of the River Bann in the North and west of the River Shannon in the South is the most impoverished region in Western Europe. Government by different regimes has made no difference to the lives of Catholics or Protestants. The unemployment figures for the past twenty years show the similarity:

* *Parliamentary Debates,* Vol. 263, No. 2. Dail Eireann, 26th October, 1972.

Percentage of Unemployment

	1951	1961	1966	1971
Republic of Ireland	7.3	5.7	6.6	8
Northern Ireland	6.1	7.5	6.1	8.1
Scotland	2.5	2.9	2.7	5.7
Great Britain	1.2	1.5	1.5	3.6

If politicians were serious about solving the common problem of relieving unemployment in the western half of the island, they could make a concerted effort without compromising their political standing with the voters at home. Like the Republic, the North has depended on foreign capital to provide new industries and jobs. Since 1945, companies from Great Britain, the United States, West Germany, and elsewhere have invested more than $800 million and provided sixty thousand jobs in the North. Given the smaller population in the North, this is, in fact, a far better performance than the effort by the Republic of Ireland. The Republic has sent a representative from the Industrial Development Authority to New York to seek foreign investment. So has Northern Ireland. And a third emissary, representing the Shannon Airport area, comes into the city to make his own separate presentation. As usual, the Irish cannot agree; parochial rivalries intrude. Needless to say, the executives of American corporations, already confused by events in Ireland, are confounded by this rivalry. It is as if the Canadian province of Nova Scotia, also in the business of attracting foreign capital, had three competing representatives in the United States. Roy Bradford, a former Minister for Development in the Northern Ireland Cabinet, once complained: "It is a waste of energy and resources that areas such as ours, struggling to improve life standards, should engage in sometimes cut-throat competition for the limited amount of mobile new industry." Bradford's appeal for economic cooperation was drowned in the rattle of Thompson machine guns.

The other unmentioned, perhaps unmentionable, subject when unification is discussed is the Republic of Ireland's steadfast policy of neutrality. The North has received some tangible economic benefits from Britain's role in NATO. Both the aircraft and shipbuilding industries in Belfast have been kept afloat by Britain largely because they are considered part of the country's defense establishment. The blighted city of Derry has received an infusion of cash and jobs from a naval base which serves American, Canadian, and British naval vessels. Would Ireland remain neutral if a majority of the voters approved unification? Would NATO forces then depart, the naval base close, the aircraft and shipbuilding industries be placed in mothballs? Or would the predominantly Catholic island, so vociferously anti-Communist, accept an American military presence in return for economic aid, like Franco's Spain? In the absence of any discussion of such vital matters, which affect the security of Britain and Europe, talk about unity is, as Barry Desmond said, "all my eye."

Unification without a massive annual British subsidy is unlikely in this century, even if Catholics and Protestants submerged their sectarian differences. And the financially hard-pressed British government could hardly be expected to continue subsidizing Ireland in the event that the British military presence was removed to appease the IRA. Merging Orange and Green would have no immediate synergistic benefits; a single national administration would leave thousands of government employees, from Cabinet ministers to veterinarians, jobless. Unemployment would certainly exceed 10 percent, unless, of course, the bloated bureaucracy was enlarged. In such a shaky economy, already overloaded with debt, the cost of providing social services on a level comparable to those of Britain, would be beyond the capacity of a central government. If Britain pulled out of the North tomorrow, and if a national administration attempted to provide social services such as health care and education to everybody on the island at the level now prevailing in the North, the average family in the Republic would be forced to pay at least an additional 30 percent in taxes, a sacrifice that even the ultranationalists might find intolerable.

A small touch of reality came to Irish politics in December, 1973, when the government of the Republic, in effect, abandoned the nationalist dream of unification by force. The Dublin government reluctantly accepted Northern Ireland's status as an integral part of Great Britain, which will remain unchanged until a majority of voters decides otherwise. A Council of Ireland was created, representing North and South, with a mandate to coordinate the legal and police systems in a way that would eliminate the safe havens of Catholic and Protestant terrorists. Moderates made much of the Sunningdale agreement, so called after a musty mansion in the Berkshire woods where the factions agreed to return to the constitutional situation that prevailed in 1920.

The Irish found it not at all paradoxical to claim that a march back fifty years in history is progress. With ruffles and flourishes, the Sunningdale settlement was signed by Liam Cosgrave, the Republic's Prime Minister; Brian Faulkner, leader of the Protestant Unionists; Gerry Fitt, head of the predominantly Social Democratic and Labour Party; and a rather puzzled-looking Edward Heath, who must have dreamily said to himself, "This is where Lloyd George came in." A friend who sat out the four-day vigil found the quadripartite gathering not without its moments of unconscious humor. As if to atone for the fact that some Irish delegates had staged a forty-eight-hour hunger strike outside 10 Downing Street in 1970, the British provided an enormous spread on the first night, washed down with lots of Bollinger '64 and vintage brandy. Prime Minister Heath, a musician of some accomplishment, had three boys and three girls sing a Grace:

> Bless this house, O Lord, we pray.
> Bless the food we eat to-day.
> God Save the Queen, preserve our host,

> And hearken to our festal toast:
> May those we welcome happy be,
> In pastime with good company.
> Benedictus benedicat
> Per Jesum Christum Dominum Nostrum. Amen

Two of the Northern delegates, portly Patrick Devlin and bearded Patrick O'Hanlon, responded with ballads like "Fiddler's Green," "Carrickfergus," and "The Boys of Mullabawn." In the early hours of the morning, when the sleepy delegates sought diversion, Devlin went from room to room singing "Help Me Make It Through the Night."

Celebration was premature because the two factions who started the fighting in the first place, the militant Protestants and the anarchistic IRA, prefer a continuation of their Holy War. The motives of these troglodytes, marching in melancholy cadence to a hymn of self-destruction, are impossible to analyze in a rational way. What can one make of those Paisleyites who triumphantly sing "O God from Whom all Blessings Flow," or Catholic nationalists who chant "God Save Ireland" over the corpses of their fallen warriors? Confronted by these rabid bands of ritual murderers an optimist can only say that the best solution would be an agreement for the two sides to disagree, a pessimist might forecast decades of guerrilla warfare. A cynic might repeat the cutting comments of James Callaghan, the British Home Secretary who examined the causes of the conflict in 1970 and said, "Here they are with all the panoply of government—even a Prime Minister—and a population no bigger than four London boroughs. They don't need a Prime Minister. They need a good Mayor of Lewisham." The rule of law applies in Lewisham, not to mention Robert's Rules of Order. And law and order has been missing for so long from Northern Ireland that it would not seem the same place if mere democracy prevailed.

8

Hibernia Ltd., Division of Multi-Conglomerate, Inc.

Disraeli, who was something of an expert on imperialism, once remarked during a debate in the House of Commons, "Colonies do not cease to be colonies because they are independent." Ireland's economic ties with Great Britain are as firm now as they were in Disraeli's day, a truth the Irish are reluctant to accept. The residents of John Bull's Other Island have never reconciled themselves to the realities of international trade, the kind of profitable pragmatism that allows an anti-Communist Wall Street banking house to finance the sale of Kansas wheat to Moscow. Something of the kind is happening while the Irish have their eyes fixed, as always, fearfully on London. One can safely predict that Hibernia Ltd. will soon be acquired in an exchange of stock, warrants, convertible debentures, and perhaps a little cash by an amorphous entity with no nationality called Multi-Conglomerate, Inc.

The degree of foreign ownership in Ireland can be measured in a number of ways. In 1972, foreign stockholders owned 19 percent of the equity in the fifty largest Irish companies. A year later, they owned 28 percent; in some companies non-Irish stockholders held control, i.e., more than 51 percent of the stock. Nor was this the supposedly passive role of a purely portfolio investment. Seagram Distillers Company, one of the large North American corporations, acquired Bushmills, the centuries-old Irish distilling company, and 15 percent of the stock in Irish Distillers, producers of, among other famous whiskeys, John Jameson. Some thirty-one Irish businesses were taken over by foreign corporations between 1970 and 1973. Hardly a voice was raised in protest.

With some regret, one must even point out that the ownership of Guinness, the makers of the national drink, is British. True, the Irish government honored the first Arthur Guinness, who founded the Dublin brewery in 1780, by issuing a stamp in his honor. And the present chairman of Guinness, Arthur Francis Benjamin Guinness, known in prim London as Lord Iveagh and in parochial Dublin as Benjy, lives in a stately house outside Dublin with his wife, the Lady Miranda, and their three children. Still, the headquarters of the company is in London, and most of its annual revenues of $600 million are derived from sales outside Ireland.

The selling of Ireland to foreign investors has been entrusted to Michael Killeen, an effortlessly smooth, charming, witty, shrewd civil servant who travels the world in his quest for new industries. Killeen heads the Irish Industrial Development Authority, a government agency with a surprisingly broad mandate and, by Irish standards, a considerable budget. In 1972, the IDA handed out more money in grants to foreign corporations than the Irish government collected in total corporate tax revenues. As of December, 1972, the agency had persuaded some 456 foreign companies to locate plants in Ireland.

Companies from the United States have invested the largest amount of money, followed by the United Kingdom, Germany, and the Netherlands. These firms now provide more than 20 percent of all jobs in manufacturing. Irish experts say the foreign-owned companies are responsible for 60 percent of the increase in Irish exports over the past decade, a vitally important contribution to a nation with a large annual trade deficit. The same experts say that the presence of the foreigners has done little but provide jobs. There has been no measurable spin-off to encourage the creation of local industry, nor is there evidence that high-technology companies like General Electric have generated any demand for local research and development. By and large, the foreign companies operate nothing more than assembly plants, attracted to Ireland by tax concessions.

The hard-selling program of Michael Killeen and his associates in the Industrial Development Authority is as basic in its way as the technique of an automobile dealer with an overly large inventory of cars on the back lot. Typical of the IDA's sales pitch is this dialogue between OE, an English tax collector, and E, his Irish counterpart, taken from an advertisement in the *Financial Times* of London in June, 1970.

OE: He got away.

E: They sometimes get away.

OE: But this time he got away for good.

E: For good?

OE: For good. He went over to you.

E: Over to me?

OE: He's yours: get all you can out of him.

E: All I can?

OE: You Irish taxmen are not very quick on the uptake, are you? I'm making you a present of him. He's successful, enterprising, one of our best businessmen. He must be worth a lot of money.

E: Not to me.

OE: What do you mean not to you? You tax profits over there, don't you, like us? You show no mercy?

E: Yes. I mean no.

OE: What do you mean, yes, you mean no? I thought you Irish were supposed to be on top of the morning and all that kind of thing. You don't sound very enthusiastic.

E: He got away from you, your successful British industrialist.

OE: He got away from me: they sometimes get away.

E: And he came over to me.

OE: And he went over to you. Why? Why? Why?

E: Because, a mhic, our government has lured him with fifteen years freedom from taxation on exports profits if he sets up in Ireland, with all kinds of assistance towards the cost of his site, his factory, his machinery, with incentives which our learned friends the Economic Commission for Europe describe, and truthfully, as going further than any other country in Europe in encouraging export industries and in attracting private capital for this purpose. Small wonder that forty percent of the three hundred new industries established in Ireland in the last ten years are British based.

From the very beginning the campaign to attract foreign investment had about it an air of desperate and frenzied improvisation. It must be said that the Industrial Development people were laboring under some considerable disadvantages. First, they were late starters in an international contest that included scores of other territories, states, and countries, from the Commonwealth of Puerto Rico to neighboring Northern Ireland. Second, Ireland lies a considerable distance away from the central distribution centers of Europe and North America. Third, the Irish knew little about the internal policies of companies abroad; they could not know whether these companies saw Ireland as simply a place to make maximum profits for fifteen years or less and then depart, or whether the location of a plant on the island was part of a long-term European marketing strategy. Fourth, and most important, the government of Ireland had failed to think through the effect this foreign invasion would have on its own economy. The attitude in Ireland was totally passive, as if the government had given up on the ingenuity of native entrepreneurs to come up with new ventures that would create an export market. As a result of all these considerations, few prospective investors, however bizarre their schemes, were turned down. The only criterion seemed to be: Will the company provide jobs? An affirmative answer brought an instant handout.

The tax concessions offered by Ireland were so liberal that profit margins for foreign companies locating there were outrageously high by American standards. Some whimsical trade patterns emerged as a result. De Beers Consolidated, the South African diamond company, prepares its industrial diamonds in Shannon for shipment around the world. At one time a Dutch company found it profitable to make plastic pianos in Ireland to be sent by air to markets in Europe. Bally Manufacturing, the company that supplies one-armed bandits to Caesars Palace and other Las Vegas casinos, makes slot machines near Dublin. General Electric does a good deal of its subassembly work there; chances are that a transistor radio or television set assembled in the United States has some components soldered together in Ireland. One of the most extraordinary aspects of the data-processing industry is that some American computer companies find it profitable to handle their softwear operations in Ireland; billing lists and punch-card data are shipped by air to Ireland, processed there, and then flown back to the United States. At one time, it was rumored, one of these companies had actually bid for the contract to print checks in Ireland for the million or so families on welfare in New York. That politically explosive plan came to nothing.

Most of the foreign-owned plants are small by American or European standards, yet they produce such a catholic range of products that it seems likely that just about any manufactured article, whatever the final destination, can make a profit under these tax-free conditions. Bubble gum, industrial cranes, transistors, bathroom scales, powdered milk, fine chemicals, and precision machine parts are just a few of the products shipped off to world markets. On my last visit to Ireland, Snia Viscosa, the big Italian synthetic textile manufacturer, had located a plant in Sligo, not too far from the resting place of William Butler Yeats. Unemployment and poverty have brought the arid province of Reggio Calabria in the south of Italy to the brink of civil war with the central government in Rome, and the Italians might have been politically wiser to locate their plant in that stricken province. One can only assume that the profit margins in Yeats's country outweigh any other consideration.

The Irish government is beginning to run into difficulties with unions concerned at the disparity between wages and fringe benefits in the United States and in Ireland. The AFL–CIO does not look kindly on countries accused of "pirating" jobs that unions say should go to American workers. I came across one example of the kind of long-distance pressure that can be applied in Kinsale, a small village fifteen miles south of Cork. In this quiet little backwater, an American company had located a plant to run up dresses. While the local women were more than happy to have even low-paid jobs, the leadership of the International Ladies Garment Workers Union in New York was outraged at what they considered an act of piracy by the Irish Industrial Development Authority. The union obtained a court order forcing the American company to pay royalties on any garments entering the United States.

Every company is close-mouthed about the profit margins of its product lines. They always claim, when asked by Senate investigators, securities analysts, or anyone else, that such figures are proprietary information. No foreign subsidiary in Ireland offered to enlighten me. Quite by accident, I came across a prospectus in, of all places, Stockholm, which explained why so many companies feel happy about doing business in Ireland. Some friends in the Swedish capital had received an invitation to invest in a plant that a Swiss company—ASL International S.A.—was about to build in an unidentified part of the Republic. ASL is a drug manufacturer with plants in Europe and one in Hong Kong that trades with various agencies of the People's Republic of China. Precisely what kind of drug the company intended to make in the Republic, Dr. Chris Zour, an executive of ASL, never did say in his prospectus, but he did invite investors to subscribe $3 million for "establishing a new factory in Ireland with all the financial and administrative help of the Irish government." Dr. Zour's communication sought to reassure potential investors by pointing out that "Due to an average 300–500% margin of profit, virtually no manufacturer of pharmaceuticals has bankrupted in the last century."

This, I thought, was an astounding claim. The profit margins of the six largest drug companies in the United States in 1973 were as follows: Searle 12.7 percent, Merck 16 percent, Schering Corporation 17.3 percent, Eli Lilly 16 percent, and Smith, Kline & French 11.9 percent. Granted that the American companies pay higher taxes, the spread between their reported margin of profit and Dr. Zour's claim seemed astronomical. Even more curious was why the Swiss company, if it was making all that money, needed outsiders to put up money for its Irish plant. ASL promised that the purchaser of one of its $500 bonds would receive an interest payment of 12 percent the first year, escalating to 24 percent in the ninth and final year. Not surprisingly, the people of the Industrial Development Authority were uncommunicative about the whole business. I began to think of it as the Swiss Connection.

Perhaps the most ill-advised aspect of foreign investment is that the government has allowed some highly undesirable industries to locate in coastal areas that could perhaps be permanently damaged by pollution. Oil companies find great difficulty in locating coastal sites for their refineries and oil storage facilities. After the massive oil spill off Santa Barbara in California, citizens of that state organized an initiative to prevent the construction of any additional refineries. In Maine and New Hampshire, local pressure has been exerted against proposals offered by a number of oil tycoons, including Aristotle Onassis. Even in England, the sinking of the supertanker *Torrey Canyon* made the British aware of the incalculable damage that can result to bird life and beaches.

The Irish, who are more in touch with nature than perhaps any other European people, seem blithely unconscious of the damage the oil industry can inflict not only on the environment but on the vitally important tourist business. In the sixties, the government allowed Gulf Oil to build a refinery and storage facilities at Bantry Bay, a deepwater harbor able to accommodate supertankers plying from ports in the Persian Gulf. This plant is not located there to provide energy for local consumption, as the Irish discovered in 1974; it serves distributors on the European mainland. A number of other American companies have served notice that they plan to build giant refineries for the same purpose, and these installations will also be supplied by those awesome supertankers. Although modern automated refineries provide minimal employment—the big installations in California provide about seven to eight hundred jobs—the Irish are more than likely to grant permission for the construction of these unnecessary and dangerous plants. Nobody in the country could explain why Ireland welcomes these projects, while the citizens of California and New England resist them with every means at their disposal. More than a few people made a passing reference to political corruption.

On more than one occasion when I lived in Ireland, I began to think of the place as a real-life Laputa, the fantastic floating island Swift created in *Gulliver's Travels*. Laputa was peopled by an illogical race that spent its time on soaring flights of fancy about matters totally inconsequential. The Irish are like that. They hate to be bothered with facts, especially if those facts crack the hard shell of their own preconceptions. And among those preconceptions is the notion that, given a chance, they can hold their own with any other people.

The trouble is, the Irish seldom prepare for that opportunity, as can be seen from an extraordinary report published in April, 1973, by the Committee on Industrial Progress, a government-appointed body asked to assess the readiness of Irish industry to compete in the Common Market free-trade area. Using data supplied by companies representing 50 percent of employment in industry and 38 percent of the national output, the commission reported, with what I thought was an admirable lack of hysteria, that many of the firms it examined did not know from one year to the next whether they were making a profit. The report went on to catalogue a series of grave and inexplicable inadequacies. In some cases, the owners had no idea of what their raw materials cost. In others, the accounts were so scrambled that audited financial statements only became available twelve months after the end of the financial year. In passing, the report noted that, although Ireland's labor costs were increasing at a rate faster than in any other country except Japan, many businesses had no technique for estimating their unit labor costs. These failings and many others the commission attributed to decades of protectionism, when the home market was reserved exclusively for native manufacturers.

In those happy Laputan days, it was normal procedure for a bank to finance a company without anybody giving too much thought to the month-by-month financial performance. Things floated along quite nicely without acrimony on either side. If the company turned out to be in the red at the end of its financial year, a price increase brought the business back into the black. The government never questioned this procedure, nor was there a predatory competitor lurking around to snatch the business by cutting prices.

If an economy running on such a loose rein seems implausible, consider that a six-month bank strike in 1970 caused not a dimple or a wrinkle in the national charts of production, employment, and distribution. The bank clerks sat out the strike in England, where they took any jobs available. The bank owners sat raging on the sidelines like cartoon capitalists. The bank customers carried on as if nothing had happened. They created the first modern bankless society. Checks were written against nonexistent accounts, and when checkbooks were not available, people used plain paper, shopping bags, and business cards. Shopkeepers, bar owners, and bookies acted as bankers. Additional coins and notes were available in banks across the border in Northern Ireland. Everyone seemed sad when management capitulated. Not to receive a monthly reminder of that mounting debt had been heaven indeed.

Ireland is fertile ground for studies in eccentricity, not least in business. The career of Tom Roche, the chairman of Roadstone, a company that sells sand, gravel, and other building supplies to the construction industry, can only be described in poetic language unheard of in the precise case studies of the Harvard Business School. Roche, with his younger brother, started out in the 1930s with a Model-T truck. He has been driving hell for leather ever since and is now considered one of the wealthiest men in Ireland. When he thought he was being gouged on fuel costs, he set up his own chain of gasoline and diesel stations. His executives were expected to be all-round men like himself, resourceful enough to keep the fleet moving or to make a good pot of tea. When it became fashionable to study management technique, a group from the Irish National Productivity Committee descended on Roche to pry out some of his secrets.* The curious, as they admitted in a lengthy report, were at a loss for an all-embracing conventional term to describe Roche's methods. For inspiration they turned to some spirited sporting dispatches sent back to Dublin by Benedict Kiely, a novelist, poet, critic, and journalist, who was on a lecture tour of American colleges.

From time to time, Kiely wrote stories on American exotica, including one on the strange hortatory slogans chanted at college football games. He was especially taken with one cheering section that roared out the letters "E-X-L-A-X" when the offensive team was within scoring range, and the equally original "P-L-A-Y-T-E-X" when the defensive squad was making a heroic goal-line stand. Inspired by Kiely, the people from the

* William Murray, *Management Controls in Action*. Dublin, Irish National Productivity Committee, 1970.

Productivity Committee wrote: "Certainly these proprietary names (and particularly the first) aptly summarize the characteristics of the two main management models in Roadstone." The Roche style of management thereafter became known as "E-X-L-A-X-I-O-N-I-S-T."

Roche has since merged his company with a European concern, an example of the kind of multinational transaction now prevalent throughout the Common Market countries. There are some special reasons why Irish companies are particularly vulnerable to mergers and takeovers. Generally, they are relatively small concerns which have reached the limits of growth in their small national market. Apart from their unique managerial styles, they are no different from the thousands of small European and American companies that vanished in the merger mania of the sixties. As with these small companies, which were usually family-owned or -controlled, the technique of merging is one way of avoiding the immediate payment of taxes on a business that must be sold. Finally, Irish companies have little or no knowledge of European tastes and preferences. They never had to sell their products in Lyons or Milan; indeed, most of them were small national monopolies that never faced competition. If they wish to stay in business, they must get a European partner who knows the markets. Inevitably, the Irish companies will end up as either minor partners or disappear completely as the larger European and American companies divide up the Common Market area into contiguous manufacturing and marketing territories. Some Irish businessmen are more than anxious to take part in this trend toward consolidation. In effect, they act as brokers for the European merchant bankers, who are always looking for the large and immediate profit accruing from a merger or an acquisition.

In Ireland, ancient heroes are cherished like good whiskey and thoroughbred horses. At one time or another, almost every

small boy in Dublin is taken out to the Curragh, a broad
expanse of meadowland, to view the footprints of Dan Donnelly, Ireland's first great bare-fisted heavyweight fighter, who,
judging from the indentations, swung mightily from the heels.
The hero worshipers then usually adjourn from Donnelly's
Hollow to a nearby hostelry in Kilcullen, appropriately named
the Hide-out, where the great Dan's arm, black and withered
now, is reverently preserved in a glass case. Besides fighting two
English heavyweights on the same day, Donnelly is remembered
for having the longest arms of any boxer in his era. "With a
reach like that," says one of Dublin's boxing experts, "he'd jab
the lard out of Muhammad Ali."

Just up the road from the reliquary is Castlemartin, the
country seat of Anthony John Francis O'Reilly, who, figuratively speaking, has the longest reach of any living Irishman.
O'Reilly, a youthful thirty-eight, is built like a man who would
have given Donnelly a run for his money, standing six foot
three and weighing in at about 205 pounds. He is known in
Pittsburgh as president of H. J. Heinz Company, but when he
strides through the streets of his native Dublin, dwarfing his low-
slung countrymen, he is treated as an authentic sports hero,
trailing a retinue of admirers and autograph hounds. Rugby,
not boxing, was O'Reilly's game. If there is any truth to the old
saw that the Battle of Waterloo was won on the playing fields of
Eton, then O'Reilly's football days presaged some mighty victories, even though his school was a modest and less hallowed
Jesuit college in Dublin. At twenty, O'Reilly was an outstand-
ing ball carrier for Ireland's international team, winner of some
notable victories against France, England, Scotland, and Wales.
On several occasions, he was singled out as one of the best
players in the British Isles, an honor that sent him to Australia
and South Africa as a member of the British Lions, an all-star
touring team. His sporting career brought no financial reward,
but it did bring fame, a lot of trophies, some fractured bones,

and a nose that, despite remedial surgery, is noticeably off center.

Unlike Dan Donnelly, who did himself in by imbibing forty-seven whiskey punches, O'Reilly's sporting prowess was subsequently overshadowed by more cerebral endeavors. While climbing to the presidency of Heinz, which he refers to as "that old pickle company," he has been involved in so many ingenious, imaginative, and controversial deals, mergers, acquisitions, and tender offers in Dublin that he is unquestionably Ireland's best-known businessman. He is by no means the wealthiest; this honor goes to the reclusive Patrick McGrath, whose father organized the Irish Sweepstakes in the 1930s. But for someone who had few assets to speak of as recently as 1969, O'Reilly has moved fast.

His role in Irish society transcends the popular image of a fine strapping hero created by the sporting life. O'Reilly has some powerful political and business friends in London, Dublin, and Belfast who solicit and respect his opinions. If he can be said to have a philosophy, it is simply this: The future of the Western world is being shaped by multinational capitalism. Because Ireland is part of this society, a fact he finds necessary to repeat fairly often when talking to his countrymen, the divided country must accommodate itself to reality. By his example in putting together a corporation with interests in both the Republic and the North of Ireland, O'Reilly is suggesting that the economies of the two areas can be integrated.

To hear O'Reilly tell it, he has just begun to get moving in the conglomerate game. He is deputy chairman and a substantial stockholder in Fitzwilton, a conglomerate with revenues of $126 million. Fitzwilton, in turn, owns 21 percent of New Ireland Assurance Company (assets $120 million) . Among its numerous holdings, New Ireland owns more than 20 percent of Solus Teoranta, the country's largest maker of electric light bulbs. Fitzwilton has five thousand employees, and in classic conglomerate style has moved into businesses abroad; it owns stock in a publishing business in England and in a company that makes coal-mining machinery in the United States. When he describes the growth of Fitzwilton and the details of his other investments, O'Reilly has all the details to hand and offers them with the enthusiasm of a small boy who has just been sent to the head of the class. He has been compared in Europe to asset strippers like Jimmy Goldsmith and Jimmy Slater, whose business styles have been influenced by their hobbies; Goldsmith was an inveterate gambler in his youth, while Slater is a fanatic chess player who put up a considerable part of the purse in the famous Bobby Fischer–Boris Spassky contest in Reykjavik. O'Reilly would not want to be placed in such company. "Goldsmith comes across a room with his hand outstretched as if he was about to take 51 percent of the assets in your left-hand pocket," says O'Reilly with just a hint of disapproval; an Irishman, he implies, would never be quite so obvious.

O'Reilly's plan to build a big international company whose performance will be monitored by stockholders in the United States and Europe is a characteristically unexpected break with tradition, and it has had the welcome effect of making O'Reilly's peers look beyond their limited local horizon. To ascribe all the changes that are taking place in Irish industry solely to Tony O'Reilly would be an exaggeration, yet his infectious enthusiasm, demonstrated success, and financial inventiveness to date have given some of his countrymen a psychological lift, an air of confidence about the future that they previously lacked. There is no question that O'Reilly feels he is a pioneer, although he has been careful to preserve, and use to good advantage on occasion, his "Irishness," by speaking Gaelic, telling hilarious dialect stories with professional ease, dramatizing facts, and relaying spicy gossip with a sly Dublin smile. In the sixties, he was approached by a Hollywood producer who wanted to make him into a movie actor; he probably would have made the grade, but such a sedentary occupation had little appeal for a man of action. Besides, he seems most comfortable in Dublin. *"Nil aon tintean mar do tintean fein,"* he will answer when someone asks why he wants the headquarters of that big company to be located in Dublin. Roughly translated it means, "There is no fireside like one's own."

Many a deal has been cooked up by O'Reilly and his friends in the penthouse of Fitzwilton House, a new office block on the fashionable South Side of the city. From there, the view of Dublin in the lambent evening air can be spectacular, but Tony has little time now for sentimentality. He pours himself a glass of white wine, points across the deserted canal at an expanse of grass and trees on the opposite bank. It is an oasis in a sea of concrete. "That's an old riding school," he explains. "We're going to put an office building there." O'Reilly is flanked by two close friends and Fitzwilton directors, Jim Mc-Carthy, a chunky ex-rugby player, who heads up the construction division, and Nicholas Leonard, a former journalist, who dreams up new schemes for Tony's delectation. As they stare out the window, their faces light up with great expectations.

For someone who is seeking acquisitions, the disadvantage of a Dublin exchange listing is that the stocks traded there are viewed by foreigners with some suspicion. In order to get a wider and more respectable market for Fitzwilton shares, O'Reilly is examining likely acquisition targets listed on the London Stock Exchange. Such a deal will doubtless have to be in cash, but he has that long reach. He is a director of the Ulster Bank, a subsidiary of National Westminster, one of Britain's largest banks. In the past, Nat West, as O'Reilly likes to call it, has looked favorably on his ventures, and he sees no reason why that friendship should cease. National Westminster is also one of Heinz's principal British banks. And Nat West's subsidiary, the Ulster Bank, and the New Ireland Assurance Company have formed a new investment banking company based in Dublin.

Even in the freebooting atmosphere of Ireland, one of O'Reilly's sweetest deals caused raised eyebrows. In 1973, through a private company, he paid $2.7 million for the voting stock of Independent Newspapers, a large publishing company that produces three national and three provincial papers. At about the same time, two of O'Reilly's companies, Fitzwilton and New Ireland Assurance, bought 40 percent of the nonvoting shares. Shareholders voted to merge both classes of stock, while O'Reilly ceded his monopoly on the voting rights for a complex but favorable stock-option plan. In essence, the plan stipulated that if the earnings of Independent Newspapers increased by 23 percent over the next three years, O'Reilly could acquire an additional 2.4 million shares, then trading at $2.60, for just a little more than two cents a share. If the earnings goal is achieved, he will then have 36 percent of the stock and a minimum capital gain of $3.4 million.

O'Reilly conducts his freewheeling business operations in Dublin more or less on a part-time basis. His other, quite separate career in Pittsburgh as president and chief operating officer of Heinz is a distinctly more conservative affair. The demands of his Irish interests have forced O'Reilly to become a regular commuter between Pittsburgh and Dublin. It is an unusual, if not unique, dualism, but the directors of the Pittsburgh company look upon O'Reilly as their great white hope. "He is the most unusual, smartest young businessman I've seen anyplace," says Vice Chairman Burt Gookin, Heinz's chief executive officer. It seems to bother the directors of Heinz not at all that O'Reilly is devoting something less than his full time to the welfare of their company. And they dismiss out of hand the possibility that a potential conflict of interest exists for someone who is making acquisitions for Heinz at the same time that he is building a multinational conglomerate based in Dublin. Outwardly, the attitude in Pittsburgh boils down to this: Better to have a piece of O'Reilly's time than the full-time services of another executive. That kind of praise cannot come too easily; there is an astringent quality to Burt Gookin and the older Heinz executives that seems to preclude effusions of any kind and also seems, to this outsider, appropriate to the faint odor of vinegar seeping into the executive offices from an adjoining plant. But when the talk gets around to Tony O'Reilly, nothing but sweet phrases fill the air. "He's a unique guy," says H. J. Heinz II, chairman of the board. "He has the disciplined mind of a lawyer, he's a highly creative marketing man, practically an M.B.A. with figures, plus being a natural Irish humanist."

Heinz first got a line on O'Reilly in 1967, when he negotiated a joint marketing venture between Heinz and Erin Foods, a relatively small frozen-vegetable company owned by the Irish government. At times, he had to shield his youthful, bubbling sense of humor and natural irreverence. He recalls one painful, interminable luncheon in a Dublin hotel when, along with a younger colleague, he affected an air of dull seriousness to impress two Heinz executives from London. After an hour consisting largely of pregnant silences interrupted by desultory platitudes, O'Reilly was beginning to feel mildly successful at behaving like a conservative executive, when he saw disaster bearing down in the form of an old friend of his, a convivial politician, who came over and introduced himself loudly with the immortal Dublin phrase "Tony, who are these two whores you're sitting with?" One of the Heinz men was so taken aback that he developed a temporary speech defect.

That O'Reilly was able to surmount such first impressions to land a job at Heinz and become its president inside four years gives some idea of his executive ability and his powers of personal salesmanship. The son of a civil servant, he went to Belvedere College, and later qualified as a solicitor at the age of twenty-two. In 1958, lawyers constituted a fairly high proportion of Dublin's unemployed, so Tony O'Reilly, although he got a job offer from a real estate company, hied off to England to try his luck. He landed a job as a trainee industrial consultant with Weston-Evans and Company and spent time as a work-study observer on the floors of some gloomy Dickensian factories.

Supreme among O'Reilly's natural gifts is a photographic memory, which enables him to recall data, dates, and events with infallible accuracy. One experience from his stint in the north of England stands out in his mind among all the others. On assignment to spot redundancies, Tony calculated that exactly sixty men could be dismissed from a giant plant without affecting productivity. He presented his findings to the managing director, who looked at him sourly. "Now look, lad," said the managing director. "I know these men are redundant. But we can't sack them."

"Why not?" asked O'Reilly.

"Because, lad," explained the boss, "that's my bloody brass band."

O'Reilly took this and other valuable lessons about the corporate decision-making process back to Ireland at a time when many of his countrymen were fleeing the island. In 1962, he was appointed general manager of the Irish Dairy Board with a mandate to develop foreign markets for dairy products. The Dairy Board was a political instrument, in the sense that the government used it to increase the income of its largest constituency, the farming community. O'Reilly spent four and a half years on the job and performed admirably. Although even under O'Reilly the Dairy Board was no model of efficiency, he created a big retail market in Britain by establishing a brand name for the Irish butter, "Kerrygold."

In 1966, O'Reilly, then thirty, was appointed managing director of the Irish Sugar Company, again a politically sensitive job because he would have a hand in determining acreage allotments for sugar beet and the price paid to farmers. Around this time, he began toying with the idea of a full-time political career. He needed no outside observer to measure the intellectual quality of the Cabinet formed by the reigning Fianna Fail Party; although sufficiently loyal not to criticize former ministers of state, he must have felt at times like a giant among leprecauns. Businessmen of consequence thought of him as a prospective Kennedy-style Prime Minister who would improve the party's rather grimy image. Although O'Reilly opted, after much thought, for the greater material rewards of business, he keeps in close touch with politicians in Belfast and Dublin. That he would have changed the style, if not the content, of politics is beyond question. He likes to tell a rather derisive story of General Michael Costello, his predecessor in the Sugar Company, who was noted for his propensity to attack head on instead of folding up the flanks. Costello visited Addis Ababa during the war between Italy and Ethiopia in the thirties. "Tell me, Haile," asked Costello of the Lion of Judah, "what's your biggest problem?"

"Deserters, I suppose," replied the Emperor.

The general puffed on his Kapp and Peterson pipe for a moment. "Well, now, do you have any tar barrels around?"

An aide to the Emperor volunteered as to how there might be a few.

"I'll tell you what to do then," said the general. "Grab the first hundred deserters tomorrow morning, stick their heads in the tar barrels, and set them on fire. That should stop the rot."

O'Reilly's weekend visits to Dublin are such crowded, strenuous affairs that one of his colleagues, Sir Basil Goulding, the chipmunk-cheery chairman of Fitzwilton, was moved to register a complaint in a baroque letter to stockholders. "Mergers, it must be faced," wrote Sir Basil in his stylish letter, "lift several legs against one lamp-post; so that those abalance there had better take care, courage or consequence. Patently we had cumulated to a large board and to special danger—one big with knowledge. In this we were saved by the breadth of the persons overlaying the length of the board and the depth of their savvy. . . . And so we now have access at intervals, but of a sudden suddenly, to a strongroom of well minted advice. A pretty anomaly is that our prime executive [O'Reilly] is not normally among those present. Instead of yielding a daily drip of running command, our tap gets turned on full cock during serial weekends, through day or night, in office, house or inn. By times the basement is awash."

One of the inns favored by O'Reilly is Snaffles, a subterranean Dublin restaurant near the Grand Canal, housed in a building that looks from the exterior like the lodgings of an elderly distressed gentleman. For the big Fitzwilton board to reach the eats, they must negotiate down a dark precipitous stairway, give the password at the door, and arrange themselves in a small room filled with a reek of old port, cigar smoke, and the drippings of a few pairs of pheasant roasting in the kitchen. This basement restaurant is always awash with talk, a lot of it deliberately inexplicable to an outsider because of the close proximity of other diners, with whom it is possible to lock elbows, especially when a two-handed attack is made on the pungent pheasant pie.

At Heinz in London, it must have been hard for the ebullient O'Reilly to stifle a small crow of delight when he was introduced to his older and more solemn British colleagues. But O'Reilly is not one to swing from the heels. From the vantage point of London, and with a rare sense of timing, he perceived that a new era was beginning for Ireland and that he could turn it to profit for his own account. In 1971, he put up $100,000 of his own money, borrowed $960,000 from the Ulster Bank, and bought control of Crowe, Wilson and Company, a small textile wholesaler that had a listing on the Irish Stock Exchange. With bewildering speed the little textile company was transformed into a conglomerate, Fitzwilton, through a series of mergers and acquisitions.

The stock market valuation of O'Reilly's conglomerate is $55 million. In 1973, O'Reilly's investment of $100,000 had increased in value by 3,400 percent. Just after O'Reilly had started making acquisitions for his heady Hibernian conglomerate, in August, 1971, he was appointed to his job in Pittsburgh. Fortunately for O'Reilly, the assignment involved fairly frequent trips to Europe, where he found time to nurture his conglomerate and make some other shrewd investments. And the old pickle company has become a big factor in Irish business. The company buys $10 million worth of dairy products in the Republic, and it purchases one-third of all the milk products in the North. Heinz is now thinking of building another plant in Cork, the home of O'Reilly's old friend, former Prime Minister Jack Lynch.

Most Irishmen are by nature cynics, and some exotic reasons are advanced in Dublin to explain the remarkable example of O'Reilly's upward mobility. Some Dubliners believe that a kind of freemasonry exists among old rugby players, that, like members of a cabalistic fraternal association, they "take care of" their own. Others think of O'Reilly as a front man for foreign investors. In a gerontocratic society, the success of any young man is particularly puzzling. But one of Tony's old colleagues, Senator Brendan Halligan, an economist who is now general secretary of the Irish Labour Party, detects a certain consistency in that career and provides a shrewd analysis. "He is a specialist in disasters. His whole career has been shaped by his ability to arrive on the scene just when things are at their lowest point. His experience in Ireland taught him this sense of timing. None of the businesses he operated for the government here were really viable, but he stayed around long enough to put a new face on them."

What especially pricks some of the more lugubrious Irish is that O'Reilly unself-consciously enjoys his wealth. His tailoring is impeccable, and he has a taste for the latest gadgetry, including cars and watches. O'Reilly's manner of dress and his habit of commenting on the clothing of others give a clue to an un-Irish concern about his appearance. "Tony was brought up awful hard," says one of his friends, an old man who can remember a very subdued young O'Reilly arriving for his summer vacation in the West of Ireland. "When he began to know what mattered, he would always say, 'I'm going to make a lot of money when I'm young. Then I'll take a look around.' "

Most Irishmen have no dress sense. It is a point O'Reilly makes so often by retelling a Dublin story about a man who visited his tailor that it must be of deep significance to him. At the first fitting, the suit seemed baggy, the coat too long in one arm, the pants too long in a leg. "Lift your right arm now, higher, higher," said the tailor. "Now the left leg, bend it down like that, turn it a little. And bring your right shoulder forward like this." The customer obeyed. Later, while walking in his new suit, two Dubliners stare in amazement. "That fellow must have had the father and mother of an arthritis attack," says one. "Aye. Just think what a hell of a job his tailor must have had fitting him."

In Fox Chapel, a suburb of Pittsburgh, O'Reilly lives rather luxuriously in a $250,000 home, complete with formal Japanese and Scottish gardens and a Catholic chapel built by a former owner, Mrs. Mary Louise Maytag McCahill. When Tony discovered that he was flanked on either side by large families, he promptly named the area "No Pill Hill." In Ireland, he bought Castlemartin, a three-hundred-acre estate near Dublin, for $400,000. Castlemartin is a classic stone-fronted Irish country house with some historic significance. In 1798, Sir Ralph Dundas, a British officer who helped put down the rebellion of the United Irishmen, made his headquarters there. The agent whom O'Reilly appointed to search for a property thought that the land was in great heart, its big green fields bordered by the River Liffey, which is still as clear as a mountain spring twenty miles from Dublin. The house, he said, "is a terrible white elephant."

At times, Tony likes to stand outside the entrance hall, which is guarded by two china greyhounds, and stare past the avenue of tall trees. In the silence of early morning, the scene is timeless. "Just think of General Dundas saddling up for an attack on the peasants," he says. One can imagine it; harnesses jingling, cutlasses drawn, the disciplined cavalry regiment setting off down the avenue to where a leaderless rabble of peasantry stood armed with nothing but pikes. At Castlemartin, O'Reilly likes to spend occasional weekends and a month in the summer with his wife, Susan, the daughter of a wealthy Australian mining executive, and their six children, including triplets, whom he collectively calls "the Vietcong." Very much the country squire when he is in residence, O'Reilly likes to stroll through the sweet thick grass, which is grazed just to ankle length by a herd of Friesian cattle, and, totally in character, he is now mulling over the idea of starting a thoroughbred horse farm. People who race horses seldom make money at the game; those who breed them almost always do.

"The Irish are a fair people," Samuel Johnson wrote. "They never speak well of one another." O'Reilly was paid the ultimate tribute by his countrymen when a thinly disguised satire about a young tycoon in a pinstripe suit was presented on Irish television. After a series of encounters in which the businessman pays astronomical sums to acquire companies, he turns to his man Friday and in a stage whisper asks, "Listen, do you have the loan of a fiver?"

It was through the sale of one of his Irish investments that O'Reilly, perhaps unwittingly, set off a bitter debate about the foreign ownership of Ireland's natural resources. Until the early sixties, it was generally accepted by experts that the country possessed no mineral wealth in commercially recoverable quantities. One of the skeptics was Patrick Hughes, an Irishman who had emigrated to Canada in the 1940s and, like so many new Canadians with an adventurous turn of mind, began prospecting for uranium. Hughes did not have much success in Canada; indeed, on one occasion in the Western Rockies he broke a leg while taking rock samples and was forced to spend the night in bitter cold awaiting the arrival of a rescue aircraft. Hughes remained very much an Irishman. He was convinced from studying old geological data that there were promising mining areas in Ireland, and in 1958, along with some other Irish miners then living in Canada, he formed a company to use as a vehicle for financing some modest exploration. When he attempted to name the company Red Hand, which is the militant armorial crest of his native Ulster, Canadian authorities balked at the subversive nature of the corporate name. Instead, the company was named Northgate, a less inflammatory but nonetheless, to Hughes, a distinctively Irish name. Northgate struck pay dirt in 1962, when some rich copper deposits were discovered in County Galway in the West of Ireland. But the native Irish, skeptics to a man, refused to believe that Hughes had a worthwhile mine. He was forced to turn to Canadians for additional capital; control of the company has since rested in non-Irish hands.

Hughes's discovery attracted some seventy foreign prospecting companies, but no other significant strike was made until Hughes again hit it rich in 1970 on the banks of the Blackwater River, not far from Tara, the ancient site of the old Irish kings. The Tara mine proved to be the largest deposit of zinc ore in Western Europe, a particularly valuable find at any time, but especially so in 1970, when experts estimated that the world's known zinc reserves would be exhausted in about seventeen years. Precisely how much ore is minable is in dispute; Tara lists one figure with the SEC in Washington, another in Dublin. The Tara mine was the subject of complicated litigation involving Hughes, the Irish government, and a number of neighboring landowners.

One of the most piquant stories involves an elderly farmer named Patrick Wright who owned land adjoining the Tara discovery. Wright refused to sell his land to the Tara company; instead, he sold the mineral rights for about a million dollars and a share in any future proceeds to Bula, a company controlled by Tom Roche, the "exlaxionist" businessman. The Wright farm is now estimated to be worth $50 million. In the meantime, the Irish government changed the tax laws, under which mining companies had been previously exempt. The Tara mine will now be taxed at levels comparable to prevailing tax rates in other countries. It was a bitter blow to Hughes, who says that he had planned to build a smelter to treat the ore in Ireland and, by so doing, create the basis for an Irish metals manufacturing industry. More than likely, the ore will now be shipped abroad for treatment.

In 1972, when litigation over the Tara mine was still in progress, O'Reilly, through one of his investment companies, paid $5.6 million for 350,000 shares of Tara. Two years later, when the proposed mining taxes became known, he chose to make a fast $5 million profit by selling his shares to Cominco, a big Canadian mining concern. The timing of the transaction angered a lot of people, including Patrick Hughes, who believed that O'Reilly should have offered the shares to him. An attempt by Cominco to gain control of Tara failed, but only because Noranda, another Canadian mining company friendly to Hughes, bought a substantial number of shares on the open market. Although nobody ended up with a controlling interest in Tara, it is clear that the ownership of Ireland's biggest natural resource is now in Canadian hands.

The Canadian ownership of the Tara mine is a controversial, not to say explosive, topic in Ireland. On a number of occasions the company's offices, located in Navan, a small town near the mine, have been bombed. More peaceful critics say that by bringing the two big Canadian companies onto the scene O'Reilly and Hughes have given credence to the charges that foreign capital is an instrument of exploitation. While a non-Irish company might pay some taxes and provide some jobs, in the long run, these critics say, its purpose is to provide the maximum return for its investors in the shortest possible time.

The debate has now broadened to a discussion about the ownership of possible oil and gas deposits lying off the coastline of Ireland. If the mining controversy is bitter, the discovery of a substantial oil reserve will undoubtedly encourage those who advocate nationalization of oil and gas reserves. At the very least, the government will probably be forced to become a partner, along with private enterprise, in the energy business. Enough precedents exist to make government ownership a respectable goal. The Norwegian government controls the exploitation and marketing of its offshore oil and gas deposits, while the many oil-producing nations in the Middle East and Africa now own outright or in part the oil and gas reserves that lie in their own territory. Resolution of the matter is of some urgency in Ireland. Oil and gas deposits have already been discovered off the southern coast and, although the big oil companies are now concentrating most of their resources on North Sea drilling, they have staked out substantial blocks off the Irish coast for future exploration.

Until quite recently, dealings between the government and the oil industry have been secret, shielded even from curious members of Parliament. Was it through simple ignorance, one wonders, that in 1959 *all* offshore and on-land oil and gas concessions were sold to three American speculators for $1,200, just about the price of a ramshackle secondhand car? Over the years, fractions of the concession passed from hand to hand, increasing in value as oil companies began a tentative mapping and drilling program. One American company, Marathon Oil, now holds *part* of the original concession, valued at upwards of $900 million following the discovery of a commercial gas deposit. The true value of oil and gas deposits is impossible to estimate, pending a full-scale exploration program. Oil experts say with certainty that because of the world energy shortage, the presence of a profitable commercial gas field off the Irish coast, and the almost daily discovery of new deposits under the North Sea, Irish concessions are extremely valuable. Only in 1974, however, when a new coalition government took a look at the curious contracts between the previous regime and the oilmen, did some of the unusual tax and concessionary agreements come under critical scrutiny. Even then, news of the original $1,200 deal was greeted with equanimity, as if it were something as normal as another mild outbreak of foot-and-mouth disease.

The natives assume that Ireland will always get the raw end of any international deal, either through incorrigible corruption or childlike innocence.

Mesmerized by the prospect of oil riches, Irish politicians have forgotten the nasty jurisdictional tangle which would ensue should drillers discover oil or gas at a spot equidistant from the shores of the Republic and the North of Ireland. Under international law, Britain could claim a share; the Republic, claiming hegemony over the island through its Constitution, would demand full ownership; the official IRA, orthodox Communists as they are, would demand instant nationalization; and the cash-poor Protestants in the North might, as Scottish nationalists are doing, cast off loyalty to the Crown and demand their own share of the energy pie. Of course, if the matter was ever settled to the satisfaction of these four parties, the Luddites and anarchists of the Provisional IRA would attempt to blow up the first drilling rig on the site.

Apart from the question of who should control natural resources, the Irish have welcomed the foreign invasion. Unlike other European governments, notably the French, the Irish have put out the welcome mat for just about any foreigner who is willing to invest some money. Nor is there any noticeable concern about an impending collision between the interests of the big multinational corporations and the aspirations of the Irish people. Silence would suggest that they are as one. If a showdown ever came, the native government would be up against powerful institutions. A comparison of the gross national product of Ireland in 1972 with the annual sales in that year of four big multinationals who are well established in the Irish economy gives some idea of the inequality:

General Motors	$30,435,231,000
Ford	$20,194,400,000
General Electric	$10,239,500,000
Gulf Oil	$ 6,243,000,000
Irish gross national product	$ 5,593,000,000

9

Threading
the Needle and
Other Diversions

If a visitor can perform the rather difficult feat of leaving aside the religious warfare between Catholics and Protestants, Ireland still has a magic, therapeutic quality. One must not demand the standards of efficiency, hygiene, truth, logic, or promptness that are advertised, although not always available, in other Anglo-Saxon countries. Ireland and the Irish must be taken on their own terms. The actor Robert Morley, in an effort to describe the improbable place in a single phrase, once said of Ireland that it was the Pope's Disneyland. This was not said in derision, I hasten to add, but in high praise. The Irish cannot for long take themselves too seriously.

My own vision of contemporary Ireland is a series of related comic scenes and encounters which move across the mind's eye like a high-speed film. I was delighted to find, for example, that within a week of settling into a Dublin hotel my phone calls, when I could reach the other party, were monitored by a helpful operator, a cable to New York was delayed for three days, and mail was occasionally delivered with the envelope and its contents solicitously separated for the busy American. The Irish secret police, called the Special Branch, are endearing men in that they make their presence known immediately. They have the religious fanaticism of Catholic employees in the FBI,

Lord Iveagh of Guinness

Michael Mullen, labor official, near Liberty Hall, union headquarters, Dublin

Fisherman, Howth harbor

Thoroughbred horses
bound for England

Patrick Hughes, chairman
of Tara Mines

A hard-rock miner

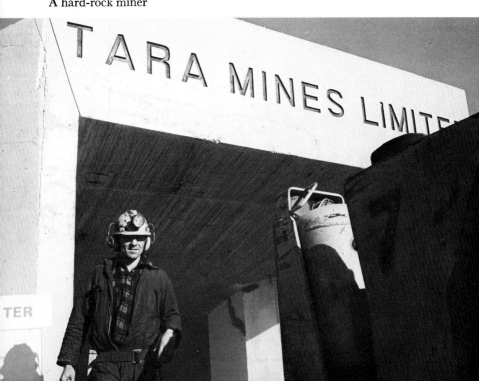

Gordon Lambert, businessman and art collector

Flour mill, de Valera's fortress in 1916

Charles Haughey, future Prime Minister?

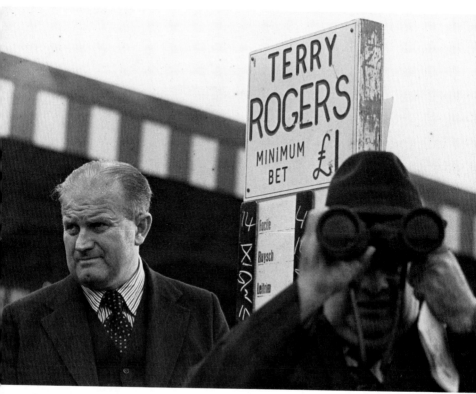

Sporting life, Phoenix Park

Children, Lower Dominick Street, Dublin

the hair styles and tailoring of the KGB, and the investigative ability of the Keystone Cops. In all fairness, they apparently had mistaken me for someone else, possibly an assistant field marshal of the IRA with the same name. When matters were sorted out, one of the Special Branch men proudly showed me his pistol, a rare treat. In the absence of potcheen, his favorite nourishment, he accepted a Jack Daniels, which he sipped thoughtfully while complaining about an ignorant uniformed policeman who had given him a ticket for speeding. A welcome like that makes the bizarre seem normal and sharpens the senses for high comedy.

The Gort fire brigade respond to an alarm by donning their Mack Sennett uniforms, mounting their sturdy bicycles, and peddling furiously to the blaze. A jeep races ahead of them with a small pump and a hose. A Miss Lonelyhearts in a Dublin paper is asked, "Is it possible to get pregnant from dancing closely with my boyfriend?" The answer, of course, is yes—a logical exposition of how one thing can lead to another. In the corridors of Leinster House, Garret FitzGerald, the Minister for Foreign Affairs, tells Conor Cruise O'Brien, the Minister for Posts and Telegraphs, that the only way to get the attention of the telephone operator is to throw the telephone on the floor. "I know," replies O'Brien. Richard Condon, the American novelist, now living in Ireland, asks a Dublin wine merchant if he can recommend the house brand of champagne. The vintner has a grand brand named Reilly. The label says Royale. During a debate about contraception on Irish television, a viewer calls in with an interesting question: "Why were the nuns in the Congo issued the pill with the approval of Rome?"

At the Royal Dublin Horse Show, the social event of the year, some nationalists, overcome with fervor, tears showing on their cheeks, stand rigidly for the playing of the national anthem, then rush to shake the hand of every bandsman. Cripples who are being gently loaded onto a jet at Dublin Airport strike up, in Gaelic, "I'll Sing a Hymn to Mary." The meaning of the bilingual sign "FIR/GENTLEMEN" on a public toilet has been transformed by the addition of an elegant "e" to the Gaelic. "Compassion and mercy shown to the lesser creation will lead to compassion and mercy to the higher," begins a press release from the Irish Council Against Blood Sports; they especially want to end the killing of live hares in greyhound coursing. Three imprisoned IRA men are airlifted by helicopter in broad daylight from the exercise yard of Mountjoy Prison in Dublin. People click their tongues and say, "Well, alanna, it's another first for Ireland." What other nation could present this eclectic scenario, the Irishman acting on his own stage?

Some of the worrying kind are beginning to ask themselves, "Who are we?" As if anyone who spent a year living in that unchanging, maddening, entertaining stew of provincial chauvinism could doubt his national identity. We are—and I use the editorial, racial "we" because I still carry an Irish passport—the indomitable, illogical Irishry.

Being Irish is a state of mind, and Irish culture is whatever a person thinks it is. Most of my countrymen do not believe that the national culture has anything to do with the preservation of the Palladian mansions or the Georgian squares built by the Anglo-Irish; Desmond Guinness, the estimable member of the brewing family, raises most of the money for his Georgian Preservation Society abroad. The Irish could not care less if these monuments collapsed or if the still beautiful environment is ruined. A Paddy Solemn in a Dublin magazine talks of the Martello Towers as "grim reminders of foreign domination; they have nothing to do with our national heritage." The Electricity Supply Board has just sliced the top off a mountain to build a pumped storage electricity plant; the somnolent remains of the seventh-century monastery of Glendalough lie threatened in the valley below. That is progress. The Irish want to catch up with Europe. The little herring fleet at Bantry Bay sets out to sea in the oil slicks of a tanker discharging its cargo from Kharg Island in the Persian Gulf. Near my own town, Wexford, a nuclear power plant is about to be constructed, a frightening prospect indeed, considering the size of the country and the disagreement among scientists about the danger of radiation. I stood on the quayside one morning and wondered whether this nuclear plant symbolized the beginning of the inevitable industrial chain: cheap power, aluminum, chemicals, polluted water, and poisoned air. Probably, but there is about twenty years' grace for anyone who wants to see this haunting, languorous country before it is raped by real estate tycoons and multinational managers.

For the pure nationalist, the restoration of Irish culture lay in the prospect that the native language would become the language of the streets and the marketplace. Those of us who grew up in an environment where Gaelic was taught through the medium of physical force are glad that the days of compulsory Irish are over. Apart from the idiotic notion that English could be displaced, or that the works of Shaw, O'Casey, Yeats, Joyce, and Beckett were written in a "foreign" language, the force-fed cultivation of Irish meant, in effect, that another barrier was placed between the unification of North and South Ireland. Civil servants, by law, had to be proficient in Irish, which excluded all Protestants and most Catholics who were educated in the North of Ireland. Cynicism about this dual language system spawned a proverb, *"Is fearr Gaelige Briste na Bearla Cliste"*—"Better broken Irish than clever English." The Gaelic lobby speaks for about eighty thousand people who are reasonably proficient in this incredibly difficult archaic language, and they are as vocal and illogical as the blustering citizen in *Ulysses*. The absence of Irish from the six official languages used by the commissioners of the Common Market is the final blow to their pride and aspirations. They wrote a furious letter of protest to the Prime Minister of the Republic, in English.

English is, of course, the mother tongue, and every Dublinman will tell you over a jorum of Jameson that his English is the purest extant. Dublin English is certainly the most colorful, scatalogical, gaseous, slang-ridden, musical use of language anywhere in the English-speaking countries. During the St. Patrick's Day parade in Dublin, I stood beside a man who watched with an evil glint in his eye the strutting of an American female marching band, an unusual display of pulchritude in moral Dublin. "I'd give anything to thread the needle with that tall one with the stick," he said with the air of a man who had seen his life's fantasy flash by.

The Irish fantasize a great deal about sex. Guilt and censorship have seen to that. Even if the Irish were like their cousins across the Channel in England in every other respect, their sexual deportment alone would mark them as a distinctively puritanical race. There are some signs that the old inhibitions are loosening up, but honest talk about sex, serious flirting, and fondling in public are still taboo for most people. On every visit to Dublin I ostentatiously carry a copy of *Playboy*. If a customs official sees it, he turns bright red and hands it back with the warning that the forbidden magazine cannot be sold. I always have the feeling that one could smuggle through a dozen machine guns by stampeding the place with a half-ton of pornography.

Sex is a serious business. A producer with a light satirical touch for the subject has no business working in Irish television. The difficulty was explained to me by Frank Hall, a television personality with whom the Irish have a love-hate relationship. I suspect that Hall was sexually liberated at an early age, hailing as he does from Northern Ireland. He is a satirist who deftly punctures the posturing respectability of the Irish, his second favorite target being the piratical politician. His favorite target, which he failed to hit because the censors jogged his arm, is sexual prudery in Irish dance halls.

Dancing is a great diversion that brings the sexes together under one roof, though seldom into bed. The ritual is best observed at a carnival—not a farewell to flesh but a nightly succession of dances in an immense marquee staked down in an open field. When the males summon up sufficient courage—liquor is necessary—they descend upon the females like a sexual press gang. The sight of a thousand sweating couples in a humid tent, with the smell of new-mown hay drifting in from the fields, is a magical aphrodisiac. What looks like the beginning of an orgy, however, is merely an overture for an endless series of jigs, frugs, waltzes, and tangos (contact dancing is preferred), which seems to satisfy the hopped-up participants. Hall wanted especially to film the contortions of a fellow whom he called "the greatest close-in dancer in Munster," a rubber-legged farmer with a hairline mustache who danced nothing but tangos, from one end of the marquee to the other, without saying a word to his partner. "If I could only show this fellow's legs," said Hall, "it would give a new dimension to the sexual expression 'in and out like a fiddler's elbow.'"

In an era when we all seem to be digesting the same canned cultural goods, Irish television, or Radio Telifis Eireann (RTE), to give the station its official name, might appear at first sight to be a minor outlet for CBS or ITV, the American and English commercial networks. RTE enjoys the advantages of both government and commercial television: income from commercial television, license fees from viewers—and the power of censorship. The station runs popular titles like *The Mary Tyler Moore Show, Mannix, The Forsyte Saga,* and *Sesame Street* for toddlers. This is partly a matter of economics, partly a demand by viewers for slickness, a quality absent from the native dramatic shows. With just over 500,000 households in the country, the cost of rerunning a foreign program is minimal.

What makes RTE different is not the few Irish-language programs (no commercials are in Irish!) but the presence of performers like Frank Hall, whose acerbic Irish comments cause station managers to banish him during national elections. Hall fits the national need for irony and irreverence, neatly expressed in a poem that begins:

> Though naughty flesh will multiply,
> Our chief delight is in division:
> Whatever of Divinity,
> We all are Doctors of Derision.

When Hall suggested that drisheen, a variety of blood pudding, was less than edible, he received threatening letters.

On Saturday nights, the Irish actually stop drinking for a spell to watch Gay Byrne, another television personality, who, unlike Hall, personifies the man in the street. At the most innocuous droplet of gossip or information, Byrne professes deep interest or amazement. He tends to be overly sympathetic to foreigners, like the Irishman in Moscow who, after viewing Lenin's tomb, said to a guard, "I'm sorry for your trouble." His accent switches readily from Synge Street Christian Brothers to Hollywood High, depending on his evaluation of guests' standing and importance. A consummate stage Irishman, when he utters words like "sex," "money," "honeymoon," "politics," "IRA," or "constipation," his mobile features compose themselves into matching expressions of shock, joy, bliss, derision, sorrow, and puzzlement. For more than a decade on his program, *The Late Late Show,* Byrne has kept his audience in suspense by refusing to reveal the identity of guests until air time. A viewer may expect anything, from Jack Benny to a dancing elephant. "Byrne drives the country mad on Saturdays," a man said to me, and I can well believe it. The audience responds to his programs with telephone calls and mail, the greatest avalanche coming after a discussion of constipation. Sex and religion, the old staples, ensure that the ratings remain high.

Television is much more rigidly censored than films. Dermot Breen, the present film censor, once said that he would prefer the word "fuck" to "Jesus" or "Christ" in a film to be shown in Ireland, although that advanced stage of emancipation has not arrived. Because Byrne's program is funded by a government that seeks no confrontation with the Catholic Church, sex must be handled with care. He once asked a Mrs. Patrick Fox what color nightgown she had worn on her honeymoon. When Mrs. Fox said she probably had worn none, the Most Reverend Doctor Thomas Ryan, Bishop of Clonfert, issued a statement that came close to excommunication for all hands at RTE. "I regard it as most objectionable and I intend to preach about it in the Cathedral in the morning," said His Grace. "I am going to ask my people not to look at the show again." Since then, Gay Byrne's ratings have progressed, so that a million viewers now watch every Saturday night to see what comes after the honeymoon.

As for another cultural matter, music, my daughter Isolde, who spends her summers in Ireland, assures me that there are certain similarities between American and Irish styles. Dublin children adore the squeaky-clean Osmond Brothers; they know all about the peregrinations of the various Beatles. I was a little startled when she showed me the words of an Irish pop song which was, as the aficionados say, "creeping up the charts":

> He was just a little man, he led a lonely life,
> Working in a bank in Santa Fe.
> She was raised in luxury, a wealthy rancher's wife,
> And he fell for all her evil schemes. . . .

I suspect that in the interests of broadening his market, the composer had substituted the American city for Mullingar or Enniscorthy.

Some time ago, I discovered that traditional Irish music, with its simple rhythms and tempos, has an astonishing resemblance to the American country and Western style. On assignment in Las Vegas to cajole the legal staff of Howard Hughes for information on the elusive eccentric, I interviewed Governor Donal O'Callaghan to see if he had a line on the casino owner. It was natural for an O'Callaghan to assume that an O'Hanlon might be interested in things Irish in the state of Nevada. He brought me along to the Desert Inn, a Hughes establishment, to listen to his favorite musical group, the Irish Dixies. We might as well have been in Cork, the home of the performers. When the Governor sang a chorus of "Come Back Paddy Reilly To Ballyjamesduff," the polyglot audience of tired gamblers loved it.

Some Irish entertainers, in search of what is called the pure Nashville sound, actually journey there to make their recordings. Larry Cunningham, who can sing, dance, and play a variety of instruments—fiddles, accordions, bagpipes, tin whistles, and spoons—is a regular visitor to Nashville, where he records, and to Lincoln Center in New York, where he performs for audiences that are not exclusively Irish. The advent of electronics and the addition of such instruments as electric guitars and organs to the traditional fiddles and harps has brought modern Irish music a wide international audience. The most interesting Irish group, the Chieftains, have developed a unique sound, which I can only describe as Irish-Oriental. The Chieftains are as disciplined about their work as a chamber music quartet. I listened to them play variations on a Mozart theme in New York with traditional Irish instruments like the harp, violin, and the uileann pipes. The result was an eerily beautiful melodic performance of grace and emotion.

Cultural purists deprecate this advance into unknown territory; they prefer the come-all-yez and the high-pitched wails of Irish tenors sitting all alone in the gloaming while waiting for Molly Malone. This brand of Irish music is repetitive, dull, and overly sentimental. The new generation of Irish, at last, can make fun of lugubrious sentimentality. My daughter, an assiduous researcher for Hibernian arcana, came across a contest for the "heaviest" musical group in Ireland, measured not by the skill and influence of the performers but by the avoirdupois of the lead singer. First came Big Tom and his Mainliners, who was soon outweighed by a specimen called Mean Tom. His advertising slogan read: "Come along and see this colossal sight of a man." Mean Tom's championship was taken shortly afterward by a behemoth from Belfast, when it was announced that no bath could be found on the island to fit Big Ivor.

The Irish cannot hear enough or read enough about themselves. Consequently, there are nine national newspapers, forty-one provincial newspapers, ten weekly magazines, eighty-one other periodicals that are published regularly, twenty-eight religious publications—of which the largest is the *Far East* with a circulation of 194,000—and numerous illegal IRA broadsheets surreptitiously circulated by hotel porters, taxi drivers, and commercial travelers. The most sophisticated daily, the *Irish Times,* is edited with a light hand—indeed, a lot of Irishmen would say too light a hand—and provides readers with a flow of items from a variety of foreign news services. The *Irish Times* has the most entertaining and disputatious letters-to-the-editor column in the English-speaking world. Such disparate citizens as Michael O'Riordan, a retired bus conductor who is secretary of the Irish Communist Party; Desmond Broadberry, the anti-contraceptive leader with eighteen children (it may be nineteen by now) ; and Conor Cruise O'Brien sound off regularly. The heavyweights are balanced by a light sprinkling of cranks and perceptive birdwatchers who claim to have seen the first tit of the year. The paper's cosmopolitan air is enhanced by learned reports from Paris on Paco Rabanne's copper breast-plates for women who usually wear A cups, or the significance of Louis Feraud's fall love affair with pleats. Naturally, one can find the latest copper prices from London, the Dow-Jones averages, and editorial wisdom on Watergate or Moscow. The editors of the *Irish Times* do not short-change any reader, especially farmers, who are given much wisdom on the state of mind of Brussels bureaucrats or the economics of rearing Charo-lais cattle. Finely tuned editorial judgment is reflected by a front page story which appeared recently about a pig that was let loose on the lawn outside the Dail. On the pig's back were painted the slogans "E.E.C. Off My Back" and "In the Red."

A visitor to Ireland ignores provincial newspapers at his peril.

Perhaps a hundred travel books have been written about Ireland, mostly by foreigners. Provincial newspapers, however, offer information about the local life style which is indispensable for anyone seeking to plumb the Irish psyche. Pick a paper at random, from the *Dungarvan Observer & Munster Advocate* to the *Anglo-Celt,* and you have the Irish under a microscope, brawling, cheering, complaining, evading, cheating; forty-one little Irish communities letting it all hang out. One of my favorite stories appeared in the *Anglo-Celt,* a crisp account of an incident in an Irish village. The full story took up four columns. This is not the kind of thing you read about in Fielding's guide, or the Shell guide written by Lord Killanin, but it is more entertaining, since it leaves the reader with a number of complex legal, cultural, sexual, alcoholic, and grammatical problems to solve.

Ballinamore District Court

WOMEN IN BED WITH CLOTHES ON

An early morning raid by Gardai on a public house in Main Street resulted in convictions at Ballinamore Court on three people, the publican, Mrs. Brigid Maguire, who was fined £4 and two men found on, who were fined £5 each.

Garda witnesses gave evidence of finding three women in bed upstairs with their clothes on and of being told by a man standing on the stairway that he couldn't go home because "his father had burned his bed."

I think I can guess where John Millington Synge would have taken this story. An Irish Balzac is what we need.

When I began to write this book in Dublin, a lot of friends told me scandalous tales, prefaced with the plea "Don't tell this story. If you do, you'll be letting down the country." This communal effort to preserve the decent, honest, and respectable image of Ireland has been remarkably successful. The Ireland that foreigners read about and most tourists see is a hybrid creation, like dwarf wheat or the Irish wolfhound. The contemporary wolfhound is a useless animal, unlike the original species that lived to kill. The new Irish wolfhound is a combination of various specimens, bred for looks and too friendly by far. Visitors to Bunratty Castle, near Shannon Airport, may see an Irish wolfhound play his role at the medieval banquet, a dinner with music, singing, and much drinking of a concoction called mead. Rory, the wolfhound, stands guard at the portcullis as the visitor enters; he follows the guests to the great hall upstairs, where he can indulge his powerful craving for mead. Rory got drunk one night and fell down the stairs; two strong men carried the enormous pet to an ambulance. When I next saw the animal, he had a splint as large as a baseball bat on his leg. He was perched in the middle of what the Irish Tourist Board says is a folk village, friendly as a well-tempered baby. The folk village at Bunratty is a hybrid, too, a museum with a blacksmith, a thatcher, a fiddler, fair colleens, a few farmhouses and cottages, farm implements, a gift shop, and a pub. The reason for the existence of Bunratty is, I suspect, that many North American travelers stop over at Shannon Airport for a very short period on their way to European capitals. It is a convenient way for the Tourist Board to show the kind of Ireland they believe the Americans and Canadians would like to see, a packaged tour of the countryside, lunch at some hotel, then the folk village, a medieval banquet, and a lick from Rory.

The Irish greyhound, a sleek, occasionally savage, and always temperamental dog, is more symbolic of the Irish character. During the winter, greyhounds compete in open country at coursing meets. It is a sport that repels many, for the live hares used are often killed. Bloodless racing is conducted at twenty tracks around the country, where dogs chase mechanical hares. The betting is frenetic. A good greyhound is extremely valuable, for he can win substantial prize money and attract foreign buyers who flock to Dublin for the annual sales. Europeans and Americans spend large amounts for animals with good track records and fine breeding. The perfect greyhound, Mick the Miller, made his appearance in the 1920s, winning classic races with such ridiculous ease that his body has been reverently preserved and can be seen in the National History Museum in London.

The elevated status of the greyhound in Ireland was explained by my friend Patrick Reilly, a breeder, owner, and expert on the species. Reilly once owned a dog of such estimable qualities that he decided to bring it to dinner if it won an important race at Shelbourne Park, Dublin's noted track. When the beast won and Reilly collected a fistful of ten-pound notes from a bookie, man and dog headed for a prestigious Dublin hotel. This noted establishment is frequented by clergymen of high rank and lissome young ladies whom they introduce as nieces. Some of the young ladies are; others are just second cousins. "You can't bring that animal in here," said the liveried head porter as Reilly mounted the steps. Money passed. Reilly reached the dining room. "You can't bring that animal in here," said the headwaiter. Money passed. Reilly led the dog to a corner table. "We both had steak," said Paddy. "His raw, mine well done. And he slept like a baby on the way home in the back seat of the car."

Needless to say, everybody I met in Ireland was either writing a book or threatening to do so. "You'll be too late," I was told when I announced that I had joined the pack. "At least six other fellows have the same idea." This was said with great satisfaction and sincerity, a tantalizing rite in Dublin, where most books are talked, not written. It was hoped that I would join the journalists for a jorum of Jameson where we could exchange notes and confidences, slander every pharisee, and talk about technique. When some of my confidences appeared in print, I could see that a lengthy stay in Ireland in convivial surroundings would mean that my book would be written by others, appearing regularly in short takes and chapters. Joseph O'Malley, the Dublin journalist and editor, may have detected some wavering on my part. He wrote an admonishing column to the effect that a novel of Joycean dimensions could be written by someone who could lock himself into a room with a typewriter and a copy of the Irish *Who's Who*. When I pointed out that the Whos who matter are not listed, he backed off a little.

Fortunately, there is one cultural tradition in Irish life that makes a writer's lot easy, a place to observe everyone who matters and a lot of others who think they do. The racetrack breaks down all differences in caste and class. Love of the horse, the legendary tough Irish thoroughbred, and the splendid prospect of making money without toil attract everyone. At the Curragh, the Phoenix Park, Leopardstown, Galway, or any one of the other thirty racetracks, the Irish and many foreigners gather in happy anticipation. Here is culture with all its old slatterliness: lords, ladies, conglomerators, the building contractors and their cousins, the tinkers, bar owners, auctioneers, accountants, touts, flim-flam artists, chancers, bankers, barristers, actors, bishops, priests, altar boys, fly boys, Cabinet ministers, Protestant ministers, Orangemen, IRA leaders, ladies of leisure, remittance men, retired pole vaulters, mingling in riotous egalitarian camaraderie. If you turn to a perfect stranger and ask, "Do you know anything?" you have made a friend for the day.

My initiation to the importance of the Irish thoroughbred began the day my father showed me how to dose a horse with cocaine. I will not disclose the secret here, except to say that the deed was done in the interests of international understanding, the owner of the horse being a British officer who had flown from Cyprus to see his gallant steeplechaser win. Had I not inadvertently administered an overdose, the horse would have strolled home, and perhaps continued on to the nearby mountains. Blinded by the drug, the horse crashed into a fence, where he lay for a heart-stopping five minutes. Later on, when the animal's eyes had refocused, the jockey turned to the downcast British officer and said, "If it was a flat race, now, you'd be counting your money."

Cruelty to animals, not to mention jockeys, was not a concern of mine in those halcyon days. Never will I forget that prince of sybarites, Ali Khan, arriving with his latest mistress to grace the racing scene. The Irish wanted to please him, as they always do with moneyed foreigners. His Highness wanted desperately to actually ride a winner, having experienced every other pleasure known to man. He was advised to enter a mount in a race for gentlemen jockeys, a two-mile affair in which most of the riders were neither gentlemen nor jockeys. Experts said afterward that they had seen every possible riding style until the prince rode past the winning post clutching the horse's mane, his flailing legs out of the stirrups. He looked like a man about to take a dive from a six-inch board. "Jesus, Mary, and Joseph," prayed my father, "I hope the clown doesn't fall off." Had he done so, I believe the gentlemen jockeys behind would have stopped, lifted him into the saddle, and escorted him past the winning post.

Such theatre would not be tolerated today. Racing is a serious business, and while the colorful characters still flock to the tracks, the official rules of racing are observed, at least most of the time. The foreign owners are a new caste, including such people as Nelson Bunker Hunt, John Galbraith and Dan Lufkin from the United States, a Japanese tycoon named Kashiyama, and an owner of oil tankers with the euphonious name of Ravi Tikkoo. One of the most ardent owners is John A. Mulcahy, who emigrated from Ireland, established a successful engineering business in the United States, sold it to Pfizer, the American drug firm, and returned home with dreams of equine glory. Mulcahy bought a farm in County Limerick, where he entertained Richard Nixon. Besides pledging $3 million to the

Nixon campaign, Mulcahy has spent enormous sums on horses, luxurious hotels, and sundry other ventures.

It was not unrelated to the arrival of some wealthy Americans that tourist facilities improved immeasurably. The Irish are undemanding hoteliers and restaurateurs, to say the least; standards of food and service, not to mention hygiene, fall far below those available in very modest American establishments. The two best hotels in Ireland are the Ashford Castle in Mayo, owned by Mulcahy, and Dromoland Castle in Clare. Dromoland was transformed at great cost from a mournful old pile into a sparkling establishment by Bernard McDonough, a businessman from West Virginia who demands that guests be treated by the staff as he is himself.

Asking an owner, trainer, jockey, stable hand, blacksmith, or any relatives of those five whether a certain horse is going to win invites lifetime disbarment from the club of real gamblers. The direct question is considered poor form; where a horse is concerned, it invites bad luck and displays a downright show of ignorance. The questioning, after appropriate libations, must begin with the elliptical "Do you know anything?" The conversation proceeds in that coded form at the bars that grace every racetrack.

Lording over the whole affair are men of commerce, the bookies with their voluminous leather bags, predictably stuffed with notes at the end of the day when they light up their Corona Coronas. The bookie is assisted by a tic-tac man, a fellow who watches the other betting boards. Like punters everywhere, the Irish aficionado is convinced that every race is fixed, or at least that it is not an event in which every animal is giving his all. Even if he is the recipient of a tip, he might think that it is a conspiracy on the part of some group to keep the money on the track in Ireland while the owner telephones his bet on another horse to a bookie in London five minutes before the race. The technique is used occasionally and is helped immeasurably by the vagaries of the Irish telephone service. Should the English bookie try to lay off his liability with a Dublin bookmaker, chances are that he will not be connected by phone for an hour. By then, the winner is safely unsaddled, the conspirators snug in a secluded lounge, breaking open the first bottle of Jameson twelve-year-old.

Of all the bookies, Terry Rogers, with his raucous voice and resplendent dress, is the master. Trained by his bookmaker father, Rogers will tease and challenge the sluggish bettors with such phrases as "Yez didn't come out here for the fresh air."

A gambler at heart himself, he once gave the gamblers a break by forecasting the winner of the Irish Derby. He had discovered that Bing Crosby had purchased part ownership of an animal called Meadow Court, which was favored to win. When it was announced that Crosby, not known for wild speculations, was actually flying to Dublin, Rogers knew that the jig was up. He placed advertisements predicting that Meadow Court would win, adding a rider that in the interests of the preservation of the sport, bettors should try to forecast the horse that would finish second. Few were seduced. When Meadow Court cruised across the finish line, the happy punters sang "When Irish Eyes Are Smiling" for Crosby, who looked very happy himself.

It is not true, as some people have suggested, that Terry will lay odds on anything. He has drawn a line on certain political contests, especially Irish elections, because the true gambler would vote for a man he hated just to win a bet. As for American contests, the Nixon-McGovern race left Terry literally holding the bag. Initial odds on Nixon were five to four, dropping to one to three as the polls showed the mounting Nixon landslide. When prayers for the last-minute entry of Ted Kennedy went unanswered, the book was closed. Terry paid off when the election results were announced. This was, perhaps, the only time when things could not have been worse.

Ireland's most elegant social week is, of course, centered

around the horse. Even though most of those present at the Dublin Horse Show cannot tell a fetlock from a crupper, there is a great deal of horse talk. Much flowery language appears in magazines in London and New York about stallions, geldings, and fillies. Visitors rush to buy jodhpurs, hacking jackets, and sundry other parts of a riding kit. Riding crops are optional. Dublin throbs with pride at the glory of it all, providing background music to taste. The military band within the grounds plays endless choruses of "Erika"; ballad singers across the road harmonize "Give the Woman in the Bed More Porter"; stouthearted rugby players roar out their club anthems. At night, men in kilts, military uniforms, and sundry dress regalia swing their ladies around to "The Skaters' Waltz" or flog the floors jigging "The Walls of Limerick." It seems quite in character that a spectator watching the jumping events keeps shouting "Up Down," perhaps the county of his birth, perhaps encouragement to a stumbling gelding. In the middle of this vortex calmly poses Miranda Guinness, wife of Lord Iveagh, so Irish now that she speaks in a soft Dublin whisper. She poses for a fashion photographer under a double bank while Sir Oliver Onions' stallion, Jeremy B, clears the fence.

The Royal Dublin Horse Show would be incomplete without an incident. In 1973, it was the eviction by police of Joe Clarke, an IRA leader who was trying to sell a booklet, *Freedom Struggle*. Clarke is ninety-four, one of the few survivors of the 1916 rebellion, and unlikely to be packing a Thompson submachine gun. The good-humored crowd would probably have bought the booklet for old times' sake. His eviction was a breach of good manners, an infringement of free speech, and a blemish on Irish culture.

Irish life and legend center around sport. National newspapers devote at least a third of their editorial content to the sporting life, appreciably more if the national team wins an important event abroad. Every sportswriter worth his expense account will toss off sports esoterica, such as the maximum height of the Connemara pony (14.2 hands), the location of the oldest yacht club in the civilized world (Cork, 1720), or the historic day of the first international heavyweight championship fight, when Peter Corcoran, a Dublinman, beat Bill Darts, the English champion, on Derby Day, May 18, 1771.

"We're the greatest sporting nation in the world, sure everybody knows that," a Dublin sportswriter said to me one evening as we made our way to the Felt Forum in New York to see how an Irish amateur boxing team would fare against some run-of-the-mill Golden Gloves champions from the New York area. Besides boxing, this sportswriter composed essays on badminton, bicycling, cricket, hockey, tennis, soccer, handball, golf, track and field, lawn bowling, and road bowling, a contest in which a small steel ball is thrown in stages from one village to another. The sad state of Irish boxing became apparent when the Golden Gloves champions, almost all blacks, toyed with the green-gloved Irishmen. "What will you write?" I asked him, knowing from his long sad face that some alibi had to be given to the readers of the Dublin newspapers. "The Americans are professionals in disguise," he answered, "sure everybody knows that."

Rugby is the one sport where political and religious differences are set aside. On the morning of an international contest between Ireland and England, Orange and Green fans top each other's stories about the epic feats of great Irish rugby teams of the past. The only note of acrimony enters when debate focuses on whether it was a Protestant or a Catholic who threw the English forward into the stands at Lansdowne Road. Amity returns when one sporting historian says to the other, "Please God, one of our lads will do it again today."

Physical strength, not skill, is the principal characteristic of native sports. Did not Cuchulain, the legendary hero, single-handedly beat two hundred, or was it two thousand, men at the game of hurling, a unique sport that can be traced back to prehistoric times? A visitor to Ireland can learn much about the national temperament by attending the All-Ireland hurling final in Dublin. Two sides with fifteen players apiece, each armed with a curved ash stick four feet in length, engage in controlled warfare. Tempers flare, and the clash of ash against ash sometimes becomes the clash of ash against skull or bone. Having played the game myself, I can display some old wounds —three broken fingers and an improperly set leg. While it is the fastest field game known, equaling on occasion the tempestuous pace of ice hockey, skill is subordinated to strength and the lethal use of the hurley stick. Jack Lynch, the former Prime Minister, was a prominent hurling star in the forties, and it is said that a lot of people voted for him not because of his political views but because he led his native county, Cork, to national championships on several occasions. I asked a relative of mine, Michael O'Hanlon, who played against Lynch, what the Prime Minister was like on the playing field. "Just like he is today," said Michael, "as cute as a fox. When the ball was at the other end of the field, he'd give you a jab in the kidneys and then say he was sorry."

Not all the sports are as savage or as popular. Take the artistic sports. "Ireland is the only country in the world where the writer enjoys the same status as a Priest." This considered judgment of Richard Condon, the American novelist, who lives in manorial tax-free splendor in the placid meadows of Kilmoganny, appeared in an Irish magazine recently, no doubt to reassure foreign readers that the Irish censors no longer burn prurient manuscripts after breakfast. The natives know better. A few weeks before Condon's encomium appeared, Francis Stuart, a controversial Irish novelist who spent World War II in Germany, was complaining in the *Irish Times* that his new novel, *Memorial,* had been seized by customs men in Cork, apparently on the grounds that it was obscene. "What hope has an Irish writer like myself of living and working here?" complained Stuart. "Should he endure indignities and calumnies, or should he depart, while a government that professes greater liberalism and concern for the arts remains passive and unconcerned?" In one sense, Condon was right; the writer is feared like the priest, and for that reason alone his stature is great.

My own theory about the presence of so many foreign artists in Ireland is that the government reasoned, quite correctly, that they would never bite the hand that granted them freedom from taxation. In one issue of *Ireland of the Welcomes,* an official government publication distributed mainly abroad, film director John Boorman and Wolf Mankowitz, an eclectic producer of film scripts, books, and an encyclopedia of ceramics, gave a collective portrait of Ireland that made the country seem like a Shangri-la of the arts. Not a word, of course, from Francis Stuart or any of the other Irish writers about dealing with anonymous creatures in the Department of Customs and Excise who assign import duty on inner tubes one day and become literary critics the day after.

The double standard makes some Irish writers furious. Heinrich Böll, who has not one but two houses in Ireland, sees only the endearing softer side of life as he looks out on the windswept shores of the Aran Islands. A few acid comments were heard in Dublin when Böll was properly solicitous about the welfare of Aleksandr Solzhenitsyn, the banned Russian writer, yet apparently unaware of the plight of Stuart, a writer of integrity who has been struggling with the agents of the Irish government for more than a decade.

Perhaps it is official censorship, the idea that putting words on paper is somehow a subversive act, which produces so many Irish writers. They are good, bad, indifferent, amateurish, or petulant. Many are undisciplined, leaning to the idea that if one puts half a million words on paper literature will finally emerge. Michael Farrell, a part-time writer, for example, spent his entire life writing an enormous historical novel, *Thy Tears*

Might Cease; it only saw the light of day in 1962 after his death.

When the Irish writer is away from the island of talk, his style is often transformed. Samuel Beckett perfected his spare craggy style in Paris, a style, I might say, that seems to be foreign and mysterious to Irish critics and the actors who occasionally perform his difficult plays. I saw a production of *Waiting for Godot* in Dublin in which the actors, veterans of the casual, naturalistic Abbey Theatre manner of stage presence and elocution, tore the tight understated language into flitters of music-hall farce. Brian Moore, another exile, who lives in the United States, writes in a style so cool, polished, understated, and yet mysteriously resonant that the Irish pretend not to understand him. Two of Moore's many novels, *The Lonely Passion of Judith Hearne* and *Catholics,* are minor classics. What disconcerts the Irish is not so much the absence from such books of fulsome language, long passages of colloquial dialogue, and only slightly disguised portraits of contemporary figures, which the Irish love in their parish-pump way ("Who is the fellow on page seventy-nine?"), but Moore's surgical dissection of the confused, wounded, self-pitying, class-ridden, pretentious, sexually haunted Irish psyche. "He's too starchy and stiff" is the general verdict, a judgment probably influenced by the fact that Moore is from Belfast and therefore not quite an Irishman.

The Irish theatre, some say, is in crisis. Part of the problem is that the Irish government has been niggardly in its financial support. The Abbey Theatre has been deserted by the best Irish actors and authors. Actors must work abroad most of the year, returning for a sentimental season when the Dublin audience can see Cyril Cusack, Richard Harris, Peter O'Toole, Michael MacLiammoir, Siobhan McKenna, and a dozen other actors of great range and power play everything from Chekhov to Shaw. It may be heretical, but it is probably as well that the government does not fully fund a national theatre and arts center.

Otherwise, Ireland would have half a dozen official censors and countless unofficial ones, interfering, goading, politicking, criticizing, offering scripts for the private imprimatur of the bishops and the czars of the Tourist Board, two groups that are overly concerned with the preservation of an image of decorum and respectability.

One of the plays the native philistines believe lets the country down is *Sive,* which would never have seen the light of day had it been tested for bawdiness by a starched-collar censor. *Sive* is a hymn to the life of the Irish tinker, written by John B. Keane, a Kerry pub owner, philosopher, and practical joker. No visitor should miss it. An American friend of mine was so overcome with the bacchanalia of it all that he hired a horse-drawn caravan, the traditional transport of the tinker, to recreate in life what he had seen on the stage. He set out with a guitar, a beautiful lady friend, a supply of Guinness, and the proper prurient frame of mind. Unfortunately, the horse shied near Limerick and he spent a week in hospital with a few broken ribs. Listening to John B. Keane can do mysterious things to a man.

Foreigners who get to know Ireland and its people treat the place with great affection. I have described its queer quirks—deviousness, amorality, inefficiency, bluster, blarney, blasphemy, xenophobia—for I am of Ireland and I know their ways. Yet I can't stay away from the place, and whenever I read about the latest row—and there is always a row in progress about sport, politics, religion, money, or the destruction of Dublin by the money-crazed speculators—I want to rush over there so that I can get involved. Never mind that travel writers advise the visitors to be wary of the Irish; "Let them approach you" is the usual advice to the visitor. Turn to the nearest native of Dublin after you check into your hotel, whether he is a bus driver, a barrister, or a bishop, and simply say, "I suppose it'll settle itself soon." This portmanteau phrase covers every element of Irish thought, from the weather to the war in Northern Ireland. You will be immediately identified as someone of deep wisdom with great respect for the healing hand of time. And you will be given honorary citizenship in the ancient land of the ever young if you leave the gathering after hours of entertaining blather with the balmy blessing "Things could be worse."

Notes on Sources

As befits a nation of poets, the Irish treat facts and statistics as raw materials for the construction of a pleasing portrait. This is nice for the artist, but it makes a diligent researcher's task extremely difficult and makes him seem like a churl when he disputes official numbers, or the lack of them. As an example, the government claims that it does not possess a list of the ten largest landowners, an astonishing omission on the part of the Revenue Commissions, as tax authorities in Ireland are known, if it is true. For the benefit of those, like myself, who are curious about such matters, the Catholic Church and the Gaelic Athletic Association rank first and second in the value of the land and property they own. Neither organization is taxed. My sources for this information, like so many people I interviewed in Ireland, prefer to be anonymous. They feel they have given away national secrets.

A great deal of the information in this book came to light in the course of innumerable interviews, formal and informal. As far as possible statistical data have been checked with at least two, and often as many as four, government agencies. When the answers differed, as happened on more than one occasion, I was forced to accept a figure which seemed logical to me. No doubt my friends in the Irish government will disagree with this technique; in the circumstances, it was the only method possible.

Perhaps the most helpful journal in filling in the gaps was the green-covered transcript of the Parliamentary debates in the Dail. At one time or another politicians asked those questions which particularly puzzled me, e.g., the additional cost to the Dublin government if it was given the administration of Northern Ireland. Where appropriate, the answers given by Cabinet Ministers have been incorporated in the text. Among other sources used for statistics were the annual reports of the Central Bank of Ireland, which always included splendidly acerbic essays on the state of the Irish economy. I leaned heavily on the published material which was extracted from the various censuses conducted between 1946 and 1971, on the annual statistical abstract, and on the reports of various government agencies, all of which are available through the Stationery Office in Dublin.

The annual reports published by government-controlled corporations such as Irish Air Lines, the Industrial Development Authority, the Electricity Supply Board, the Irish Tourist Board, and the Agricultural Credit Corporation present a refined analysis of the most important sectors of the Irish economy. Reading between the lines one can detect the broad strokes of government policy.

Some invaluable sources are available outside the government orbit. The annual economic survey of the Organization for Economic Co-Operation and Development is indispensable, as are the occasional surveys conducted by the British magazine *The Economist*. *Who's Who, What's What and Where in Ireland,* published in 1973 by Geoffrey Chapman, London, in association with the *Irish Times,* is the first attempt to put between covers the people and organizations who comprise the power structures of the Republic and Northern Ireland. Although attempting to be comprehensive, the book has a number of startling omissions, the most notable being the absence of Patrick McGrath, Ireland's wealthiest businessman. The *Encyclopaedia of Ireland* (Allen Figgis, Dublin, 1968) is an excellent sourcebook, with some sprightly essays by eminent scholars.

Two other general sources are essential. The Economic and Social Research Institute in Dublin publishes an astonishing array of highly professional studies and surveys covering almost every aspect of Irish life, from the class structure of Dublin to the internal movements of the population. I have found that when no other source is available, the Institute can provide a lead. The annual reports of the Irish Congress of Trade Unions present an unadorned view from labor's side; the proceedings of the ICTU's annual conference contained in the reports are highly entertaining and most valuable on the reasons why the Irish trade-union movement keeps the IRA at arm's length.

In order to understand the constitutional and economic barriers to the unification of Ireland, readers should be familiar with the following documents: *The Future of Northern Ireland, a Paper for Discussion,* Her Majesty's Stationery Office, 1972, London; *Northern Ireland Constitutional Proposals,* Her Majesty's Stationery Office, London, March, 1973; Kevin

Boland, *We Won't Stand (Idly) By*, Kelly Kane Limited, Dublin, undated.

The essential source on the power of the Catholic Church in Ireland is still Paul Blanshard's *The Irish and Catholic Power*, Beacon Press, Boston, 1953. A highly partisan approach is taken by J. H. Whyte's *Church and State in Modern Ireland 1923–1970*, Gill and Macmillan, Dublin, 1971. For a discussion of the constitutional and political problems surrounding the legislation of contraception, see Vol. 1, No. 3, *People*, published by the International Planned Parenthood Federation, London. An important contemporary survey of the numerical strength of the Irish Catholic Church, at home and abroad, is published in *Social Studies, the Irish Journal of Sociology*, March, 1972.

Copies of the legislation protecting the operations of the Irish Hospitals Sweepstakes are available in the files of Hospitals Trust (1940) Ltd., on file in Dublin Castle. Some of the companies controlled by the Sweepstakes' operators, such as Waterford Glass, also file financial statements at the same location. Most of the sources for the information on the Sweepstakes have to remain anonymous.

The *Irish Times* is the indispensable newspaper of record for anyone interested in Irish affairs, covering events in the Republic and the North of Ireland with commendable neutrality. Most other publications have axes to grind. The *Irish Press* is useful because it is the partisan organ of Fianna Fail, the island's largest political party. The views of the Catholic hierarchy are presented in the *Irish Independent*, the more extreme Protestant point of view in the *Protestant Telegraph*, while the Belfast *Telegraph* gives a more muted picture of Protestant thinking. In recent years the Manchester *Guardian* and the London *Observer* have devoted a considerable amount of space to the reporting and analysis of Irish affairs. The *Irish Post* in London and the *Irish Echo* in New York reveal the states of mind of Irish emigrants in those cities.

Profiles, a Dublin magazine which ceased publication in 1974, contained a great deal of worthwhile material on political affairs. Many of its unsigned articles reflect the views of prominent politicians. *Social Studies, the Irish Journal of Sociology*, presents the opinions and analyses of Catholic priests, although occasionally a lay note is allowed to intrude. Business and economics are covered sketchily, if at all, by Irish publications. *Business and Finance* occasionally penetrates the veil of secrecy which businessmen draw about themselves, while *Hibernia* nibbles around the edges of some rather strange dealings on the Dublin Stock Exchange.

Index

ABOUT THE AUTHOR

Thomas O'Hanlon was born in Wexford, Ireland, in 1933, and was educated at an Irish-language school in Dublin. He wrote for newspapers in Dublin and London before coming to the United States in 1957, where he contributed to a number of publications, including *Queen's Quarterly* in Canada, *Dun's Review,* and the *Wall Street Journal.* He received what he calls a "fellowship to the Michael J. Quill school of cultural camouflage, eccentricity, and Irish evasiveness" while serving as a paid listener and writer for the American union president.

In 1965, Mr. O'Hanlon was appointed associate editor of *Fortune,* and in 1970, a member of its editorial board, contributing articles on such diverse subjects as Howard Hughes, international oil, the automobile industry, the Irish Sweepstakes and the assassination of a union leader. During his research in Ireland for this book, he conducted more than two hundred interviews with politicians, clergymen, nuns, crooks, gunmen, gamblers, conglomerators, cattle dealers, and "a fair cross-section of the Irish power elite." "To get to the heart of the matter in Ireland," he says, "you must talk to a subject's best friend and worst enemy, somewhat like the triangulation method Saint Patrick used to explain that three really means one." He and his wife, Grainne, have a daughter, Isolde, and live in Neponsit, New York.